THE
Westminster
Pulpit

VOLUME IX

THE
Westminster
Pulpit

VOLUMES IX

The Preaching of
G. CAMPBELL MORGAN

WIPF & STOCK · Eugene, Oregon

Wipf and Stock Publishers
199 W 8th Ave, Suite 3
Eugene, OR 97401

The Westminster Pulpit vol. IX
The Preaching of G. Campbell Morgan
By Morgan, G. Campbell
Copyright©1954 by Morgan, G. Campbell
ISBN 13: 978-1-60899-318-5
Publication date 1/15/2012
Previously published by Fleming H. Revell, Co., 1954

G. Campbell Morgan Reprint Series

Foreword

IF IT is true that the measure of a person's greatness is their influence, not only on his own time but on future generations, G. Campbell Morgan must be regarded as a great person. His greatness is seen not only in the wide impact of his ministry on both sides of the Atlantic, but in the fact that his books are still read and studied sixty-five years after his death. Named one of the ten greatest preachers of the twentieth-century by the contributing board of *Preaching* magazine, Morgan made the Bible a new and living book not only to the congregations who listened to him, but the vast multitude of persons who read his books.

Fox sixty-seven years Morgan preached and taught the Scriptures and served churches in England and the United States. What is remarkable is that his commentaries and expositions of the Bible still speak to persons of a new millennium. There have been many changes in the world since he faithfully preached and taught the Scriptures, but the wide appeal of his books testify to the timelessness of his message.

Although he held pastorates in the Congregational and Presbyterian denominations, he had an ecumenical appeal to persons of all denominations and traditions. The mystic

Thomas á Kempis once wrote, "He to whom the eternal word speaks is delivered from many opinions." In one of his sermons, he referred to the words of Amos that there would be a famine for hearing the word of God (Amos 8:11). The timeless work of G. Campbell Morgan addresses that hunger, as his books enable his readers to get beyond opinions to the living Word.

Wipf and Stock Publishers have rendered a great gift to the religious world in reprinting dozens of Morgan's books. This growing collection makes his books more available, so that readers have an option other than searching the internet for used, and often expensive, copies. Among this collection is the classic *The Great Physician* and commentaries on the Gospel of Matthew and John. Persons seeking a living faith and a meaningful encounter with God would profit from reading any of these Morgan books.

Near the end of his ministry, in a sermon entitled "But One Thing," Morgan commented on how Portugal changed the words of a coin after Christopher Columbus discovered America. No longer did the inscription say, *Ne Plus Ultra* (nothing more beyond) but *Plus Ultra* (more beyond). It is the hope of the G. Campbell Morgan Trust that the reprinting of these books will bring readers to the "more beyond," and an even deeper encounter with the Word in Scripture.

THE MORGAN TRUST
Richard L. Morgan
Howard C. Morgan
John C. Morgan

CONTENTS

CHAPTER		PAGE
I	PLAYING THE FOOL	9
II	AMBITIONS	23
III	SOUR GRAPES	38
IV	FOUR MISTAKES ABOUT CHRIST	51
V	THE UNCHANGING ONE	65
VI	THE PROBLEM OF HOW TO BEGIN	78
VII	THE MADNESS OF JESUS	92
VIII	THE HEALING OF LIFE	106
IX	FORGIVENESS	120
X	THE RESURRECTION	134
XI	THE WAY OF RIGHTEOUSNESS	147
XII	JEHOVAH OF HOSTS—THE GOD OF JACOB	161
XIII	THE TRAGEDY OF LIFE WITHOUT FAITH	175
XIV	THE JUSTIFICATION OF THE SINNER	189
XV	THE SUPREME INSPIRATION OF FAITH	203
XVI	CHRIST JESUS, THE LORD	217
XVII	CHRIST AND SINNERS—IDENTIFIED AND SEPARATE	232
XVIII	THINGS SHAKEN—THINGS NOT SHAKEN	246
XIX	TRIBULATION, KINGDOM, AND PATIENCE	257
XX	THE HARVESTS OF THE WORD OF GOD	269
XXI	THE ASCENSION	281
XXII	LIFE IN THE LIGHT	293
XXIII	SONGS IN PRISON	304
XXIV	WAITING FOR GOD	316
XXV	THE LOOKING OF JESUS	328
XXVI	THE WAGES OF SIN—THE GIFT OF GOD	340

THE
Westminster
Pulpit

VOLUME IX

CHAPTER I

PLAYING THE FOOL

. . . behold, I have played the fool. . . .
I SAMUEL 26:21.

THAT IS AUTOBIOGRAPHY; CLEAR, TRUTHFUL, INCLUSIVE. In half-a-dozen words we have the story of Saul, Israel's first king, like the nations. Under stress of circumstances, men often tell truths and whole truths, which, if they had time to think, they would never utter. God's method of crisis is that of the commonplace. His method of examination is that of the unannounced. When for a moment a man is off-guard, in all probability you will know more truth about him than in all his attempts either to reveal himself or to hide himself. The ever-present consciousness, habitually, carefully hidden, flashes forth. Later, he may apologize and say he did not mean what he said, that he was not at the moment responsible. The fact is that he was surprised into saying what he was constantly thinking. In all probability Saul had never said that before and would never say it again; but he had been thinking it for a long time, "I have played the fool." It is an error to suppose that a man does not know the truth about himself. In that sense also, God hath not left Himself without witness. There is no escape for any man as long as reason continues, from the bare, naked, unadorned truth about himself. He may practice the art of deceit so skillfully as not only to hide himself from his fellow men, but in his unutterable folly to imagine that he has hidden himself from God; but he has never hidden himself from himself. In some moment of stress and strain, he says what he has been thinking all the time. So with Saul.

Saul had slept deeply that night, for the record tells us that "a deep sleep from the Lord was fallen" upon him. He was awakened from his slumber by the voice of David calling to him from the opposite mountain. Waking he became keen, acute, neither dulled by food nor drugged by wine; everything was clear and sharp about him, as it so often is in the waking moment. Ere he knew it, he had said, ". . . behold, I have played the fool. . . ." That is the whole story of the man.

Let us consider then the man who spoke; the opportunities that came to him; how he played the fool; in order that we may finally inquire what this story has in it for us.

Let us look at the man as he is revealed to us in the passage we read, and as he is revealed in all those chapters from beginning to the sad and dire calamity in the midst of which they end.

In the first place, he was a man of good family. His father Kish, a Benjamite, was a "mighty man of valor," that is of substance, wealth. Saul looked upon life from the viewpoint of good family connections, that viewpoint from which every young man would desire to look upon life; a viewpoint which should compel a man to thank God every day he lives.

I observe, in the second place, that Saul was a man of splendid physique, ". . . a young man and goodly: . . ." says the record, standing head and shoulders above his fellows, a man with all the advantages of height, and health, and handsomeness. Let no man undervalue these things. I know perfectly well what may be in the minds of some of you, especially those who lack those qualities. You will remember that Isaac Watts wrote:

> Were I so tall to reach the Pole
> Or grasp the ocean with my span;
> I must be measured by my soul
> The mind's the standard of the man.

Quite right; but let no haggard and thin man pretend he does not admire the magnificent physique of his friend!

In the record, I also find that this man was a man of simple life, a yet greater advantage; living at home, interested in his father's affairs, and bound to his father by the ties of very sincere and honest affection. When we are introduced to him, he is about his father's business. In those long wanderings in fruitless search after the lost asses of his father, there is a revealing touch in the fact that at last he said to his servant, ". . . Come, and let us return; lest my father leave caring for the asses, and take thought of us." Saul had all the advantages of actual work and responsibility in rural surroundings. No sane man would live in a city if he could escape it. As Bismarck said, "Great cities are great sores upon the body politic."

Further, he was a man of modest disposition; a man who, when he was saluted by the seer in those remarkable words which suggested to him that all desirable things in the kingdom were for him, replied that he was a Benjamite, the smallest of the tribes, and a member of the family that was least in the tribe. In that answer was revealed the pride of modesty.

Once more, he was a man of slumbering courage. Its manifestation came after a little while, in his action when the nation was insulted by Nahash. The story I am not going to tell for you know it. Simply let me say of the man Saul that he was a man of that courage which farms until occasion demands and then strikes with passion and force in defence of national life.

That is the man who at the end said, ". . . behold, I have played the fool. . . ."

Let us look again at the opportunity which came to him. It was a unique, remarkable, surprising opportunity. He was called to kingship, to a position of responsibility and authority in the life of the nation. The people had clamored for a king; it was an evil clamor, it was a clamor that proved their degeneracy; it was a clamor according to God's interpretation of it to His servant Samuel, which demonstrated the fact that they had rejected Him from being King. Nevertheless, they had clamored for a king and in working out His own purpose, following that principle which always characterizes the Divine activity, that of giving people what they ask for and thus compelling them to work out their own desires to ultimate manifestation, He granted them a king; but He chose the king, He selected him. The call to Saul was clear, definite, solemn. What a scope for his powers! What a chance to bless men from that high position of authority. What an opportunity to cooperate with God in such a way as to prove to the people that God was still King. What an opportunity to exercise authority under the authority of God in such a way that through his authority the authority of God might be manifested anew, and the heart of the people turned back to Him from Whom they had wandered. It was a great hour and a great call.

Notice further, not only his opportunity in itself, but in its equipment. His first equipment was himself. He was such a man as he was, and in that fact lay great value for the doing of the work to which God had called him. Whenever God calls a man to high vocation, it is not merely true to say He will confer upon him what he needs for the fulfilment of that vocation; it is also true that He has chosen the right man for the work. If God calls a man to preach, it is not merely true that He will give him his message and equip him for his preaching, it is also true that He has called a man who can preach. The call of God is always answered by the capacity that lies within a man; it is made to that. Saul had himself; he was kingly in himself. He was equipped in his own personality, having within it the capacity for kingship which God recognized in the moment in which He called him to the place of kingship.

He had more than that; he had God with him. Said Samuel to him, ". . . God is with thee," and as he turned from Samuel and went on his way, he was conscious of some strange change, ". . . God gave him another heart: . . ." and he became another man. More than that. ". . . the Spirit of God came mightily upon him, . . ." and on his journey home he joined a company of the sons of the prophets who were traveling; and lo, the Divine afflatus possessed him, and he saw visions and lifted up his voice and uttered words of Divine truth.

There were other forces at his disposal. He was equipped in the matter of the men who were about him. His preparation for his work is demonstrated by the friends he possessed, and by the foes he discovered. Samuel was with him, and there is no more radiant verse in the story than this, pregnant with suggestiveness, ". . . there went with him the host, whose hearts God had touched." He was prepared for kingship by the fact of his foes. Who were they? The sons of Belial, worthless, base fellows. You may often know what a man is by discovering who his foes are. When the sons of Belial are against a man, you may believe in him.

This is the man who at the end said, ". . . behold, I have played the fool. . . ."

Let us now ask how he played the fool. Going over the old, well-known story in the most rapid way, I want to speak of the manifestations of his folly, and that in order that we may try to find the secrets thereof.

The first manifestation came very early; soon after his anointing. When they sought him on that subsequent day of popular election which was to ratify the Divine election, he was hiding away; and in that hiding away there is the first manifestation of weakness, the first evidence of folly. I am going to say to you quite frankly that I know a great many will join issue with me here. I have heard it declared by men for whom I have the profoundest respect, that the hiding away was a new demonstration of his modesty, but I ask you to remember that there is a modesty which is wholly evil. If God has called a man to kingship, he has no right to hide away. If God has called a man definitely, anointed him, equipped him to take charge of the Empire, if that man out of any sense of modesty shall hide away and try to escape the responsibility, therein is the first evidence of his weakness. So it was with Saul.

I notice next that this man manifested a strange new form of military pride. For the first time there was established in this nation a standing army, and I begin to see the line along which his kingship is going to move. Saul created a standing army of three thousand men, he himself taking charge of two thousand while the remaining thousand were with Jonathan. Note the sequence; the whole story is graphically told. Jonathan smote the garrison of the Philistines and

Saul blew the trumpet in Israel. Israel heard that Saul had smitten the garrison!

I watch him a little further and observe that he has become restless, impatient, self-dependent. Samuel has not come; then we can do without Samuel; offer the sacrifices! He violated a principle, and despised a command in the rush of his restless impatience.

I follow him a little further and find another story, the story of his rashness in taking an oath which imperiled the life of Jonathan which would have resulted in his death if the people had not interfered and rescued him.

I go a little further and find another illustration of his failure; his disobedience in the matter of Amalek and his lying afterwards.

The most glaring revelation of his folly is that ruthless, persistent, undying hatred of David; hunting him, as David himself did say, like a partridge upon the mountains.

The last manifestation of his folly is that in which we see him in the night time commerce with the underworld of evil, and trying to find out the hidden secrets through the muttering of a witch. A man with whom God was, who received from God a new heart and became another man, who was mightily clothed with the Spirit of God so that he joined the ranks of the prophets. What a morning of promise! At last, in the darkness of the night he is seen creeping stealthily to find a muttering witch, dealing with evil spirits. He was startled and surprised in the darkness of the night, for there also he found God, and to her surprise, the witch found God for Samuel came. That is the last phase of his folly.

These are but the manifestations, the symptoms, the results. The tragedy of the man's life lies deeper. His hiding away, his military pride, his impatience, his self-dependence, his rashness, his disobedience and lying, his hatred of David, his traffic with the witch; these are all manifestations of something deeper. Wherein then lay the folly of this man? I shall answer my question fundamentally and processionally. I shall speak of that which is fundamental and then ask you to notice how that expressed itself in the man's history.

I am almost afraid to tell you the fundamental wrong because it has so often been said and because the saying of it is not the sort of thing that troubles men as it ought to do. It is so old a story. The fundamental wrong of this man was that he failed to submit himself to the one King. Lack of loyalty to God; that was it. That is nothing new, of course. That is what we hear so constantly; so constantly that all the keen edge goes off the truth, and men are not troubled by it as they should be. In that terrific hour when the prophet told him of his rejection, we have these words, which are quoted often enough, ". . . to obey is better than sacrifice, and to hearken than the fat of rams." Therein lay the man's failure, that he had not obeyed, that he had not hearkened; ". . . I have played the fool. . . ." Created by God, being in myself all that I am by God's creative act, called by God to high, dignified destiny, equipped by God with all that was necessary for the fulfilment of that destiny; ". . . I have played the fool . . ." in that I have forgotten God to Whom I owe myself, my destiny, my equipment. He had trusted in his own strength, he had trusted in natural advantages; but he had forgotten that his own strength was God's gift to him, that his own natural advantages came to him from God. He had forgotten God.

Mark the manifestation of it. No longer in the events chronicled but in the processes which are revealed. This man failed entirely to exercise the true function of kingship.

This man in his government of Israel was a warrior and nothing more; he was never a shepherd. He manifested from the first only one kind of concern about his people, concern about the frontier, concern about enemies. It had its place; it was necessary that he should make war upon the Philistines, and this he did successfully through a long period. I am not affirming that he was wrong in being a warrior; the times demanded it, and the command of God was that he should deliver his people from Philistia. But that concluded his kingly activity. He had no care for the people; he lacked the shepherd heart. It was Homer who said, "All kings are shepherds." These words of Homer are certainly vindicated by the biblical revelation of what kingship means. Kingship is always shepherdhood in the Divine economy. There is no greater psalm in all the five books, celebrating the Kingship of God, than that old and familiar one which we so constantly recite, "The Lord is my Shepherd." That is the supreme song of Jehovah's Kingship. This man Saul lacked the shepherd heart and the shepherd quality.

Then observe, as he passed on through the years, his neglect of his true friends; his neglect of Samuel, his cruelty and injustice to Jonathan, and the persistent, devilish hunting of David to which we have already made reference. He became a man, self-conscious, self-dependent, self-assertive, self-centered.

These evidences of the man's folly are simply revelations of the things resulting from that central, fundamental wrong; for if he had not forgotten God but had been obedient to Him, then in communion with Him he would have been not a warrior alone, but a shepherd also. If he had not forgotten God and ceased to be loyal to Him, he would have known the value of Samuel and Jonathan and David. The man who forgets God is self-centered. Every man lives under the government of God or of Himself. The man who forgetting God, neglecting Him, disobeying Him, living without Him, finds his soul circumferences around the center of his own desire, lust, passion, will and waywardness. That man inevitably in some hour of crisis will be compelled to the confession, ". . . behold, I have played the fool. . . ."

So finally, let us gather from the story some of the things it ought to say to us immediately. I suggest to you, first of all, that the story of Saul teaches us that advantages are not insurances of success. You may have all the advantages and yet at last be a disastrous failure. Advantages as to family, and physique, of natural disposition characterized at once by modesty and courage are all valuable; but a man may have all these and yet play the fool. I say that almost with bated breath lest I be misunderstood. Do not undervalue your family relationships. When next you think of your advantages, head the list, if indeed it be true, with this: my father lived a clean life before me and left me the legacy of his example; and my mother prayed for me through all the days. But remember, your father's example and your mother's prayers are not enough. A man may have had these things also, the highest spiritual family advantages, and yet he may play the fool.

I observe, in the second place, that the story of Saul teaches that opportunities do not crown men. You may have heard the call of God, a kingdom may be waiting for you to govern it, rule it, administer it. You may have with you the comradeship of the good. These things are all valuable, indeed they are all necessary if life is to be fulfilled. But a man may have the whole of them and play the fool. A man may have heard in his soul the call of God to the ministry, to the mission field, to professional life at home, to commercial life at home, for I maintain that in these things God also calls as distinctly as to other things. You may know you are where God put you. Saul knew it, the anointing oil had been upon his head, he had made no mistake. The profound, spiritual conviction is yours that you are exactly where God would have you be. Yet you may play the fool, spoil your life, miss your kingdom, weaken your volition, end disastrously. So thinly separated from opportunities crowning a man, every opportunity for that which is high, noble, wonderful, is an opportunity for terrific failure. The greater the opportunity that comes to you, the greater the possibility of disaster, unless you find the secret of life and obey it.

I learn, quite simply and finally, from this study that there is one thing necessary. The one thing necessary for the fulfilment of life is that of surrender, loyalty, obedience to God. Apart from that there can be no proper understanding of life. Apart from that there is no wisdom or power to deal with life.

I know full well as I speak to you how the minds and hearts of some of you will rebel against such a statement as that; that a man may tell me he knows himself and his capacities and powers and knows perfectly well the true way to deal with these to assure success to himself. Well, I pray you think again, and think more deeply, and recognize the fact ere it be too late, ere disaster come, that no man knows himself perfectly, finally. If you would have witnesses to the thing I am now saying, they are here; I cannot call them, cannot ask them to speak, but they are here; men who are going grey, men who have been weathering the storms and finding out themselves. They will tell you that the most astonishing hours that have ever come to them were hours in which they discovered in themselves things they never dreamed were there; things sometimes of good and sometimes of evil. The last words of the old Greek philosophy were great words, "Man, know thyself." It was great because it brought every man face to face with himself and so to the discovery that he was greater than he had ever known, so great that he could not know himself. Infinitely more true to the experience of human life was the word of the Psalmist in the Hebrew psalter, in that marvelous one hundred and thirty-ninth Psalm, opening as it does,

> O Lord, Thou hast searched me, and known me,
> Thou knowest my downsitting and mine uprising,
> Thou understandest my thought afar off.

Then the Psalmist said,

> Such knowledge is too wonderful for me;
> It is high, I cannot attain unto it.

"Such knowledge, . . ." that is knowledge of myself. I do not know myself. When a man has learned that lesson, then he is prepared to submit himself to the One Who knows him, and so the great psalm which opens with the affirmation,

> O Lord, Thou hast searched me, and known me

ends with the prayer,

> Search me, O God, and know my heart:
> Try me, and know my thoughts:
> And see if there be any way of wickedness in me,
> And lead me in the way everlasting.

That is the language of the wisdom of the man who realizing God's knowledge and his own ignorance, will submit himself to God at the beginning of life, when the flush of dawn is upon the sky and high hope is singing its song in his heart. The man who will begin there will never end by saying, ". . . I have played the fool, . . ." for "The fear of the Lord is the beginning of wisdom." Apart from his surrender, loyalty, obedience to God, there can be no proper understanding of life, no adequate wisdom or power to deal with life.

There are many manifestations of the fundamental folly. I will content myself with grouping those suggested by the story. A man plays the fool if he halts when God calls him to some pathway of service. Has he called you, my brother, did you hear the call? Why are you hiding? End your folly, and march according to the Divine command.

A man plays the fool when he neglects his best friends. What are these new friends that make you neglect the old ones? How is it that we have missed you recently from the fellowship of the saints of God? God set round about some of you a band of men whose hearts He Himself has touched. Why neglect their company? I believe in the communion of saints. I believe in the value of keeping in the comradeship of the saints. I do protest that unless I maintain my comradeship with the saints, I shall wander from the path of the just. I owe more to the spiritual sympathy and help of the children of God than I can ever tell. How many a man have I seen drift out of the Christian church and out of Christian work because he has neglected the friends that God provided.

A man plays the fool if he marches upon the Divine enterprise when God has not commanded him. That is only the reverse of the other truth that a man plays the fool when he halts when God commands. Go upon no enterprise at your own charge. Await the Divine command, for therein is the Divine covenant, and the Divine covenant provides that thou shalt find the resources needed to meet the command. A march without God is a march of unutterable folly toward final disaster.

A man plays the fool if he disobeys in even the smallest matter. To obey is better than sacrifice. The religious excuse is the most damnable of all excuses. To disobey God in the interest of religion is to blaspheme.

A man plays the fool when he attempts to justify the wrong he has done. It is upon the basis of confession that God can forgive sin and reinstate a man in righteousness. That is not merely a Divine enactment and requirement. It is a moral necessity. When a man justifies wrong, tries to excuse it, he is playing the fool; for he is keeping the evil thing that has already threatened to ruin him.

A man plays the fool unutterably when he allows some hatred to master him, as Saul did in the case of David.

There is some man here who is saying, ". . . behold, I have played the fool. . . ." What shall I say to that man? What that man supremely needs is help that comes down to his level, takes hold of him, touches him in pity but also in power, bends over him in infinite compassion, but also with force that will remake him.

That is what Browning felt when he wrote his great poem:

'Tis the weakness in strength that I cry for! my flesh that I seek
  In the Godhead! I seek and I find it. O Saul it shall be
A Face like my face that receives thee: a Man like to me,
  Thou shalt love and be loved by, forever! a Hand like this hand
Shall throw open the gates of new life to thee! See the Christ stand!

To every man tonight who is saying in the deepest of his soul almost in despair, ". . . behold, I have played the fool, . . ." I say, ". . . See the Christ stand!" He has come to the foolish to make them wise, to the ruined to redeem them, to the lost to find them, to the impure to purify them, to the dis-crowned kings to crown them, to the souls that have unutterably and disastrously failed to realize within them the original intention and lift them into the place of fellowship with God.

CHAPTER II

AMBITIONS

... desire earnestly the greater gifts. And moreover a most excellent way show I unto you. Follow after love. ...
       I CORINTHIANS 12:31; and 14:1.

WE ARE ALL FAMILIAR WITH THE WORD "AMBITION." Coming to us from the Latin, it has acquired a significance quite other than that of its first meaning. Quite literally, it simply means going round. In process of time, it came to signify going round for votes. Today, it stands for that mood of the soul which makes a man go round for votes; today it stands for earnest desire, especially desire for honor in some form. Thus it will be seen that the word originally described a method, an action; while today, it is used rather of a purpose, an inspiration.

  The question which has been under consideration this month by our young people has been: "What would you consider the greatest honor that could come to you; and why?" It will immediately be recognized that the purpose of the question was that of discovering the ambitions which are inspiring their lives, or which ought to inspire their lives; for it is possible for a person to cherish an ambition which is not an inspiration but which is a dead weight. The answers which I have received have been most interesting, and in some ways I cannot help saying remarkable; but I will come to them presently.

Let us first take time to consider this subject of ambition, as to its place, its peril, and its power in human life. This we shall do in the light of the text selected. I recognize that there are far larger values in this text than I intend to deal with. There is, however, exactly the light we need if we are finally to understand the proper place and power of ambition in human life.

In considering this, therefore, we will first of all dwell with some technical care upon the word of which the apostle made use, and which the revisers have translated "desire earnestly"; and King James translators, "covet." It is one word in the apostolic writing. It is the Greek word from which two well-known words in our English language have been derived. I refer to the words "zealous" and "jealous." Zealous is a word full of suggestiveness, its root idea being that of fire, of passion. Zeal is the driving force in endeavor; jealousy is that which guards the way. Thus in our two words, we have two aspects of the same central thought. The activity suggested by the word is that of mental approbation which expresses itself in strenuous endeavor. The idea is expressed exactly by our modern use of the word "ambition." It is a strong desire to obtain position, power, honor, in the best sense of that word honor.

There is a prevalent notion that ambition is wholly evil. You will remember what Wolsey said to Cromwell:

> Cromwell, I charge thee, fling away ambition.
> By that sin fell the angels; how could man, then,
> The image of his Maker hope to win by it.

Or, again, Mark Antony:

AMBITIONS

> . . . The noble Brutus
> Hath told you Caesar was ambitious;
> If it were so, it was a grievous fault;
> And grievously hath Caesar answered it.
> Here, under leave of Brutus and the rest
> (For Brutus is an honourable man;
> So are they all, all honourable men),
> Come I to speak in Caesar's funeral
> He was my friend, faithful and just to me;
> But Brutus says he was ambitious;
> And Brutus is an honourable man.

In each of the quotations the conception is that ambition is evil. This is not necessarily so. The fundamental principle of society is that of individual self-preservation and self-realization. There will be no perfected society that is not made up of perfected individuals. A chain is as strong as its weakest link. A castle is as strong as its least-guarded door. If in society there are links that are weak, society is weak. If in the great household of men there are individuals that are imperfect, then the household of men remains imperfect. Perfect units are needed for the perfect unity. Therefore, the ultimate purpose of individuality is not individuality, but the realization of the commonwealth. The ultimate reason why every man must be perfect is not that the man should be perfect, but that the community should be perfect. Therefore, every individual must aim at high things, noble things, and desire honor. This is ambition in its simplest, purest form; and this is not evil, but wholly good.

There is one brief prophecy in the Book of Jeremiah, a simple prophecy among the great utterances of the prophet of thunder and of tears, a prophecy uttered to one man, to Baruch, the man associated with Jeremiah in his work. The heart of the prophecy is contained in these words: ". . .

seekest thou great things for thyself? Seek them not; . . . ." Jeremiah did not tell Baruch that he was not to seek great things; he told him he was not to seek great things for himself. There in a flash we have the revelation of the difference between true and false ambition.

That reveals the peril of ambition. When the whole is lost sight of and its well-being is not sought, ambition becomes deadly. Then action growing out of it becomes cruel and ruthless. When a man seeks great things for himself, what cares he how many suffer so that he succeeds; how many are downtrodden so that he may rise; how many are flung out by the whirling wheel, so long as he arrive at the goal? Such ambition is the spawn of hell, the progeny of Lucifer who fell from his high estate by ambition that was entirely self-centered.

When a man seeks great things, not for himself, but in the interest of the community, then ambition is godly, sacred, pure, the inspiration of all that is noble.

To desire honor for oneself without reference to its effect upon others is wholly evil. Along that line all despots have climbed to the thrones from which they have crushed and cursed humanity. But to desire honor for oneself in order that the honor gained may be made the occasion of help and blessing and healing is the very way by which—I say it reverently, but I say it—our Lord and Master has climbed to the throne of universal empire and will at last heal all wounds, end all weariness, wipe away all tears, and lead the race into the beatific Kingdom of God.

Therefore, true ambition is a great and gracious power. To desire, to covet in that sense, is necessarily to strive. Thus it becomes the secret power which contributes to the realization of the commonwealth itself.

The great subject of the apostle in this letter was that of

the Christian church; he was dealing with its unity and its diversity; with the fact that it is unified by the indwelling Spirit of God, with the fact that it is diversified in all those gifts which the Spirit of God bestows upon the individual members of the church; all which gifts are bestowed in order that those possessing them may exercise them, not for the benefit of themselves, but for the benefit of the church. Whenever Paul dealt with the church in this world, he dealt with it as realizing and revealing the Kingdom of God, the true social order, that which is to be established here in the world. Paul ever saw the church in this world as the instrument of the Kingdom and its revelation, because within itself the Kingdom principles are realized. Therefore, to members of the church he said: "Covet, desire with passion, the best gifts, not that you may hold high position and become famous, but that you may minister to the good of the whole church, and that the commonwealth may be realized most perfectly because of the gift which has been bestowed upon you."

In the church, therefore, and in the Kingdom of God, individual members are to be ambitious; they are to desire gifts as capacities for usefulness; and the very possession of such gifts is honor of the highest kind. In the Christian atmosphere, everything is conditioned by a man's relation to his fellow man. In the atmosphere created by the teaching of Christ and the presence of His Spirit, honor consists in the ability to serve. True honor within the church of God, within the Kingdom of God, is the possession of that, the use of which helps others and blesses them. Finally, the apostle teaches that the one true way of ambition is the way of love.

From that survey of the subject, let me turn to the answers to the question. I have received one hundred. A few missed the point of my question. One or two filled up their paper preaching against the sin of desiring any honor at all! That was due to their very limited conception of what honor means. If honor meant what they thought it meant, I should agree with all their preaching.

The majority, however, answered quite naturally. My purpose now is to group these answers generally, selecting one or two for special treatment in order that I may say some final words of counsel and help.

There were certain conspicuous facts in the answers received. The first was the almost remarkable unanimity of unselfishness of motive. To be mathematical, out of the hundred, that was true of at least seventy-nine of the answers. The answers that were of a more personal nature, nevertheless, revealed desires on a singularly high level. Among the hundred answers, there was one note of despair, and to that one note of despair I shall come in the last five minutes. The others I have grouped, and will deal with them so, saying one or two brief words in each case.

Twenty-two young people declare in one form or another that the highest honor which could be conferred upon them would be that of ability to help those who are in need. In many ways this desire was expressed among those twenty-two answers; but the desire to help the needy, the wounded by the way, the weak, the crippled, was found in answer after answer, and when I read them alone quietly, they moved my heart singularly.

The chances are everywhere! You can realize your ambition if that is it. Do not make the mistake of nursing an ambition, which does not become an inspiration to activity. Do not sit down and sigh for some great opportunity of helping the needy in some large and magnificent way. Remember Charles Kingsley at this point:

> Do the thing that's nearest,
> Though it's dull at whiles;
> Helping when you meet them,
> Lame dogs over stiles.

That is a perfect and magnificent piece of Christian philosophy. Never shall I forget sitting in this pulpit and listening once to Dr. Broughton as he preached from a group of texts. When he read them, I remember I could not think what he would make of them ". . . as He went . . ."; ". . . as He passed by . . ."; ". . . as He was in the way! . . ." That great sermon was intended to show that nearly all the works of Jesus were wrought as He was going to some place, on the way. Thank God for your ambition to help. You will have a chance before you get home if your eyes are open. By the way, the ambition may be in part realized; and if you will begin then that ambition will be the dynamic of service that moves in rhythmic harmony with the highest intention and activity of God.

Nineteen answers expressed this same desire only perhaps in a more essential way; to be able to win souls for Christ. Can there be any higher honor than that?

Again I say to you knowing how difficult it may seem to you to be, yet it is true; your chances are all about you. I venture to say to anyone who has that ambition, if you will dare to begin with all courtesy and sanity, with all manliness and womanliness and naturalness, you will be surprised to find that the very people you were afraid of have wondered why you never spoke about Christ before.

Eight declared that no greater honor could be conferred than a distinct call to enter the mission field.

I want to suggest to those who wrote that, that they take time to consider quietly whether it may not be that they have had the call. I will say no more about it than that. If not, unless you are quite sure about it, keep and guard as a sacred thing the sense that it would be an honor if it were conferred upon you. Remember, that if He is not calling you to go to the mission field, He is calling you, as His child, to hold the ropes for those who are there and to help in the great work that they are doing.

Six declared in different ways that their supreme ambition was that of pleasing Christ.

Five expressed the same thing in another way, by definitely saying that no higher honor could come to them than to hear Jesus say at the end of life, ". . . well done. . . ."

How inclusive that is! And yet how searching! Let me say to my own heart and to such we may rest assured that Christ will never look into our eyes and say ". . . well done . . ." unless it has been well done! Then let us also remember that in order that things may be well done, He says, ". . . lo, I am with you all the days. . . ."

Six answers, all of them from women, touched my heart. They said that there could come to them no greater honor than that of having committed to them the care of little children either in the homeland or in heathen countries. That is a great, gracious, beautiful, motherly desire, coming up out of the hearts of these girls and women.

Let me say to these that there are crowds of little children that they may care for near at hand. It is a great ambition. The first word of the final high commission of Jesus to Peter, in the shimmering light of morning, as it played upon the Galilean Sea, was this: ". . . Feed My lambs."

From thirteen came the answer that the highest honor that could come to them would be that of love, issuing in marriage; with the dignity of fatherhood, motherhood, and home. I thank God for every answer so honestly written. The theme is too big for me to begin to deal with here. Let me only say to all who feel that, the sense is a sacred one; guard it. You have noticed, if you have read the Song of Solomon carefully, that three times in the course of the great love song, the voice of a singer is heard who is not one of the chorus, but who sings a recitative, and these are the words:

> I adjure you, O daughters of Jerusalem . . .
> That ye stir not up, nor awaken love,
> Until he please.

Thus in the midst of the music there is a pause, and the voice of the singer is heard in warning. At the end of the marriage, following the wooing, before the betrothal, and in the midst of the united life, that revealing caution is uttered. I would that interrupting charge could be written in letters of gold and hung in every hall in which young people assemble. In the presence of the glory of love, it warns them not to trifle with that most sacred thing in life. It is a great ambition. I thank you, my brothers and sisters, who wrote for my eyes without your name appended that thought which you nurse within your heart; the great honor of the marriage relationship, of the making of home, and of caring for your own children. Never allow anyone in your presence to speak even flippantly of the great subject. Cherish the ambition; only do not wake up love until it please, and ever remember that the crowning glory of parenthood is the exercise of one of the most distinctively divine powers bestowed upon humanity.

All of these were expressions of desire that life may be of help and blessing to others.

Then I had a group of those that were more personal, but none the less high and beautiful. There was one answer which gave me pause; I am not quite sure about it, and therefore, I do not want to be unfair. One man wrote and expressed the wish that the day might come when his name should appear in the King's birthday list of honors, giving as his reason that such an appearance would be a proof of integrity on his part recognized by the nation. It made me pause, because I am not sure that its meaning is always as it appears. That is what it ought to mean. I take his wish at that high level. Perhaps that was the most selfish thing I read, yet the motive was not low; it was high.

One was a pathetic answer; hardly an answer, yet sincere. "The highest honor that could come to me would be that someone could make it possible for me to believe in God." That is pathetic, but it is full of hope. A man who will write that is on the highway to the light. As I have often said before, and I say again, the agnosticism that is an agony, is a birthpang; presently there will be the light! The agnosticism that is a pleasantry is a profanity. When a man flippantly tells me he is an agnostic and smiles, I know him to be an ignoramus and a fool, for agnosticism is never the final resting place for the honest man. I would counsel that one to cherish the ambition and make the ambition find an answer.

Someone quoted the verse from Proverbs, "A good name is rather to be chosen than great riches. . . ." That is scriptural. Nothing could be better than that, only it must be remembered that Scripture must be defined by Scripture. What does Scripture mean by a good name? A good name is like ointment poured forth! The woman breaking the alabaster box of ointment upon the feet of Jesus is the illustration. The biblical good name is not a name of hard equity and righteousness. It is like ointment poured forth. It is the good name of the soul that gives, serves, and spends.

Someone else wrote this, and here again is a strange piece

of wistfulness. "I should consider it the highest honor possible if only I could see a miracle wrought through my faith and my prayers!"

Here, again, is a soul feeling after great things, and again I say, guard the ambition, only consider the statement most carefully. Remember this: "More things are wrought by prayer than this world dreams of," and understand that you cannot measure the influence of your prayer by anything that appears. That is not a demonstration of the greatness of prayer which is startling and wonderful. Think again in this realm, my friend. I would not dampen that ardor or speak slightingly of the desire, but I would ask you to consider it.

Then I got one that was touching and beautiful. I think a hundred could have written it, but one girl wrote: "The highest honor that could come to me would be to know that in my life my mother's prayers are answered!" I know what your mother prayed for you; I know what mothers pray for us; I am with you! If presently, for it has not been so yet, if presently all my mother prayed for me can ever be true of me, that is the greatest honor I want. Cherish that ambition, live toward it, strive toward it! That ambition will be the inspiration of great living and of great service.

Another wrote, "The highest honor that could come to me would be to be loved and trusted by all in sorrow." Is not that fine? Let me ask you a question. Who is your neighbor? That question was asked quite cynically of Jesus, and you remember how He answered it. He did not tell the man who His neighbor was; He gave him the parable of the good Samaritan. Do you want to be loved? Then love! Pour out your love on some needy soul, and the answering love will satisfy you.

Another answer was written by a woman. "The highest honor that could come to me would be to have good health and a strong spiritual life." I am ambitious for these things.

I wondered as I read that, how much pain lay behind it, how much weakness and suffering. If I could find that woman and talk to her alone, I would say this to her: "Whom He loveth He chasteneth." There is a profounder meaning in your pain and weakness than yet you know! God grant you His peace!

It seems to me it is good thus to ask ourselves what our ambitions really are, and then to ask why we have such ambitions. I suppose soldiers are ambitious for the Victoria Cross. Well, they can buy them! They are worth about 7½d., I believe, as metal. But it is not the Victoria Cross men are eager for, but the thing that it signifies; the heroism that deserves it! If we have discovered what our ambition is, let us submit that ambition to the apostolic test. Love must lie at the heart of it, or it is a perilous and evil thing. If the ambition stand that test, if the reason why I desire this or that thing as an honor, is the love within me, then let me cherish my ambition, cling to it; let me be jealous and zealous in the prosecution of that which will issue in the realization thereof.

If our ambitions do not stand the test, what shall we do? Begin all over again by coming to the Christ Who sees the whole. His ambition was to reach the throne of universal empire as Saviour. The throne of universal empire, as empire, did not satisfy Him; He had that; but He ". . . emptied Himself, taking the form of a servant, being made in the likeness of men; and being found in fashion as a man, He humbled Himself, becoming obedient even unto death, yea, the death of the cross." What took Him thus down? Ambition! "Wherefore also God highly exalted Him, and gave unto Him the name which is above every name; that in the name of Jesus every knee should bow, . . . and that every tongue should confess that Jesus Christ is Lord. . . ." The name He won and bore aloft to the throne of imperial, universal power was Jesus, and the name Jesus He bears because ". . . it is He that shall save His people from their sins." His ambition was to sit upon the throne, not as sovereign merely, but as Saviour. To that Lord, let us come, and to that One, let us yield ourselves, that we may re-adjust our ambitions.

Now in conclusion, someone wrote upon the answer paper these words from Jean Ingelow:

> To strive—and fail. Yes, I did strive and fail.
>   I set mine eyes upon a certain night
> To find a certain star—and could not hail
>   With them its deep, set light.
> Fool that I was. I will rehearse my fault;
>   I, wingless, thought myself on high to lift
> Among the winged. I set these feet that halt
>   To run against the swift.

That is a note of despair which suggests there was honor coveted and not won; ambition cherished but never realized; and the writer seems to me to be settling down upon that terrible disappointment.

Seeing you chose to express yourself in poetry, let me answer you in poetry. Let me ask whoever wrote that answer to take Robert Browning's *Grammarian's Funeral*, quaint, peculiar, strange in many ways, but wonderful poetry. Read this, and read it all:

> That low man seeks a little thing to do,
>   Sees it and does it;

> This high man with a great thing to pursue,
>   Dies ere he knows it.
> That low man goes on adding one to one,
>   His hundred's soon hit;
> This high man, aiming at a million,
>   Misses an unit.
> That, has the world here—should he need the next
>   Let the world mind him!
> This, throws himself on God, and unperplexed
>   Seeking shall find Him.

That is finer philosophy than the other. What did you tell me, that you set your eyes upon a certain night to find a certain star, and you could not hail them with its deep-set light? You did better than you knew probably. The only wrong you have committed is that of imagining that you did not attain that toward which you were aiming. It is the aim, the ambition, and the consecrated activity that grows out of it, which matter! No, who is there here among us who has ever seen anything of the real glory luring him or her to the heights who has already reached them?

We had better get back to the Bible. This man Paul when he had been three-and-thirty years following Christ, wrote his autobiography in a love letter, for the Philippian letter is preeminently a love letter. In the third chapter we have these words, and here is nothing finer in literature:

"Not that I have already obtained, or am already made perfect: but I press on, if so be that I may lay hold on that for which also I was laid hold on by Christ Jesus. Brethren, I count not myself yet to have laid hold: but one thing I do, forgetting the things which are behind, and stretching forward to the things which are before, I press on toward the goal. . . ."

Mark his attitude, dear friend of mine who wrote that poetry. Take heart! The night is black, the stars are not seen, but they are there! Keep your eyes toward them, and presently, ere you know it they will be seen! Or, it may be that you will never see them, because while you look, the morning will break and the stars are never seen when the sun is shining!

CHAPTER III

SOUR GRAPES

In those days they shall say no more, The fathers have eaten sour grapes, and the children's teeth are set on edge. But everyone shall die for his own iniquity: every man that eateth the sour grapes, his teeth shall be set on edge.
JEREMIAH 31:29; 30.

What mean ye, that ye use this proverb concerning the land of Israel, saying, The fathers have eaten sour grapes, and the children's teeth are set on edge? As I live, saith the Lord God, ye shall not have occasion any more to use this proverb in Israel. Behold, all souls are Mine; as the soul of the father, so also the soul of the son is Mine; the soul that sinneth, it shall die.
EZEKIEL 18:2-4.

DIVINE RELIGION HAS NO MORE INSIDIOUS AND DEADLY FOE THAN misrepresentation, whether in the lives of those who profess it or in the interpretation of its sacred writings.

Nothing can be more disastrous in its effect upon men than a false doctrine; that is, a misinterpretation of what God has said to men, resulting as it must in a false conception of God and of man's relation to Him. And I am growingly convinced that amongst the most pernicious misrepresentations are those which are popular, general, superficial, based upon some isolated passage, and resulting from a conception due to superficial observation. General, popular, superficial, are words I have used of set purpose. These general impressions, resulting from a glance at things upon the surface and expressing themselves in some passage of Scripture, which seems to square with the opinion formed as the result of such superficial observation; these, after all, are far more deadly and perilous heresies than those more familiar ones of the Christian church against which we so often protest.

It is to one such misinterpretation that I desire now to direct attention, because it is so common, and because it is in many respects doing harm. I refer to the popular quotation and interpretation of that proverb which occurs in both of my texts; ". . . The fathers have eaten sour grapes, and the children's teeth are set on edge." Let me say immediately that the statement is not true. It is constantly quoted today, glibly quoted, in the course of conversation in order to clinch an argument. It is constantly quoted in order to prove the helplessness of a man because of his relationship to his father. A man has yielded to certain courses of vice, certain habits of meanness, and either he himself or someone else will say in excuse for him, ". . . The fathers have eaten sour grapes, and the children's teeth are set on edge." That is to say, this man cannot help these things because he has inherited the tendency from his father.

It is constantly quoted also in regard to that most pernicious and evil doctrine that God punishes children for the sins of their fathers. Neither of these statements is true.

Let us consider, then, first the history of this proverb; ". . . The fathers have eaten sour grapes, and the children's teeth are set on edge"; in the second place, God's answer to the proverb as we have it here in Holy Writ. From that twofold consideration, let us finally attempt to state the resulting truths which are of importance to ourselves.

Let us first take the proverb itself. What is its place in Scripture? There is a reverent yet mischievous worship of the Bible which leads people away from its spiritual value and corrective force. Let me give you a characteristic illustration of what I mean. It is said that the Abyssinian church, having canonized all the names in the Bible that were the names of good men, proceeded to canonize Pontius Pilate because his name is in the Bible, and he became Saint Pilate." That is a very grotesque illustration of what I mean. Sermons have sometimes been preached upon this proverb as if it were true, because it is in the Bible. Let us see how it comes to be in the Bible. It is found twice and only twice—once in Jeremiah and once in Ezekiel. The prophecy of Jeremiah having been uttered somewhere about the time of Ezekiel's, perhaps a little earlier, I refer first to it. This particular proverb is found among those which Jeremiah uttered in the last days before the fall of Jerusalem. It was a wondrous ministry that ministry of Jeremiah, because it was a ministry foredoomed to failure. Others of the prophets spoke the great Word of God, always in hope that the Word might be listened to and obeyed, and that there might be some improvement in the circumstances of the people as they turned to God; but Jeremiah had to face the certainty that men would listen to him, and then laugh at him, and sin again. Nevertheless he had to go on proclaiming the great message. It was a ministry of failure. If we study his prophecies carefully, we discover this most interesting and wonderful fact, that in the darkest days, when Jeremiah was in the dungeon, his prophecies broke out into their most optimistic notes. The prophecies of hope were uttered from the dungeon. It is in the midst of these prophecies of hope that this particular proverb is to be found. At the close of chapter thirty-one, the great message of hope is singing itself out; through all the darkness the prophet was looking toward the light, from the midst of adversity he was gazing upon a restoration. "Behold, the days come, saith the Lord, that I will sow the house of Israel. . . . Behold, the days come, saith the Lord, that I will make a new covenant with the house of Isreal. . . . Behold, the days come, saith the Lord, that I will build the city. . . ." These are the opening words of three strophes. He was looking on to wonderful days that are yet to be. But, remember, he was in the dungeon, he was in the prison, he was in the midst of the most dark and evil hours of the history of Judah. "Behold, the days come. . . . Behold, the days come. . . . Behold, the days come. . . . In those days ye shall no more say, The fathers have eaten sour grapes, and the children's teeth are set on edge. But everyone shall die for his own iniquity: every soul that eateth the sour grapes, . . . it shall die." He was looking to the days of restoration when men shall return to true conceptions of God, and he declared that in those days false proverbs shall cease.

I turn to Ezekiel, and there I find the text again. Ezekiel received his great call to prophetic ministry six years before the fall of Jerusalem, but never exercised his ministry in Jerusalem. Away yonder in Babylonia on the banks of the River Chebar, in the midst of the influence of Babylonish things where he saw those mystic representations of God, the revolving wheels, the burning electron, there this wonderful prophet of hope exercised his ministry. While he was doing so, there visited him certain elders from Jerusalem who came to talk with him about the situation. The prophet received the elders of Israel, and among other things, he said to them, "Why do you use this proverb in Jerusalem? The fathers have eaten sour grapes, and the children's teeth are set on edge. What do you mean by it?" All chapter eighteen is in refutation of that proverb.

When the proverb was born I cannot say, but here it came into use. This is its first appearance in biblical history, and its last; but it has persisted in the speech of men until now. The days in which we first find the proverb were days of national ruin, days of national disaster, of spiritual deadness and moral turpitude. There is an acidity about it that bites. It is striking and suggestive. I can hardly recite it without feeling my teeth are on edge; "The fathers have eaten sour grapes, and the children's teeth are set on edge." I go back to the day of Isaiah, the great prophet of the theocracy, and I hear him singing a song of a vineyard, and the owner of the vineyard says he has planted a very pleasant vineyard with a very fruitful vine. ". . . he looked that it should bring forth grapes, and behold it brought forth wild grapes." I wonder if someone took hold of that thought of the vineyard, and said, "Yes, and the fathers have eaten the wild grapes that are green and acrid. The fathers in the days of Isaiah not only produced wild grapes; they ate them; and as a result, the children are suffering, their teeth are set on edge." The men of Israel, whoever formed the proverb, were using it in that sense of excuse for their sin of reflection upon God. It was the utterance of a word of despair, "We cannot help it. Jerusalem is going to pieces. Zedekiah is playing the fool; punishment is falling upon us. We cannot help it. . . . The fathers have eaten sour grapes, and the children's teeth are set on edge."

The proverb is used today in exactly the same way. That use of the proverb persists in the most remarkable way through the millenniums, and we hear it still. Sometimes it is used with more flippancy than in the case of these men;

sometimes with the same despair. Many a man will look into the face of the Christian worker and say, "Look at me. See what I am. I cannot help it. My father has eaten sour grapes, and my teeth are set on edge." Another man will say, "What does God mean by this? I am suffering for my father's sins."

It is important that we should consider God's answer to the proverb. First, its presence in Holy Scripture is due to the fact that it had to be denied. It is only to be found in the Bible in order to be contradicted, in order that, like a base coin, it might be nailed to the counter forever as counterfeit and untrue. Yet it is current still. Let us listen to the answer. Jeremiah answered the proverb in two ways. First by foretelling a day in which it would be abandoned altogether; and second, by giving it the lie direct. Now notice carefully the two verses. First we have the prophecy of abandonment. "In those days they shall say no more, The fathers have eaten sour grapes, and the children's teeth are set on edge." He was looking on, as I have already said, to the days of restoration, to the days of the new covenant, and though the most part of Jeremiah's prophecy may be unfamiliar to many Christian people, that part of it is quite familiar by reason of the fact that it is quoted in the New Testament. "I will put My law in their inward parts, and in their heart will I write it; and I will be their God, and they shall be My people; and they shall teach no more every man his neighbour, and every man his brother, saying, Know the Lord, for they shall all know Me, from the least of them unto the greatest of them." In those days, the days of the New Covenant, men will not use a proverb like this, said Jeremiah. In those days of repentance, repentance on the part of men and consequent repentance on the part of God; those days when men, repentant, shall turn to God, and God, repentant, shall turn from judgment back again to mercy; those days in which there shall pass away forever more false conceptions of God; this proverb will have no place in current speech.

Thus, by predicting a period of abandonment, Jeremiah denied the truth of the proverb; and then proceeded to emphatic denial, by statement of the opposite truth, that everyone shall die for his own iniquity. Then, in order that there may be no mistake, he borrowed the figure of the proverb itself; ". . . every man that eateth the sour grapes, his teeth shall be set on edge."

Then when we turn to the prophecy of Ezekiel, perhaps uttered a little later than this of Jeremiah or it may be almost at the same time, we have a remarkable illustration of biblical exposition. In Jeremiah 31:30 are the words: ". . . every one shall die for his own iniquity: every man that eateth the sour grapes, his teeth shall be set on edge." Ezekiel 18 is a sermon on that text, an exposition of it. Let us consider that eighteenth chapter of Ezekiel in order to see what are the things the prophet said in answer to this proverb.

First of all he laid down one fundamental fact; ". . . all souls are Mine. . . ." At the close of the chapter he stated a final fact; "For I have no pleasure in the death of the sinner." Between that fundamental fact and that final fact he elaborated his argument, taking illustrations from life.

What is this fundamental fact? God says, ". . . all souls are Mine; . . . the soul of the father . . . the soul of the son . . ."; equally, separately, individually. God declares in that word by Ezekiel that He is not distanced from any man by the distance of that man's father. All souls are Mine; that of the father, and that of the son. God is as near to the son as to the father, to the father as to the son. The father may have as close relationship with God as the son; the son may have as intimate dealings with God as the father. That is indeed fundamental, for if that be grasped, the whole difficulty is dealt with, and that is why it is placed at the forefront of the argument. ". . . all souls are Mine. . . ." Every soul can have direct, first-hand, immediate dealing with God. It sometimes seems almost too wonderful a statement to find in the Old Testament. It is the culminating doctrine of the New. In other words, full of mystic beauty and tender poetry, it is the thing that Jesus told a woman of Samaria who was a sinner, making His application of the fundamental truth that in every life there is individual possibility for worship; neither in Jerusalem, nor in this mountain set apart, not here nor there by appointment, but where, anywhere, the spirit of a man goes out to God, there God is.

Therefore, no man is shut off from God by the distance of his father, and no man is brought near to God by the coupling-link of his father. ". . . all souls are Mine . . ."; the soul of the father, the soul of the son equally.

Then he proceeded to that remarkable argument by illustration, in which he does not merely take individual men, but takes them in the line of their descent. Remember, he was dealing with a Hebrew people, an Eastern people, who understood a great deal more about the solidarity of the race than we do; who believed in the peculiar continuity that runs from father to son down through the generations; who realized that a son is linked to that which is gone and responsible for that which is to come—a great truth, but a great truth which may be abused, as it was here. With that in mind, notice how the prophet traced the descent. He said in effect, here is a man, a good man, and a true man, and a righteous man. He lives. That man has a son. He is evil; he turns from his father's ways of goodness. He dies because he is evil. Watch still the line of descent. That evil man has a son who is good. He is true, he is righteous. He lives. Now we talk about the principle of heredity skipping one generation and going to another. That may be quite true. But God says, however true that is, there is another truth, and that truth is that every single man stands in immediate relationship with God and can have dealings with God. He will be judged ultimately not by the things inherited but by the things he did, in view of the immediate force at his disposal, which is the force of his right of access to God. A good man lives because he is good. A son turns to evil courses; he is not spared for his father's goodness but is judged for his own acts of evil. He has a son who turns back to goodness; he does not die for his father's evil; he lives because of his own goodness. All of which means that to turn from evil is to live; to turn from right is to die.

The prophet then went a good deal beyond the question of descent; he dealt with purely personal things. Here is a man who says, "I am handicapped by what I did; I am not blaming my father, but I am blaming those years that the canker-worm has eaten. There is my past. There is my sin. I cannot get away from it. It masters me still." To that man God says, "I put Myself between your past and you; and if you will turn from that past to do right, you will live."

Another man says, "Yes, I know I am going wrong today; but I used to be right; therefore I am still all right." God says, "No, you will be condemned, whatever you did yesterday, because of the sin of today." If my past was one of wrong and I want to turn to right, God comes between me and my past. If my past was right and I turn to wrong, God cuts off that past of right and does not reckon it, but deals with me for what I am.

If that be the answer to the proverb according to Jeremiah's statement and Ezekiel's argument, what is the answer according to Christ? The answer according to Christ is the fulfilment of what these men foretold. It is stated in Jeremiah's prophecy that He will introduce a new covenant whereby the law shall be written upon the heart. That new covenant is fulfilled in Christ. Infinitely the most beautiful poetry in Ezekiel's prophecy is the story of the river that flows from the temple of God. Is there anything more beautiful in the story than this: "Everything shall live whither soever the river cometh"? In Christ that mystic prophecy has been fulfilled, for through Him the river of the water of life is flowing freely. Everything liveth wherever the river comes. In Him men are brought to a recognition of God and of their right of access to God. In Him men are brought into actual dealing with God. So that for a man to sit down and excuse his sin, or utter his blasphemies against heaven, or wail in an agony of despair in the words of this proverb, ". . . The fathers have eaten sour grapes, and the children's teeth are set on edge," is to deny the teaching of the Bible, and to deny the message and the mission of the Christ.

Let us attempt in a closing word to gather from this meditation one or two essential truths. I put the first into this very definite form. God never punishes children for the sins of their fathers. Nowhere in the Old or New Testaments is it stated that God punishes children for their father's sins, except the children continue in the sins of their fathers. I know the passage that has been quoted, and I go back deliberately to it in the Book of Exodus. In connection with the giving of the law to the people, in the fifth verse of the twentieth chapter I read, ". . . I the Lord thy God am a jealous God, visiting the iniquity of the fathers upon the children"—but we must not stop there—"upon the third and upon the fourth generation of them that hate Me." Continuity in the sin of the father will bring continuity in the judgment and punishment of the child. And then, as if in very deed, as one of the prophets said, "judgment is ever one of God's strange acts," mark how the rest of the world runs—"and showing lovingkindness unto thousands of them that love Me . . ." and that does not mean thousands of individuals, but of generations. But there must be continuity in love. Where there is continuity in sin, there is continuity in judgment. Where there is continuity in love, there is continuity in mercy.

I pray you remember in passing in this connection, for the subject has many side issues, that a distinction must be made between punishment and chastisement. It may be in that larger operation of God with the race, that I do suffer pain as the result of sin in some of my forefathers, but that is not punishment. I am permitted by that very suffering to share in the healing process of the race. Punishment is the pain of disease; chastisement is the pain of excision. The difference must always be borne in mind. Because we are members of a race, a sinning race, most humbly and reverently, and yet with all confidence may I say it, those of us who name the Name of Christ and who enter into fellowship with Him who came to bear the sins of others, are permitted to have fellowship with His sufferings, to make up that which is behind in the sufferings of Christ. There are men today who understand that in their suffering, resulting from the wrong-doing of their fathers, they are not being punished, but they have come into co-operation with the great passion of God through which He is cleansing not a man alone, but a race, and is moving toward the establishment of His ultimate Kingdom. God never punishes a child for his father's sin except a child continue in that sin.

That leads me to another word. Someone says, "All that is true, I grant you. But there are some children who continue in their father's sins because they cannot help it." That is quite true. I admit that. That is the operation of the law of heredity. It is a perfectly true thing. We cannot escape it.

That is to say, it is true if we shut God out of account; if we put God merely at the back of a process of law, and know nothing of Him in personal, actual experience. If God is merely One through whose propulsion all things proceed, and I am merely one "within the grasp of law," it is no use talking to me. I cannot help it. There is fire in my blood. There is poison in my mind. The devil in solution was transmitted to me, and I cannot fight against it. If there is no Christ and no Bible and no Christian religion, then heredity is the last word, except, perhaps, as we may balance it by environment. But in the name of God we have our Bible, we have our Christ, we have our God; and the Bible declares that God is the deepest fact in human life for every man. The writer of the letter to the Hebrews said, ". . . we had the fathers of our flesh to chasten us, and we gave them reverence: shall we not much rather be in subjection unto a Father of spirits, and live?" A most wonderful word revealing the relationship of every man to his own father and to God. My father was the father of my flesh; he was not the creator of my spirit. I am related to my father in the flesh. He transmitted to me the forces of the flesh but had nothing to do with the creation of my spirit. My spirit in its first creation was of God. God has bound Himself to humanity in a strange and marvelous mystery, whereby He is the creator of the spirit in the case of the procreation of every human being, an appalling and a wonderful mystery; He creates the spirit. If you inherit your tendencies in that delicate and marvelous thing, your flesh, your body, from your father; underneath it is yourself, your spirit life, which your father did not generate but which God did create. Am I to be bound by the accident of flesh and blood, or am I to hear a voice that bids me turn back again to the Father of spirits, that through Him I may receive the power that shall be superior to everything else, and live? Blessed be God, it is ever strangely marvelous and majestic and inexplicable; but it is the operation of the spiritual law. The good man lives; the bad man dies; the good man lives.

Before the prophet had done, he who looked upon the face of God upon the banks of the Chebar must sing of mercy as well as of judgment. Before the prophet had concluded he sang, "The Lord loveth not the death of a sinner." Therefore, to turn to Him is to find power for life against all the evil that inheritance gives to me. And more, against my own past, for if I have done wickedness and will turn to Him, I shall live.

Let me gather up all the things that are in my heart in final words, and let me apply them. If your teeth are on edge, do not blame your father. Whosoever eateth sour grapes, his teeth shall be set on edge. If your teeth are on edge, you have eaten the sour grapes.

"Yes, but my father did eat them, and I had a tendency to sour grapes before I was born." Is that so? Then God is greater than your father, and the forces that He places at your disposal are greater than all your tendency toward sour grapes.

"Yes, but I have eaten them myself. I plead guilty. God help me, I am guilty. I have eaten them. My teeth are on edge, and I have contracted a liking for sour grapes! Though I hate them, I must have them."

God is greater than one's liking. Get back to Him. He will put Himself between you and your father, and between you and your past, for the river of God is flowing, and there is life wherever the river comes.

CHAPTER IV

FOUR MISTAKES ABOUT CHRIST

Is not this the Carpenter . . . ?
MARK 6:3

John the Baptizer is risen from the dead, and therefore do these powers work in him.
MARK 6:14

Jesus therefore perceiving that they were about to come and take Him by force, to make Him King, withdrew again into the mountain Himself alone.
JOHN 6:15

. . . they, when they saw Him walking on the sea, supposed that it was a ghost, and cried out.
MARK 6:49

WE ARE OFTEN TROUBLED ABOUT CHRIST, THAT SO MANY DIFferent views of Him are held, and yet that is almost the inevitable sequence of the wonder of His Person. The fierce conflicts that have raged around the Christ—as to Who He is, whence He came, what is the real meaning of His mission—all are due to the finite nature of the mind of man in its attempt to grasp the infinite wonder and glory of the Person of the Lord Christ.

We have read these chapters in order that we may see that exactly the same things were true in the time when He was in the world. He was manifested among men, Himself a man, but a perpetual enigma to men. In this one brief chapter, brief by comparison with the whole fact of His ministry, Jesus is described as a carpenter, as a prophet, as a king, and as a phantom. These opinions were all wrong and they were all right. In every one of them there was an element of truth; but in each case, only one truth being recognized and discovered, false deductions were made. The mistake in each case was due to the limiting of Christ which resulted from an attempt to express all the truth concerning Him in the language of one particular manifestation of His presence and His power.

Let us then consider first the opinions that were given here; second, the mistakes that were made here; in order, third, to discover the lessons that are suggested here.

We need not tarry very long in examining the opinions. The story is familiar to all of us. Yet let us take time to recall the surroundings in each particular case. In the first, "Is not this the carpenter, the son of Mary, . . ." we have the opinion of His kinsfolk, the opinion of the people who in all likelihood were most perfectly acquainted with Him within the narrow circle of His human life. Eighteen years of that life had been spent in Nazareth. There He had grown up in the sight of the men and women of that little township just off the great highways, but yet so near to them that the men and women living there were in all probability familiar with the things happening in Jerusalem and the towns adjacent, for these highways between Jerusalem and other great centers lay at the foot of the hill. Nazareth was a small township, so small that we are led to imagine from the actual wording of the criticism, that Jesus of Nazareth was the one carpenter;

"Is not this the carpenter. . . ." They knew Him perfectly well. He had grown up in their midst. They had seen the natural and beautiful boy advance to young manhood, until He came to be about thirty years of age. Now, after a brief absence, He had gone back, as a Teacher. It was not at all strange that this young man should begin to speak. The strange fact was the method and the marvel of His teaching. The picture is very striking. In that little synagogue, the men who knew Him best, looking, listening, and amazed, until, interrupting His speech, as the story suggests, they said, "Whence hath this Man these things?" What is the power that lies behind this strange manifestation of wisdom and these strange and wondrous works of which we hear in Nazareth? Then they began to account for Him, "Is not this the carpenter . . . ?" And observe how particular they were to place Him, how particular to show that they knew all about Him, "The son of Mary, and brother of James and Joses and Judas and Simon? and are not His sisters here with us? . . ." If we would know the tone and temper in which the question was asked, we must include the next sentence, "And they were offended in Him." They stumbled over Him, because they could not understand Him.

In that criticism they declared a truth that we are always thankful they did declare, that Jesus was a carpenter. They knew Him, as a man who wrought with His hands for the support of His own earthly life, through the larger part thereof. "Is not this the carpenter . . . ?" they were quite right, and they were sadly wrong.

Let us pass to the next scene. The fame of Him was spreading through all the country round about, increased by the mission of His apostles. They had been sent out, and we are told that they cast out devils and anointed many sick with oil and healed them. The fame of Jesus was thus spreading, and it reached the court of Herod, and Herod immediately said, "John the Baptizer is risen from the dead...." Herod had not seen Him. Herod never did see Him until the final hour, and then he never heard His voice. Christ declined to speak to him. But he heard the story of His power. These words of Herod reveal the impression made by the story of the work of Christ on a man who was immoral. To satisfy the vengeful nature of a wanton, Herod had beheaded John. An evil man can behead a prophet of God, but he cannot bury him. The prophet will follow him and will be with him in the night. If there is blood on your hand, you can say with Lady Macbeth, "Out, damned spot," but you cannot cleanse that hand. Herod heard of a prophet, heard of wonders wrought, and all the superstition in his guilty nature mingling with the moral cowardice of the man, he said, "John the Baptizer is risen from the dead...." The first opinion was due to the unfairness of the jealous. The second was due to the cowardice of the immoral.

Then we come to the story of that wonderful feeding of the five thousand, a kingly act in the true and full sense of the word kingly. It is said here of Christ, a thing so often repeated of Him, that He saw the multitudes, and He was moved with compassion for them. Why? Because they were as sheep without a shepherd, and it would be quite as accurate to say, a nation without a king; for God's kings are all shepherds. The true qualification for kingship in the economy of God, as the Bible reveals from beginning to end, is the shepherd qualification. They were as sheep without a shepherd, and "He taught them many things"; and then He fed them. There had been no movement towards His crowning while He taught them, but the moment He fed them they wanted to crown Him. They said, "this is the King we have been looking for"; and they would fain take Him by force and make Him a King.

Mark only gives us the picture of Jesus suddenly dismissing His disciples and returning to the mountain, but John tells us the reason; "Jesus therefore perceiving that they were about to come and take Him by force to make Him King, withdrew again." They desired to make Him a King upon the basis of His ability to satisfy their material hunger. They reasoned, He is a King, He is kingly, He can feed, and so they would crown Him. That view was that of the desire of the selfish.

We come to the last scene, the most difficult to deal with in some ways. We will look at it in its simplicity and naturalness. He retired to the mountain to pray, and the disciples, in obedience to His command, pointed the prow of their boat to the other side. The wind was contrary, and they were distressed in rowing. Then He went after them from the height to meet them by appointment on the other side of the sea. He walked across the waters, with no intention whatever of coming to them in the boat. He would have passed them by, which distinctly means that it was His purpose, that it was His intention to pass them. They saw this figure moving over the waters, and they cried out for fear and said, "It is an apparition, a phantom." This was the dread of the perplexed.

He is a carpenter. That opinion was due to the unfairness of the jealous. He is a prophet. That dread was the outcome of the cowardice of the immoral. He is a king. That view was based upon the desire of the selfish. It is an apparition. That was language resulting from the dread of perplexed hearts.

Let us turn, in the second place, from this brief glance at the circumstances and the opinions, to consider the mistakes. But just let it be recognized that there were elements of truth in all these opinions. When these men of Nazareth said, "He is one of us," they said a true thing. He is One of us. They were perfectly correct as to His relationship to Mary and as to the relationship borne to Him by the men and women they knew. He was one of them, so much one of them that they had never dreamed that there was anything beyond immediate kinship in His nature. I think that we might take out of the old prophetic writings one word and inscribe it in imagination over the door of the shop in which Jesus had wrought and used the tools of His craft for eighteen years; "There was the hiding of His power." There was no halo round His brow, no peculiar flash in His eye that suggested Deity, nothing in His appearance to make these men think for one single moment that He was other than a peasant. He was One of us. It was perfectly true. There was nothing in His appearance to make men imagine that He was anything other than they were.

When King Herod said, "John . . . is risen from the dead," there was an element of truth, not in that supposition of John's resurrection, but in the thing that made Herod quake, the consciousness that there was still a voice bringing him face to face with moral standards. John had made Herod tremble in olden days when he had listened to him. Herod had been almost persuaded to righteousness by John. There is one little phrase that indicates this. Herod "heard him gladly." Herod was now merely the wreck of a man, wholly sensual. John was dead and buried, but a voice was sounding. Herod had not escaped the law, he had not escaped that prophetic note that makes men tremble. He was perfectly right in thinking of Jesus as a prophet, stern indeed, enunciating the severest of all ethics.

The people who desired to make Him King were perfectly right. He is King, and He is King upon the basis of His shepherd character; and as King He will provide for all the necessities of those over whom He reigns if they do but obey His teaching. That, however, is the order. He taught them and then fed them. He is the one King Who really provides for the material needs of men, Who will feed them and feed them perfectly.

I watch the disciples as looking at the strange figure moving over the waters through the darkness of the night they say, "It is an apparition!" Here was something coming toward them that they could not fully apprehend, something upon which they could not put their measurement. They forgot the tossing waves and howling wind, the material and present difficulties, in the presence of this new and mystic difficulty, the difficulty of a personality that they could not apprehend, could not measure, could not weigh. There was an element of truth in what they said. Christ is still an enigma. We cannot say the final thing concerning Him. He still moves over the rough waters, surprising and startling men; and men see Him as He passes, but not clearly, and catching some mystic going of the Christ, they are still filled with perplexity.

Wherein, then, lay the mistake in each case? In the limitation of their views placed upon the Christ Himself. If we could gather these four opinions and express them in one statement, I think we might be near the whole truth about the Christ. I put that carefully, because I am not sure that it is correct. Yet, think of it for a moment. What were the things that these men discovered? His nearness, His severity, His authority, and the infinite mystery of His being. That surely is the Christ; near, "One of us"; severe, so that no sinner could escape Him, though He robe Himself in purple and hide Himself in the court. King so that He will enunciate His moral ethic, and to the people who obey it, He will be the Provider of all their material need; and yet, an infinite Mystery, baffling the attempt of the centuries to place Him, breaking the mould of every philosophy that attempts to include Him, forevermore appearing in some new guise, some new wonder, some new marvel of His power. Just as the disciples think that they have understood Him and seen the ultimate of His wonder, He dismisses them across the water, and hies Him to the mountain, and then startles them by walking over the water that baffles them. The element of the mysterious in the fact of the Christ perpetually breaks upon the consciousness, and men come to recognize that they cannot say the final thing concerning Him. Near, One of us, a carpenter; severe, so that immorality is always dragged into light. King, with an ethic the severest that men have ever dreamed of, and a power the most generous that humanity can ever hope for. Yet ever beyond us, a mystery, an apparition.

In either of these cases, the recognition of all would have prevented the false conclusion. If they could have mingled with that conception that He is One of us, the very thing the disciples said, "He is a phantom," and known that beyond the manifest was the mystery of His being, then they would have listened to His teaching and not have been offended. Or if the disciples, when they saw Him only as a phantom and hardly knew Him, could have remembered the One Who in love bade them pass from the sea to the mountain, they would have been delivered from all false fear. If Herod could have known the nearness of this Man to him in all the sympathy of His heart, in all the authority of His kingship, and in all the infinite mystery of His being, then he would have left the court and found his way to this King of kings, not merely to submit to Him but to receive from Him all He could bestow. The mistake was in limiting the Christ. A recognition of the whole truth would have prevented the false conclusion in each case.

What then are the lessons suggested by these things said concerning the Christ in this sixth chapter of Mark? The first is that the opinion a man has of Christ invariably reveals the man. The men who attempted to place Him as a carpenter did so because they were jealous and were not prepared to be honest enough in the presence of the wonders they confessed of word and work to find out the deeper secret. The fear that shook the heart of Herod like a tempest in the night at the rumor of Jesus was the result of his own impurity. The desire to make Him a King as a wholesale food-provider was based upon personal selfishness and the materialization of life. The fear of the phantom in the case of the men who were in the pathway of obedience, with their prow pointed to the shore He had indicated, was the outcome of their own doubt and their own questioning. Every criticism of Christ is a revelation, not of Christ, but of the men who make the criticism. Whenever a man shall attempt to place the Christ and leave Him as One of us, it is a revelation of the fact that he has lost a sense of the spiritual. Whenever a man is afraid of the Christ, and dare not name His name, and endeavors to escape the message of His prophecy and kingship, it is because in that man's heart there is something of impurity; the only man that dreads the Christ is the impure man. When a man shall eliminate from the teaching of the Scripture and the church, all supernatural elements and attempt to make Christ merely the leader of a party that shall feed men on this earth, it is because in that man's heart there is enshrined a selfishness which is wholly and utterly of the dust. When we who name His Name are afraid of Him, the fear is the outcome of our own doubting and our own questioning, and our lack of courage. All criticism of Christ is a revelation of the attitude of those who criticize.

This chapter is a wonderfully living chapter. All these things are still being said about the Christ. We are still being told that He is One of us. Men are still attempting to place Him on the human plane. We are still being told that it is

John risen from the dead, an ethical Teacher, with a severer note, and a fuller program, but nothing other. We are still being told that Christ's chief mission is to feed hungry men and women with material bread. We are still being told that Christ is an unreal personality, an apparition, a phantom. Such mistakes arise from imperfect knowledge of the Christ in every case. There is always the element of truth and always the neglect of the whole truth. The truth? Yes, nothing but the truth; but not the whole truth. He is One of us; He is an ethical Teacher; He does care about hungry men and will provide for their need; He is an infinite mystery. But He is not merely One of us, He is more than all, and the very universality of His appeal to humanity is a revelation of His wholeness and His greatness. We can find no other teacher, no other leader that appeals to humanity as such. We cannot take any great leader of whom we may think away from the place in which he lived and see him perfectly fitting and at home in another locality. It is unthinkable to imagine that Oliver Cromwell could have delivered France. He belonged here, and you cannot put him anywhere else. It would be an utterly vain piece of imagination to bring Abraham Lincoln and put him into this country. He belonged to the New Land, and God put him there, and he did his work there, but he was local. But this Man—man of my manhood, bone of my bone, flesh of my flesh, human of my humanity—you may put down wherever humanity is and men will gather round Him and find in Him their head tribesman, their chief of clan, their great ideal. The universality of His humanity is demonstration of the fact that He is something more, infinitely more than merely one of us. Ethical teacher, He assuredly was, but infinitely more. And if not infinitely more, then nothing to me—I freely say it to you. I speak as a witness; if Jesus has done nothing for me than give me an ethical system, then that appals me, that reveals my paralysis and leaves me helpless. But He is more, oh troubled sinner. Thank God if you have come so far as to tremble in the presence of the Christ. He is more than an ethical Teacher, He is a Saviour. He is One Who, if Herod will but have it so, will purify Herod's polluted soul. He is One Who, if you will but have it so, will break the power of canceled sin. Infinitely more than an ethical Teacher, One Who communicates to men the new forces that will remake them and enable them to fulfil the ideals of His teaching. A food Provider? Surely yes, but first a Teacher, and we have no right to claim that the Christ shall fulfil His function of supplying material need save in the order of His own revelation. He must be the crowned King, and He must be crowned, not upon the basis that He will care for the body, but upon the basis that He includes in the grasp of His purpose, eternity, and the spiritual things. Not temporal in His power ultimately, but eternal and therefore temporal. He will not remake the social conditions of today by dealing with the decaying material at His hand. He will remake the social conditions by bringing to bear upon them the regenerating forces of God. Unless men submit at that point, they have no claim upon the fulfilment of the function of His kingship for the feeding of men. The multitudes will make Him King by popular acclaim, and He will escape to the mountains. But for the little group, and the growing number, and the ultimate assembly of souls who crown Him Lord in the spiritual and central and fundamental realm, for them He will build the city and bring in the ultimate triumph of righteousness.

But is He an apparition? Let me answer thus. Every day I live and think and preach, I am more conscious that I cannot say the last word about this Christ. I would be very sorry to attempt to tell anyone exactly what my Christology is. Only this I know, that whenever I come into the presence of this human life, so real, so definite, so warm, so tender, so actual, I have to bow and confess, My Lord and my God. Charles Wesley, you remember, put the whole thing into a daring phrase, "God contracted to a span, incomprehensibly man." Let us not be afraid at the mystery, but touch the manifest. Let us no longer stand away at infinite distance from the Christ, afraid of the things that cannot be encompassed in human thought or expressed in human speech; but let us get near to the Jesus of these Gospels as He appears before us, eyes wet with tears, face often beaming with the smile of a great gladness, touching familiarly and healing in His touch, putting His arms about the children, his heart full of infinite compassion; let us get near to Him and know this, that the One Who moves across the storm-tossed waters with the appearance of an apparition is the One Who will look at us and say, "Be not afraid, it is I."

The last word is this. These mistakes about Jesus limit Him in His power. Observe what is said about the men at Nazareth. ". . . He could there do no mighty work. . . ." Why not? ". . . because of their unbelief." If we make Him only the Carpenter of Nazareth, He can do no more for us than the Carpenter of Nazareth. We put our limitation upon Him, and He is limited by our limited conception. He had no word for Herod, never spoke to Him; one of the most appalling and awful revelations of the New Testament. Herod never met Him until Pilate sent Him to him; and when He came, He uttered never a word. He refused to be crowned because He was limited by their conception. He could not exercise the power of His Kingship upon that desire. Finally, He could not pass the disciples by. We are inclined to say that is full of comfort! It is not. Study the story carefully. He would have passed them by and better for them that He should. Had He passed them by, what then? Then, they would have learned by weathering the storm in His power, some lesson of His power. He is always passing us by. You know the old story of the woman who saw three women at prayer. She dreamed that the Lord passed by, and to the first He came and bent over her with tender caress; to the next He spoke but a word; but the last He passed almost roughly. The dreaming woman thought, "How tenderly the Lord loves the first; the second is not so dear to His heart; and with the third He is evidently angry." Then the Lord, in her dream, came to her, and said "Oh woman of the world, how wrongly hast thou judged? That first woman needs all of My care and tenderness to keep her following at all; that second woman is of stronger faith, and I therefore am hastening her preparation for yet higher service; but the last one I can absolutely depend upon; and by the very processes by which I deny her My voice, I am preparing her for the highest service of all."

He would have passed them! We are not ready for Him to do so! Then in great pity He will stop and come on board. But, ah me! if I could only let Him have all His way. We limit Him in His power when we limit our conceptions of Him. Let us never forget this. Let me give you the whole philosophy by quotation. D. L. Moody said, in this country many years ago, in his own homely, straight, and magnificent way: "Christ is just as great as your faith makes Him."

Then, what shall we do? We will attempt to know Him better. Paul's last great letters thrill with one desire for all his children in the faith; that they might know; and the measure of our knowledge of Him will be the measure in which we are able to put our trust in Him. We come to the fuller knowledge by following the light of the knowledge we have.

As we walk in that and obey it, He will appear fairer and fairer, greater and greater, until He fills the whole horizon; and when He does that, then faith in that great Saviour will result in great victories wrought by Him for us and through us to the glory of His name.

CHAPTER V

THE UNCHANGING ONE

Jesus Christ . . . the same yesterday and today, yea and for ever.

HEBREWS 13:8.

THERE IS NOTHING MORE CERTAIN OR MORE IMPRESSIVE THAN the transitory nature of all earthly things. We change our calendars, and become conscious as we do so, that we ourselves have changed. Then we glance around us, and we find that there has been change everywhere. And even while we are in the act of thinking, we have changed again, and all around us is changing even as we look.

Now, this fact of change is at once the salt and the poison of life. It is the salt of life preventing monotony, that deadly foe of the soul. It is the poison of life paralyzing effort, that vital ally of the soul. Change is of the very nature of life and is necessary to life. Change takes on the guise of death and checks the movements of life. Thus are we perplexed, and earnestly do we desire to find some center of permanence and some secret of perennial freshness.

We need a center of permanence, not an anchorage. An anchorage means limitation and monotony. An anchorage belongs to a ship and is a hindrance to the ship. The tug of the ship to be away from the shore and out upon the sea is of its very nature and being, and the anchor holds it back. We are not asking for anchorage. The only sense in which the figure of the anchor is warranted is when it is used, as it was used by the writer of the letter to the Hebrews, in such form that it is contradicted in the very suggestions it makes.

In an earlier part of this letter he said: ". . . the hope set before us; which we have as an anchor of the soul, . . . both sure and stedfast." Yes! but let us finish the quotation! ". . . entering within the veil." In that phrase he has contradicted his own symbol finely, intelligently; not blunderingly. It is the figure of the anchor cast, not where the shoals are, but within the veil; the place of finality, the place of satisfaction, and eternity, and God. Thus the figure breaks down, but in the magnificence of its breakdown, it is fitting in every sense and at any and every time. The anchorage which we need must have some element, sure, unshakable, persistent, continuous; and because we are persons, let us at once say, some Person, never destroyed, never weary, never changing.

And we ask not merely a sign of permanence, but a secret of freshness; not excitement, that means reaction and yet more deadly inertia; but some element growing, developing, surprising the soul. And once again, because we are persons, we need some Person always alive, full of initiation, and ever equal to realization. Where shall we turn for these things?

We look within, and if there be one place where we fail to find the stability for which we cry out and the springing freshness we desire, it is within. We look to our friends, and the story is tragic. The air is full of farewells to the dying. We look to circumstances, and there is neither anchorage that holds nor freshness that satisfies the soul. Where are we? Great God! Where are we? We must find anchorage in that broader sense of the word somewhere. Where shall we turn?

Such thinking inevitably recalls those lines of the last

hymn which Henry Francis Lyte ever wrote, the hymn he wrote two months before he crossed the bar and saw his Pilot face to face; a hymn which in his intention did not refer to the closing of the natural day but to the close of life:

> Abide with me! fast falls the eventide;
> The darkness deepens; Lord, with me abide!
> When other helpers fail, and comforts flee,
> Help of the helpless, O abide with me!
>
> Swift to its close ebbs out life's little day!
> Earth's joys grow dim; its glories pass away,
> Change and decay in all around I see,
> O Thou, who changest not, abide with me!

When Henry Francis Lyte wrote those lines as expressive of his own experience, he wrote a hymn for humanity; one of the few, rare hymns throbbing with the elemental things of the human soul and capturing the heart and conscience of men everywhere; we do not wonder that the hymn is sung today around the world.

What warrant had he to write that hymn? The warrant is found in my text. The man who wrote that hymn was a man who believed that Jesus Christ is the same yesterday and today and forever.

In the declaration of this text is found the perfect answer to the two-fold cry of the human soul. Let us remind ourselves then of the eternal freshness of Christ. He is always alive; ". . . I am alive for evermore . . ."; always beginning some new thing, "I am the Beginning . . ."; always realizing and consummating that which He does begin, ". . . I am the Ending. . . ." Let us remind ourselves of the unchanging nature of Christ. He is never destroyed nor can He be; never weary, however weary we may be; never changing, for love never faileth, and love altereth not when it alteration finds. He is unchanged in the fact of His perpetual freshness, so that no soul has ever found it to be monotonous to walk with Him or talk with Him or think of Him or sing of Him; He is perpetually breaking in upon the soul with new surprises, in some amazing and lightning flash, or as the freshness of a morning in the springtime. He is the same yesterday and today and forever.

The text is in itself the message with which I would greet and hearten my own soul and that of each of those who may be reached by my words. I do not propose to defend this statement of the writer. I affirm it anew and pray that its music may strengthen our faith, may brighten our hope, may deepen our love. Jesus Christ is the same yesterday and today and forever. Let us then attempt to listen to the music as we consider Jesus Christ yesterday, Jesus Christ today, Jesus Christ forever.

Sometimes, in order to gain a better understanding, we must tarry long enough to be mechanical and so to catch the true meaning of the thing which is written. Therefore we pause to notice the peculiar title employed at this point by the writer of the letter. Jesus Christ! These were the usual names which this writer used in reference to our Lord but generally in separation from each other. In this letter, He is constantly referred to by the human name, the simple name of Jesus. In this letter also, over and over again He is referred to by the august and dignified title of Christ. Jesus was a Hebrew name. There were hundreds of boys who bore that name in Galilee and Judæa for it is but the Greek form of the old Hebrew name Joshua. The name had peculiar associations, setting it apart and differentiating it from all other names in that it was a name that was coined for the man who first bore it by his great predecessor, Moses. Yet it had become common, and so attention is fastened in the first case upon the fact that our Lord is essentially of our own nature and of our own being, of our own emotions and of our own temptations. Jesus is one of us. Our thought is first brought face to face with that fact. But we must remember that this name is not introduced in this letter until we reach what we speak of as our second chapter and ninth verse. The one referred to there as Jesus was introduced at the beginning of the letter in other terms and by other designations. At the commencement of this letter, He is described as Son of God, heir of all things, through Whom God did fashion the ages; the effulgence of His glory, the very image of His substance, the One Who upheld all things by the word of His power. So was He introduced, and then, presently, this Person is named Jesus! Another statement that will help us to apprehend the mystery is that of John, in what we call the prologue to his Gospel, in which he says: "In the beginning was the logos (Word); and the logos (Word) was with God; and God was the logos (Word); and the logos (Word) became flesh!" That is Jesus!

The other name, Christ, is the Messianic title indicating the fact of the office, the work, the mission of this mysterious Person Who was human and yet was infinitely more than human. He, the King-Priest, is introduced by this title at the third chapter and the fourteenth verse, having been introduced at the beginning of the letter in the way which we have already considered.

Now in this text the two titles are brought together, and the combination is rare in the letter. Only on two other occasions did this writer thus link them. When he spoke of the Lord as the One through Whom the will of God for our sanctification is accomplished, he called Him Jesus Christ. When a little later he spoke of Him as the One through Whom God makes us perfect to do His will, he called Him

Jesus Christ. And here, when he was referring to Him as the unchanging One, he named Him by the human name and by the Messianic title. The Person to Whom he referred is the One Whom he had already introduced as Son of God, the effulgence of His glory, the express image of His Person, the One through Whom all things were made, the One Who fashions the ages. It is to this Person that we are introduced, and He is declared by the writer of the letter to be the same yesterday, and today, and forever.

If we are to understand Him, we must consider the yesterday in its limited sense and remind ourselves again of what are described in the New Testament as the days of His flesh. That is the focal point of revelation. The mystic and the infinite Son of God is revealed by this veiling of deity in human flesh.

I am impressed first of all by His appeal to humanity in itself, by what He was in Himself. I am not thinking now of His appeal to humanity in His teaching. Shall I not be accurate when I declare that the teaching of Jesus Christ did not appeal to humanity and that it does not appeal to humanity yet? Humanity must be regenerated before the teaching of Christ makes any vast or powerful appeal to it. I know full well that there are certain parts and portions of the teaching of Christ, expressive of His outlook upon the ultimate purposes of God for this world, which make their appeal to humanity; but when He deals with those things of the soul in which He demands a purity which is awe-inspiring, when He begins to appeal to the human heart and to show it its own disobedience, humanity is still in rebellion against His teaching. There are a thousand men who praise the Sermon on the Mount for its broad outlines who dare not face its personal investigations. Not by the teaching of Christ were men attracted but by what He was in Himself. Today, two millenniums after His earthly manifestation, there is no literature in the world that appeals to men as do these gospel narratives. He came into the midst of human life making hypocrisy impossible while He stood confronting men. Men unveiled themselves, or unmasked themselves, in His presence. They could do nothing other than show themselves. They were often angry as they unmasked themselves, but they were compelled to the act. They were more often comforted as they unveiled themselves. But the supreme fact, the first fact that impresses us is that here was a Man Who moved among men and whenever they came into His presence, they were seen for the men they really were; veils were rent, masks were torn off, duplicity was at an end, hypocrisy perished; they stood naked in the essential facts of their character wherever He came! In His human nature, the very deeps of humanity called to the deeps in humanity, and the deeps in humanity answered the deeps of humanity. Moreover, His appeal was not that of a clan, not that of a tribe, not that of a nation, but that of the race.

I look back at Him once more, and I observe His appeal to humanity in its need. I will cover the whole ground of humanity's need by the use of two of the most commonplace words in our language—sin and sorrow. Observe how He appealed to each. He never excused sin. He never admitted that sin was necessary. There is not a single sentence in the teaching of Christ that suggests that sin is a necessary part of a process by which God is moving to something higher. He never excused it, never admitted that it was necessary. But something else is true. He never abandoned it. He never admitted that it was incurable. In the vocabulary of Jesus there never could have been such an absurd contradiction of terms as we sometimes make use of when we speak of "necessary evils." If necessary, not evil; if evil, never necessary. In the vocabulary of Jesus, such an absurd contradiction of terms as "hopeless cases," never could have been brought together with regard to humanity. No case was hopeless to His eyes. Of those men and women that came into contact with Him in His life, none were hopeless. When He confronted them, they were saved over and over again by faith, not theirs in Him but His in them and by His wonderful confidence in them.

As to sorrow, He never ignored it. It was a great reality to Him. Dear old Faber, that saint infinitely greater than his ecclesiastical convictions either before or after his going to Rome, sang the very truth as he sang that the sorrows of earth are most keenly felt in heaven. While Jesus walked the ways of men, all the sorrows of Palestine that His eyes looked upon settled on His soul and wounded His heart. But He never submitted to sorrow. He never admitted that sorrow was the final thing. In the world you shall have tribulation, but your sorrow shall be turned into joy!

He saw the dark clouds and the sweeping rain! But He forevermore said, "I do set My bow in the cloud! . . ." He knew the sun, and that the light of it flashed upon the rain drops, symbols of tears and agony, made them radiant with the colors of heaven in hope and joy. Sorrow for Him was never final. It was real, graphic, terrific, evil. He knew it. He was ". . . a Man of sorrows, and acquainted with grief: . . ." But he never bowed His head beneath sorrow and yielded to it, never came to despair. He moved breast forward against sorrow for Himself and humanity. He mastered it; He transmuted it!

I look once more at those days of His flesh, and I notice the perpetual surprises of those who were about Him. He was constantly surprising them. I think I may dismiss the whole story, for the purpose of our present meditation, by saying that He trained His disciples by surprise after surprise, surprise after surprise. They thought they knew Him, and they were glad they did and went with Him. Then He startled them by something He did or said. They were halted and then discovered its value and went on a little further. Now they understood Him! Then He wrought some new wonder and they cried: "Who, then, is this?" He was so human that they called Him Jesus of Nazareth. Yet out of that human personality there were always breaking lights and glories and powers and revelations and surprises. How are we to account for this? We account for it because of the longer yesterday. The "yesterday" includes all the infinite mysteries of the far-flung splendors of the ages about which we can only dream and about which we know nothing. In the beginning was the Word, and when tabernacled in human form, walking human pathways, mixing among human beings, lights gleamed, and glories flashed, surprising the heart of the men who were about Him. Jesus Christ yesterday!

And now what of Jesus Christ today? There is a difference, and we must face it. The difference is that He is now gone out of sight, as He said He would in those Paschal discourses from which our lesson was taken, and for a while we shall not see Him. He is gone out of sight. But He also said, ". . . a little while and ye shall see Me." In that promise there was no reference to a second Advent. He was referring to something that was to be immediate; something to which they actually did come and that soon. Those men who heard Him talk in the Upper Room, Peter, James, and John; Philip, Thomas, and Jude; the men who spoke in the Upper Room, those men lost Him. He passed out of their sight. Then came Pentecost, and they saw Him as they had never seen Him, though they could no longer see Him. He said to them: ". . . It is expedient for you that I go away. . . ." I do no violence to the thought conveyed if I change the word. "It is better for you that I go away." Why better? Because this Eternal One, localized in flesh, was limited by that localization; because in the midst of His Ministry He was compelled to say, ". . . I have a baptism to be baptised with, and how am I straitened till it be accomplished!" Passing out of sight, the sight of sense, in His coming again by the Holy Spirit to the consciousness of such as put their trust in Him, He came into nearer association, came to be the Companion of the spirit-life of men, that inner spirit-life which no man can see, either of himself or of his neighbor, by the eyes of sense. "No man hath seen God at any time. . . ." We all agree that no man hath seen Him at any time. No man hath seen man at any time! Do you agree? It is true. You have never seen me, I have never seen you. We look upon these outward forms, these are but tabernacles. Thank God if we have learned the lesson, that the body, marred, spoiled, broken, laid to rest, was but the tenement house. Jesus said to these men in effect. "I am shut outside you by living in this body, while you live in these bodies. I will go away and come again, and come right into the true spirit-life of you and reveal Myself to you by the Spirit, as you never can know Me while I remain outside you." We can have closer fellowship with Jesus than with each other. I am shut out from the final fellowship of my nearest and dearest friend in this world. I must wait for the larger spirit-life that lies beyond. I can have no final spiritual fellowship with my earthly friends, but with Him I can have full spiritual fellowship.

Thus He came again to these men and to us. He is known today through the writings, through spiritual interpretation, and through the saints who in their fellowship with

Him are transformed into His likeness and reveal Him to other men. Thus, He is the same. The only thing that is different is the accidental. The essential abides. Through that which I have just described, not carelessly but carefully, as the accidental of the days of His flesh, the essential and abiding was revealed.

I look again to the yesterday, to the days of His flesh, and I declare that He is the same, making the same appeals to humanity. That is the deep secret of the victory of Christianity. All our hindrances are due to the fact that we quarrel about forms and methods of expression and neglect the central authority of the Christ Himself. Oh! shame on us! shame on us! He is the same. Let us remember that whenever we are tempted to quarrel!

He makes the same appeal to humanity. Take that little Testament of yours! Nay, take much less. Take Mark alone, the first and simplest narrative. Print it, give it away. Read it to men everywhere. Read it to them when they are quiet, when they are thoughtful. Let them look, let them listen. So let them see this Jesus. They will come to Him. He will attract them whether they are black or white, whether learned or illiterate, whether high or low, bond or free, rich or poor. When they see Him, they forget black or white, high or low, rich or poor, bond or free, for they have found in Him their own humanity. Humanity ever goes out to the humanity in Him. That is the story of the success of missions.

He makes the same appeal to human nature. He will not excuse sin. He will not excuse my sin. He will never allow me to say in His presence that I was bound to sin. We cannot say it, we dare not say it in His presence. We say it to each other. We say it to our own souls sometimes. "We could not help it." We know we lie when we say it! But when we are alone with Him we dare not look into His face and say we were bound to sin! We know it is not true. All modern philosophy in so far as it says that sin is necessary is a lie against which this Christ of God proceeds, and he will deny it in the human conscience ere His mission is completed. Man need not sin.

But it is also true that we cannot say in His presence that our sin is incurable. It is not incurable. He believes in us. He has perfect confidence in humanity. He is producing the same effects today as of old, effects which I shall not enumerate, but summarize in His own sweet word, "Rest." "Come unto Me, all ye that labour and are heavy laden, and I will give you rest." In that word I find, righteousness, peace, joy, the things of the Kingdom of God.

He is the same today in His mysteriousness, still surprising the soul, still breaking out upon us at some point in life, amazing us and then explaining His own surprise and moving us a little further on toward the final knowledge.

So let me end, with only a brief sentence or two. He is the same forever. The phrase that the writer actually used was most suggestive. "Forever," is altogether too mechanical. It is trying to say everything. We cannot say everything. Let us dare to be poetic in company with the Bible. Jesus Christ, the same yesterday and today and to the ages! They come, they pass, they go! The year has broken, the year has dawned. It is for us a new age, but a hand breadth, but a span; but it serves to illustrate everything that is suggested by the phrase, to the ages.

We are always at the beginning of a new age. Behind us are ages; before us are ages! Now the writer says that this One Who came into human history and human life, and Whom He names Son of God, Jesus, Christ, is the same to the ages! At the beginning of this letter he declared that this

One fashions the ages, determines their nature, limits their duration, includes their forces.

Heaven will never be monotonous. There will always be new satisfaction for the heart. We shall never become satiated with the things spiritual. The unfathomed deeps and distances of the ages lie before us, but He will lead us through them. Therefore am I no longer afraid of the vastness of the outlook.

That Living One is in our midst now, calling us to rest. He is the center of all that is permanent, the spring of all that is fresh. Dare I be afraid? Amid the shock of battle, the stress of life, and the overwhelming perplexities of things, Jesus Christ is the same yesterday and today and forever.

March on my soul, without fear or faltering, for the Pierced Hand holds the scepter of the universe! All is well!

CHAPTER VI

THE PROBLEM OF HOW TO BEGIN

The fear of Jehovah is the beginning of wisdom....
PROVERBS 9:10.

THERE ARE HOURS WHICH SUGGEST NEW BEGINNINGS. AT THE dawn of the year, on our birthdays, when we leave school or college and enter upon life's business, we find ourselves almost invariably and inevitably beginning again. To use the very old and familiar figure of speech, we turn over a new leaf. The figure is poetical and it is warranted. In our life story we turn the page and begin a new chapter; and it is impossible to do it, if we have any moral sense and any spiritual sense, without wanting to begin all over again. We are conscious at such times that in very many regards our lives have been characterized by folly, and we desire that they should be governed by wisdom. We look back along the pathway and see the mistakes we have made, sometimes ignorantly but often wilfully, and at the parting of the ways, we earnestly desire that in the days that lie before us there should be fewer mistakes made either ignorantly or in waywardness. We have turned over a new leaf, and we desire that the writing upon the new page shall be more legible, more worthy of the great Master, having fewer erasures necessary, fewer spoilings of the meaning by indistinctness, more of truth, more of beauty, more of glory.

How are we to begin? That is the supreme question of such hours. It is not a simple question. The measure of our honesty is the measure of our perplexity. The measure of our sincerity is the measure of our fear. May I venture to add to these statements another; the number of our years is the measure of our fearfulness. We are more afraid than we used to be of new resolutions and new beginnings by reason of the many failures of the past. Still we desire to begin again. How are we to begin?

In my text is the answer. "The fear of the Lord is the beginning of wisdom. . . ." In the last of the set discourses on wisdom in this Book of Proverbs, the preacher made that declaration. It is not to be confused with an earlier statement. I open the Book of Proverbs and I read, "The proverbs of Solomon the son of David, king of Israel." The introductory words run on to verse six, constituting a preface. Then the preacher summarized the whole intention of his discourses on wisdom and of the proverbs which he had collected, and the summary is found in these words, "The fear of Jehovah is the beginning of knowledge; . . ." In the last of the discourses we have the words of our text, "The fear of Jehovah is the beginning of wisdom. . . ."

The difference to which I want to draw attention is not the difference between the words "knowledge" and "wisdom," but a difference between two words which are the same in our translation but which are not the same in the Hebrew; "The beginning of knowledge" and "the beginning of wisdom." The word translated "beginning" in the first declaration is a word which means first, but not in time alone; it means first in order of time, of place, of rank, of value; first in importance. You will observe that the revisers have suggested an alteration in the margin so that the first of these verses should read, "The fear of the Lord is the chief part of knowledge." The thought of the first declaration is that the fear of the Lord is the supreme value in wisdom. Of course in that larger declaration, the thought of the text is included. We are now dealing with beginnings, and that is the exact meaning of the word of my text, the beginning as the starting point, the commencement. The fear of the Lord is the starting point in wisdom, is the commencement of wisdom. The commencement of the way of wisdom is the fear of the Lord, for the fear of the Lord is the abiding secret of the way of wisdom.

Let us first consider generally this subject of beginning. In doing so I would remind you first that a beginning is not a beginning. There is always a past. There is always something that has preceded what we call a beginning. I might summarily dismiss this by saying that a new beginning is impossible. A beginning is never a beginning. We may illustrate the truth in any sphere of life. What is the beginning of a tree? There is no beginning that is not related to a past history. The young tree that we plant in our garden; that is the beginning of the tree there, but it is not the beginning of the tree. If we plant an acorn, that is not the beginning of the oak tree; the beginning of the tree which will come from the acorn is the tree from which the acorn came. We travel back until we discover that every tree is related to mysteries as infinite and far-extending as is the mystery of our own life. Take the beginning of a bird. Some of the older men and women will remember the great days when Hastings lectured on Christian evidences and that curious and interesting question which he perpetually propounded to those who held contest with him; which was first, the hen or the egg?

We begin our backward journey, and there is no beginning. A beginning is not a beginning. Enough of illustration on the lower level. There is no moral beginning either of sinning or of doing righteousness. You did not begin to sin when you sinned. Behind that beginning to sin was the thought, the conception, and behind the thinking and the conception, tendencies assaulting the soul; that mystic stuff of which thoughts and dreams are made lay behind. There is no beginning. There is no beginning for the doing of right. Behind the deed is the thought, and behind the thought is the will, that infinite majesty of personality. I am less and less surprised as the years run on, and I know better, to find that I cannot know myself. I am less surprised that the psalmist said of God, "Thou understandest my thought afar off." And then added: "Such knowledge is too wonderful for me; It is high, I cannot attain unto it." There is no beginning. Being has no beginning. The only beginning is that of form; the form of being may have a beginning; but that which takes the new form existed before in some other form. The new form is but a resultant of things that lay behind it. It always has to do with a past. I will turn over a new leaf, and I will begin again. I cannot. All the past is there. The new leaf is in the one volume and must constitute a part of the one story. The way of wisdom must take into account that past. It was this tremendous sense of the past that made Nicodemus look into the eyes of Jesus in the night and ask the question that was neither rude, flippant, nor irrelevant, ". . . How can a man be born when he is old? . . ." It was not a foolish question. It was a question coming up out of the deepest sense of personality, the essential, the elemental. It was a question of the soul. ". . . How can a man be born when he is old? . . ." What of those years that have run? How can I begin? If we are to discover the secret of wisdom, we must take the past into account, for a beginning is not a beginning.

In the second place, I remark that a beginning is not lonely, independent, self-contained. Whatever may seem to begin, begins in the midst of environment, in the midst of surrounding forces that touch it and will claim its attention. There is nothing which begins and which, in its beginning, is separated from all the forces that are outside itself. Every beginning is made in the midst of forces which are destructive and constructive. The tree begins its growth and its development; and there are evil things waiting to fasten upon it and destroy it, and there are great and generous forces waiting to give it new strength and enable it to come to perfection of being. To those forces, that which is begun will respond, rejecting sometimes, receiving sometimes; rejecting the evil things and receiving the good sometimes; sometimes rejecting the beneficent things and receiving the evil things. These are the mysteries of life. If we leave that lower realm of illustration and climb to the higher, we shall immediately see how true all this is. We make our new beginnings in the midst of forces destructive and constructive. They are in waiting for us tomorrow; no, they are right here in the sanctuary! Some of the most disastrous moral and spiritual catastrophes have happened in the sanctuary of God in the hour of vision and light and glory. When we turn over the new leaf and decide we will begin again, we must begin remembering that we cannot begin alone or independently; a beginning is not self-contained. Beating through the air, advancing upon us, are forces destructive and constructive, and the whole activity of a new beginning is concentrated at that point. A new beginning in the moral and spiritual realm is the readjustment of life to forces that surround, both constructive and destructive; the opening of the soul to the constructive, and the shutting of the doors of the soul to the destructive. The way of wisdom must take into account the forces which surround the life. There is another question, one which Nicodemus did not ask but which is quite as pertinent; how can a man live his own life in the midst of these forces? When I have turned over this new leaf and begun again, how am I going to realize my own personality in the presence of these forces? Any answer to the question of how to begin must take in this great fact of environment.

I have one other thing to say about the beginning. A beginning is a beginning. We do start new things when we begin. Being has no beginning, but its form and its expression have, and in the creation of a new form, a new expression, new forces are sent out, the issue of which no man can see. Whenever a man makes a new start, a new beginning, he is starting something that will run on from the propulsion of that beginning, whether good or bad. This fact creates the supreme responsibility of life. In that hour when we turn aside to the thing that is base, and low, and mean; beginning that from which we had previously turned away, we are starting things, the ultimate issue of which we cannot see. Equally is it true that when we form resolutions on the side of good, in that hour we start forces for good, the ultimate of which will be known in the future and never perfectly here. Every new beginning is in that sense a beginning, and the things that follow will take direction and shape from that beginning.

In the new beginning of which we are now thinking, the new moral and spiritual beginning, that new direction is supremely in mind. What do we mean by turning over a new leaf? That the order of our life is to take a new shape, a new form, a new color, a new tone. We are looking ahead. When a man desires to walk the way of wisdom, he must take tomorrow into account, for the way of wisdom is supremely a passion for tomorrow. Here then we have another question that we ask; how can a man give the right direction, the true form and fashion and shape to the future? Every beginning must take into account three things, the past, the present, and the future. How then shall we begin?

That brings us to the declaration of the text, "The fear of the Lord is the beginning of wisdom. . . ." The supreme thing in every hour of new beginning in moral and spiritual life is that of some principle of action which will set us in right relationship with the past, with the forces that lie about us in the present and with the future. That principle must be more than intellectual orthodoxy. It must be vitally actual. It must be a principle which, being observed, brings us into the place of moral and spiritual power. We must find some principle which deals with all these facts not merely ideally, but dynamically, not merely from the standpoint of revealing to us a philosophy, but from the standpoint of communicating to us potentiality, which shall be sufficient for this terrible mystery and fact of the past, for these tremendous powers of the present, and for that weird and yet alluring mystery of the future.

When I pondered this text and had come to this part of my message and my burden, I said to my soul, "It is so old a statement, how can you deal with it?" I then asked two questions, and I will now ask them aloud. They are the questions of a man who presumably had never heard the statement before; the questions of a little child. First, "Who is the Lord?" And second, "What is it to fear the Lord?"

Who is the Lord? I have no answer to this inquiry other than that of biblical and Christian revelation. That answer is a threefold one as I understand it. He is the Creator and therefore the One Who knows perfectly that which He has created. He is the Preserver of all such as He has created and therefore the One Who cares for that which He has created. Finally, He is the Redeemer and therefore the One Who must love that which He has created and which He has preserved. There is nothing new in all that, but if some of us can put our lives into right relationship with it all, that will be something new; that will be a true beginning.

He is the Creator, therefore knowing. Already in my sermon I have made a quotation which I want to use again, from that wonderful, classic psalm than which there is nothing finer in the Bible in this regard and nothing approaching it outside the Bible:

> O Jehovah, thou hast searched me, and known me,
> Thou knowest my downsitting and mine uprising.
> Thou understandest my thought afar off.
> Thou searchest out my path and my lying down,
> And art acquainted with all my ways.

". . . Thou understandest my thought afar off." Thought is the most wonderful thing in my personality, mystic, strange, the thing that supremely puzzles me; it is the vehicle through which temptation assaults me, and I cannot help its assault; it is the vehicle through which high aspirations come to me, and I cannot help their coming. ". . . Thou understandest my thought afar off." The Lord is the Creator, and I am the created, a realized thought of God. He thought me, planned me, and fashioned me. He distanced Himself from that which is physical in me by the distance of my parenthood. He kept Himself near to me in the essential mystery of my being which is spiritual. For in me, as in all other men, He breathed the breath of life. Therefore He knows me perfectly.

O the comfort of it? Did you expect me to say the terror of it? By no means; the comfort of it! "Thou God seest me." In the olden days they printed those words, framed them, hung them up in the nursery, and too often interpreted them so as to suggest that God is a sort of moral policeman. Print it again, frame it, bedeck it with flowers, and then sing it to the children: "Thou God seest me." He watches over us as the master Workman, Who, according to the ancient history, when He had completed man saw that His work was very good. The Lord is my Creator, understanding the mystic mechanism of my being. As to physical powers, I am fearfully and wonderfully made. More marvelous still are my mental capacities. The supreme, august, majestic dignity is that spiritual life which is akin to Deity, offspring of the Most High. I do not know myself; Thou Lord, knowest me perfectly. Then indeed, "The fear of the Lord is the beginning of wisdom. . . ."

He is Preserver also, caring for all that His hands have made. Here we approach a statement where there are difficulties, but let us think carefully, let us think broadly, let us come to no hasty conclusion. There are men and women in London tonight for whom it seems as though God did not care. There are little children in London tonight for whom it is very hard to understand that God cares. But we must remember that the plane of human suffering which is unrelieved by Deity is a plane from which God is excluded by man's rebellion. The blame of such suffering is not upon God's provision but upon man's dealing with God's provision. There is in this world of ours such plenty that there need be no crying out in the streets and no poverty; but when man forgets God and breaks His law, then suffering follows. In the provision of God there is perfect supply for the preservation of humanity. Remember further, that disease and suffering are not in the economy of God; they are overruled within that economy, mastered within it, held in the grip of the Divine government, but they are not the will of God. Let us talk no blasphemy about disease being the will of God. Disease is never the will of God. The Lord is the One that preserveth the life which He has created. He created the morning for us, He created the darkness for us, giving His beloved sleep and in sleep giving to His beloved; making season follow upon season for man's well-being. We often measure Him by our own incompetence, and we imagine that several wet weeks in succession demonstrate the fact that the throne of God is vacant and that humanity is to be ruined. It is not so, and those who know God never blaspheme Him by criticizing His weather. He preserveth the life of man and beast! He is the Preserver of such as He has made.

Finally, He is the Redeemer. I am not going to discuss the problem. There is a problem, the problem of evil, of sin. The fact that man has lost his vision of this God, and the consciousness of this God, and relationship to this God, and that rivers of evil surge through the centuries destroying human life; the fierce fires of wrong persist in human history and permeate humanity, blasting, scorching, destroying. We have to face the fact that man, most mystic and mysterious in his being, is a rebel, and that thus revelling against God, he is banished from consciousness of God and fellowship with God. What then? God has not left humanity; God has not abandoned humanity! God has found a way by which His banished ones may return, because His is love which alters not when it alteration finds. God's is the love that follows and associates itself with sinning souls in comradeship in order that such may be healed and restored, and that at infinite cost; cost so marvelous that we cannot attempt to speak of it in any terms that are current in the common speech of humanity. The Lord is the Redeemer.

What then is His fear? Subjectively, it is recognition of His might and of His holiness. It is admission of the righteousness of the claim He makes upon the human soul. It is reverence for Him and a desire for conformity to His will. "In all thy ways acknowledge Him. . . ." The fear of the Lord subjectively is that acknowledgment of God, that recognizing of Himself and of His claims, and that desire for such adjustment to that central infinite truth of all the universe and of all life which shall be for the glory of Him Who is at once Creator, Preserver and Redeemer. It follows that objectively the fear of the Lord is submission, adjustment, obedience. I do not mean that fear of the Lord is acceptance of truths about Him, or subscription to creeds which men have written. I am not undervaluing either the one or the other, but there may be both without the fear of the Lord. The fear of the Lord, I repeat, is first of all recognition of Himself and admission of His claim, reverence for Him; and then the answer to it that comes out of the volitional center of the life, the answer to that of which the soul is convinced.

Here someone will say in his or her heart, "This is all in the realm of mystery; let us get back to the realm of simplicity." Then I inquire, "Do you believe in God in any form, do you believe in Him in any manner?" Then the fear of the Lord is the answer of your life to that which you believe; it is the taking of your life and putting it into true adjustment to that of which you are convinced. Is He Creator? Then I venture to say in the name of common sense, if on no higher ground, your business is to find His thought for you and to obey it. Is He Preserver? Then I affirm that the supreme business of your life is that of worship and of faithfulness in recognition and in response. Is He Redeemer? Then the supreme business of your life is that of yielding yourself to that redemption, the handing over of the soul to the Redeemer. "The fear of Jehovah is the beginning of wisdom. . . ."

I claim, in conclusion, that this declaration of the ancient preacher is justified, philosophically, historically and experimentally. It is justified philosophically. Note the relation of Jehovah to the things which we said at the commencement must be taken into account in the way of wisdom; the past, the present, and the future. As to the past. What relation has the Lord to the past? Let the whole business be stated briefly once again by declaring whatever your past, or mine, He antedates it. Let me speak now to those who may not agree with all my attitudes towards the Bible. I want to ask you before you take my Bible and tear out its first page, to make up your minds what you propose to substitute for that page. We were among the trees a little while ago, tracing them back, and we lost our way. We were among the birds following them back, and there also we lost our way. Follow the pathways again; then take the Bible up and read; "In the beginning God created. . . ." If some other cosmogony satisfies you, I have no right to dictate to you; but so help me God, nothing else can satisfy me, but that does satisfy me. "In the beginning God . . ." I do not mind which way you travel; it may be you will say that the birds came after the trees and that something preceded the trees, and you travel back until you come to primordial protoplasmic germs. I will go with you, but now what is at the back of that? "In the beginning God created. . . ." He antedates all your pasts and can control your past.

What of the present? What of the forces that assault the soul, luring it both to good and evil? He encompasses the whole of them and can control them. Nothing is out of His grasp. Not heaven alone but hell also is within His government. The Book of Job, that wonderful Book, teaches us how the Adversary of man is compelled to tell the sum of his devilry before God before he is permitted to exercise his power against man. That is always so. Milton when he made Lucifer, son of the morning, say, "It is better to reign in hell than to serve in heaven," made Lucifer express not his badness only, but his madness also, for Lucifer cannot reign in hell. God reigns in hell. "Though hell be nigh, yet God is nigher, Circling us with hosts of fire." All the forces in the midst of which we make our new beginnings are atmosphere in Deity and are controlled by God on behalf of all such as fear Him.

What of the future? He possesses it and can order it. He sees the end from the beginning. The final consummation, in one gleam of gold the New Testament has revealed and in one only, when Paul having climbed to the greatest height of all his apostolic thinking, said, "Then cometh the end, when He shall deliver up the Kingdom to God, even the Father; when He shall have abolished all rule and all authority and power." That is the great and wonderful consummation about which the Bible has said so little that we dare say but little. That is made sure by the government of God. The future is His.

Where then shall I begin? "The fear of Jehovah is the beginning of wisdom. . . ." There is my past, ". . . How can a man be born when he is old? . . ." God stands between me and my past. Around me are the forces of today; How can I deal with them? God will deal with them, so I can deal with them in fellowship with Him. There is the future, what am I to do with tomorrow? There is hope in God for that also is His. Faith in God about the past; fellowship with God about the present; hope in God about the future. "Being . . .

justified by faith, . . ." that is the backward look. ". . . We have peace with God . . ."; that is the present. "Rejoice in hope of the glory of God"; that is the future.

In proportion as our lives are put into right relationship with Him, we mount His chariot and ride triumphantly toward the goal of the ages and if the wheels be sometimes splashed with blood and the conflict leave scars upon the man who fights, what does it matter! Life is not feeble, frail; it is mighty, mysterious. The way of wisdom is the way of infinite, glorious victory, and the beginning is the fear of the Lord.

The declaration is justified historically in the experience of all the souls who have known the fear of the Lord. Hear me again—it is a sentence I would like to elaborate, but I will not—in the history of all the nations that have feared the Lord, the declaration of the text is vindicated.

Finally, it is vindicated experimentally. At this moment, the answer of the soul intelligently to the declaration vindicates its accuracy, and the experience of the soul in obedience vindicates its accuracy. By which I mean that we know full well that to fear the Lord is to walk in the way of wisdom. We know full well that if we will act in the fear of the Lord, we shall have found the highway at the end of which is the perfected life and the city and the home of God.

CHAPTER VII

THE MADNESS OF JESUS

And when His friends heard it, they went out to lay hold on Him: for they said, He is beside Himself.

MARK 3:21.

THE FIRST MATTERS THAT ARREST OUR ATTENTION ARE THAT this was said by the friends of Jesus, and that it was intended to be a friendly saying. These friends of Jesus meant exactly what we sometimes mean when we say of some person in certain circumstances and for certain reasons, "Well, the kindest thing you can say of him is that he is insane!" It was the mother and the brethren of Jesus who thus went out to lay hold on Him and bring Him home, because they had come to the deliberate conclusion that He was beside Himself. Thus it was those who knew Him most intimately, as men and women know each other in this world by the light of ordinary observation, who said this thing. They had lived with Him through all those wonderful years as He advanced from babyhood to boyhood, and from boyhood to young manhood, and had wrought as a carpenter in the little workshop in Nazareth; and I venture to suggest that their criticism was in itself an assumption of His previous sanity. This was something new which caused them to say: ". . . He is beside Himself"; and so they went after Him to bring Him home.

When our Lord commenced His public ministry, these people accompanied Him in that first year in which He traveled up and down between Galilee and Jerusalem and exercised His ministry for the most part in Judæa. When at the death of John the Baptist, He set His face toward the Tetrarchy over which Herod reigned, His brethren journeyed with Him. They were with Him in Capernaum and saw His first sign, that of the turning of the water into wine. There is no proof anywhere in the New Testament that they had any hostility to Him personally. I think it is proven that they were a long time before they became His disciples, and in the account of that very journey to Capernaum to which I have made reference, the evangelist is careful to tell us that He went with His disciples, His mother, and His brethren, thus separating the groups; but there is no evidence of hostility to Him. Later on in His ministry, His brethren endeavored to hurry Him to Jerusalem for manifestation and claim of Messianic authority, but even then there is no proof that there was any real hostility to Him in their hearts. So far as these records reveal, for a year prior to this event, they had not been with Him very much, if at all. As a matter of fact we have no record of their having been in close association with Him from the time of the sign at Cana. Now, the reports of His more recent doings had reached them, and this was the decision to which they had come as they heard about Him; they said, ". . . He is beside Himself"; and prompted by love for Him and friendship for Him, they traveled, as I think, from Nazareth to Capernaum, to bring Him home. In the Gospel of Mark the sequence is quite plain. He tells us in my text of the fact of this attitude toward Him, then goes back to give an account of what the Lord was doing in the house in Capernaum, and presently resumes the narrative and says that His mother and His brethren arrived seeking Him and sent Him a message; and the people told Him, ". . . Behold, Thy mother and brethren without seek for Thee." They had come because they thought He was beside Himself and in great love for Him to try to persuade Him to go home and rest. It was then that He said, "Who is My mother, and My brethren," and looking at the little group of disciples added, ". . . whosoever shall do the will of God, the same is My brother, and sister, and mother." So much for the setting of the criticism.

I am going to ask you to follow me along two lines of consideration. First, let us consider the reasonableness of their suggestion, that He was beside Himself, and second, let us consider the reasonableness of what they counted His madness.

We must endeavor to put ourselves into their place and hear what they heard, in order to know what they meant when they said, ". . . He is beside Himself." Let us remind ourselves, therefore, of some recent events. When He left Judæa and set His face resolutely to Galilee, He first went to Nazareth, traveling from Judæa toward Capernaum, which henceforth was to be, for a period at any rate, His headquarters. In Nazareth He went into the synagogue, and I think we are justified in imagining that they were present that day, that they saw Him, and knew what He did. There in the little synagogue in Nazareth so familiar to Him, in which He had been brought up and which it had been His custom to attend, He read from the roll of the prophet Isaiah the Messianic prediction and then deliberately declared that that Messianic prediction was fulfilled that day in their experience because He was there in their midst. Then He taught them and in such fashion that they wondered at the grace of His words. Then, suddenly, the tones of His teaching changed, and He said to them: "You will say to Me,

Physician, heal Thyself; do here in Nazareth the things that we have heard Thou hast done in Capernaum." In answer to that supposed criticism He said: ". . . No prophet is acceptable in his own country." Then he began a discourse characterized by rebuke with the result that the attitude of the men of the synagogue changed toward Him. They passed from admiration to anger and took Him to the brow of the hill deliberately determining to murder Him. He passed quietly through them unharmed and left Nazareth.

Then there came news to them that one day in a house in Capernaum He had done a strange new thing. He had positively claimed the right to forgive sins. He had said to a sick man whom they had brought to Him, ". . . thy sins are forgiven"; and the rulers had objected: "Why doth this man thus speak? . . . he blasphemeth; who can forgive sins but one, even God?" Then the news reached them of His rupture with the rulers. That had occurred, and doubtless they knew it, in Jerusalem in some measure, but now it was repeated in this Galilean district. This rupture was due to two or three things. He seemed to be setting Himself to violate the Sabbath. He never violated the true sanctions of the Sabbath but those false sanctions that were destroying the true sanctions. Then He was neglecting ordinances; neglecting in company with His disciples the fast-days that were appointed; He was not fasting; and most appalling of all, He was consorting with sinners. All this was resulting in rupture with the rulers.

Then they heard that He had now, for some strange purpose which they could not understand, taken twelve of His disciples and appointed them to some close relationship with Himself; they were to leave all ordinary work, and they were now always to be with Him, and presently, He said He was going to send them out to preach and to do what

He was doing, cast out demons. They heard all these things.

Look over the whole ground again from another standpoint, and mark the unusual elements in the things He was doing and saying. His teaching was characterized by the strangest sort of other-worldliness. He was always talking as though the other world were the supreme world, of the spiritual life as the supreme life. He had given the great Manifesto and men were talking about it, but He had said such strange things. In that Manifesto there were visions and pictures of a great social order; but then in the Manifesto He had talked about praying for things and getting things by praying for them. A most curious thing about the present hour is that thousands of men are glorifying the Manifesto of Jesus, as it describes a social order, who, nevertheless, ignore it when it speaks about obtaining things by prayer, about knocking at the gates of God.

Then they heard the stories about Him and were amazed at His lack of diplomacy. He was no diplomatist or He never would have broken with the rulers. If He really is the Messiah come to establish the Divine Kingdom, what is the meaning of this lack of diplomacy? Look at Him again, and see the strange disinterestedness of everything He did. What was he getting out of it all? Nothing! He was not even conserving His work, apparently. Then there was the fact of His ceaseless activity and His restlessness; He was never long at one place. Within the last two months, eminent Christian scholars—I will not deny their Christianity though for the life of me I cannot understand it—have been discussing this very question, the sanity of Jesus; and they are basing their discussion upon these very things. They say, "See how restless Christ was, crossing the sea and coming back again; one day filled with joy, the next day filled with sadness." Positively men are saying again in this day what these friends of the olden days were saying of Him, He was beside Himself! It is a suggestive fact and an interesting one, and it helps us to understand them. Then they heard of His carelessness about Himself. He had no time to eat, He was always giving Himself to others. They said, ". . . He is beside Himself."

The phrase itself is a very suggestive one. The English phrase suggests personal eccentricity. "Beside himself" suggests a person standing by the side of himself; that the man who ought to be at a given place is not there; he is beside himself, by the side of himself. That little English phrase carries exactly the sense of the Greek word meaning a person standing outside himself. The paradox is illuminative and suggestive. It describes a man ec-centric instead of con-centric; a man not quite responsible; the central inspirations of conduct are out of place somehow; there is something wrong with Him; He is beside Himself.

Now let me ask a question. Do we wonder at their conclusion? Much as I object in some ways to the form of my next question, I am going to employ it: If He came to England in bodily form, and did in England exactly what He did in Judæa, what would you say about Him? I do not ask you to answer, because I know; that is, unless you have the vision He had, unless you have been admitted to His deep secret. If you are living according to the spirit of this age, if you are mastered by the maxims of the hour and are swept by the wisdom of the day, you would say of Him, and you would think in the saying of it you were speaking in the most kindly way possible, He is beside Himself, He has lost His balance, He is eccentric, He is fanatical.

Let us now take our second line of inquiry. In contradistinction to everything I have suggested to you, I want to declare first of all the reasonableness of the life and ministry of Jesus. I shall ask you to observe first of all the worldliness of Jesus. I have spoken of His other-worldliness, now think of His worldliness. Remember His worldliness was manifested in such ways that the men of that age said of Him, "A gluttonous man and a wine-bibber; the friend of publicans and sinners!" No one will imagine that I am saying that He was a gluttonous man and a wine-bibber; that was but the superlative way in which hostility spoke of the fact that He was not an ascetic, that He lived an ordinary human life, that He entered into home interests, that He was pre-eminently worldly; of course, not in our modern theological sense. He loved this world, its flowers, its birds, its children, its mountains, its desert places; He was so worldly, so near to the heart of nature, that He was not afraid of loneliness. He was a Man Who walked amongst men, one of their own number, and so free from anything that marked Him as spiritually aloof, that sinning men and women crowded after Him; and they never crowd after Pharisees, even today. It is the human touch that arrests the human race.

In the second place, I ask you to observe that His methods were characterized by unceasing beneficence. He went about doing good. Everything He did was good in that sense. His activity was that of ceaseless benevolence and beneficence; the doing of good, not merely the wishing of good. Wherever He went He was doing good, helping someone always. All His signs were signs which brought blessing to men. I have made reference already to John's question, ". . . Art Thou He that cometh, or look we for another?" Carefully consider His answer: ". . . Go and tell John the things which ye hear and see; the blind receive their sight, and the lame walk, the lepers are cleansed, and the deaf hear, and the dead are raised up, and the poor have good tid-

THE MADNESS OF JESUS 99

ings preached to them." Let me not spoil that by adding anything to it.

I ask you to look at Him once more and to observe not only His worldliness and the beneficence of His activity, but His dignity, His quietness, His unobtrusiveness. He did not strive, nor cry aloud, nor lift up His voice in the streets. The crowds knew Him from north, south, east, and west, but not because He was clamant, and noisy, and ostentatious. They were drawn by the things He was doing, the quiet things. If you journey with Him imaginately through the fields, and the walled-in towns, and the country towns, and the great cities, you are impressed with the quiet self-possession of this Man; there seems to be no touch of insanity about Him.

Look again, and let us try to see what He saw. Let us inquire, and we may do it at this distance quite reverently, what were His inspirations, what lay behind all His methods. Whether these strange, wonderful things of familiarity with the world, of perpetually doing good to others, of quiet dignity; or those strange things of disinterestedness, or unceasing and restless movement to and fro make Him seem sane or insane. What lay behind them all? I declare to you that the inspiration of all the life of Jesus was threefold. First, His knowledge of God and the real meaning of the Kingdom of God; second, His knowledge of man and of the real meaning of human failure; third, His knowledge of Himself and of the real meaning of His mission in the world.

His knowledge of God and of His Kingdom. His knowledge of God as truth and grace, as the God of infinite holiness and light and the God of infinite compassion and love. His knowledge of the Kingdom of God. He saw through everything to the Divine purpose and the Divine possibility.

He saw the Kingdom of God, the empire over which God reigned and ruled and in which all were submitted to Him, and He knew that it would be a Kingdom of righteousness, of peace and of joy, a Kingdom in which there should be no place for oppression nor cry of distress. Wherever He went He saw that Kingdom of God for He saw the God Whose Kingdom He so passionately desired.

That meant that He saw clearly man and his failure. He saw man in his essential relationship to God and in his capacity for God, and, therefore, in his unutterable ruin. There is nothing more remarkable in these stories than the fact that this is what Jesus saw. He saw humanity as no other man of His time or of all time has seen it, save only those who share His life and have His vision. Matthew admits us at one point to the secret. I quote again the old familiar words, ". . . Jesus went about all the cities and the villages, teaching in their synagogues, and preaching the gospel of the kingdom, and healing all manner of disease and all manner of sickness. But when He saw the multitudes, He was moved with compassion for them. . . ." Why? ". . . because they were distressed and scattered, as sheep not having a shepherd." No one else was moved with compassion. Why not? Because no one saw their ruin for no one else saw their possibility. Wherever He looked He saw men and saw them ideally, in their true relationship to His Father, saw them in the breadth and beneficence of the Divine Kingdom, and saw that they were not there and knew what they were missing. Instead of righteousness, He beheld iniquity; instead of peace, He found strife; instead of joy, He saw misery. The inspiration of all the doing of Jesus was His contentment with the perfection of the Kingdom of God and His consequent discontent with everything in the midst of which He found Himself.

Then superadded to that clear vision, that double vision, there was that constant consciousness that mastered Him, to which incidentally He made reference again and again. Every evangelist records the fact, and John becomes rhythmically, monotonously, insistent upon recording the fact that He spoke of Himself as sent by God. He was the Son of God, but He was sent by God into the world for the accomplishment of a mission which He Himself did in varying phrases clearly declare: ". . . the Son of man came not to be ministered unto, but to minister, and to give His life a ransom for many"; ". . . the Son of man came to seek and to save that which was lost." Time and again such speech passed His lips revealing His own inner consciousness. Thus, in a world characterized by failure, He proceeded to His work and resolutely refused to adopt the methods of human wisdom and human strength and human cleverness which had resulted in all the chaos in the midst of which He moved; He walked the ways of men, Himself one Man perfectly responsive to that Kingdom of God which He saw; and He lived perpetually obeying its behests and carrying out its commands and doing the will of God.

Do we wonder at His other-worldliness when we think of Him as holding perpetual communion with His Father, seeing through all the mists the established Kingdom? Do we wonder at His worldliness as we recognize that this earth with all its misery was still Divinely beautiful to Him, so that, as He Himself did say, God clothes the grass of the field, and garbs the lily with more delicate beauty than that in which Solomon in all his glory was arrayed? A sparrow falls and sickens and dies, and has as Comrade in its dying, God. When that man bending to his toil, overwhelmed with it, bearing the burden and heat of the day, wipes from his brow the sweat and dust of toil, and with it some hair of his head, God has numbered that hair! Nothing was little or away from God. Do you wonder at His other-worldliness, that all His speech took on the accents of the eternities, and that His brow was ever so high lifted as to catch the flaming glories of the spiritual? Do you wonder at His love of the world, that all its trees and flowers and birds and children were near and dear to Him? In this world He knew nothing of divorce between the material and the spiritual. For Him every common bush was ablaze with God, and He saw men sitting round plucking blackberries! Do you wonder at His worldliness or at His other-worldliness? Do you wonder at His freedom from diplomacy when diplomacy simply meant arrangements between men who had forgotten God and did not know Him? Do you wonder that once when in the midst of lamentation and complaining at the unreasonableness of His own age, He thundered against the persistent rebellion of the cities in which He had done His work, His lamentation and thunder suddenly merging in the worship of God and His words, ". . . I thank Thee, O Father, Lord of heaven and earth, that Thou didst hide these things from the wise and understanding, and didst reveal them unto babes . . ."? Do you wonder at His disinterestedness? Are you amazed at the ceaselessness of His activity, its restlessness, and His carelessness of Himself?

He was concentric. He was the only Man of the vast multitudes of His day Who was not beside Himself. It was they who were beside themselves; they who, because no longer related to the center, God, were no longer in true relationship as within themselves. That is why He said to them in differing phrases, yet again and again the same thing, "He that findeth his life shall lose it; and he that loseth his life for My sake, shall find it." He was the lonely concentric; all the rest were eccentric. He was the one Man not beside

Himself, and therefore by the standards of all men who were beside themselves, beside Himself. In an eccentric world, a concentric man will ever seem eccentric.

It did not end with Jesus. I most reverently say it did not begin with Him. I read you a strange Psalm. It is one of the finest pieces of satire and irony in Hebrew poetry. Mark the movement of the psalmist as he laughs at the wisdom of the world, amassing wealth and passing to Sheol, and then exults in the wisdom of the simple-hearted, that rest in the wisdom and love of God. I repeat that to an eccentric world, the concentric man ever appears eccentric. It was so before Jesus came. It was so after He came. There was a day when Paul was talking to two kings and a queen, and one of the kings burst in upon the discourse saying, "Paul, thou art mad; thy much learning doth turn thee to madness." Who was mad; Paul or Festus? The Pope of Rome said that Luther ought to be in bedlam. The men of his own church said Xavier was mad. All England laughed at the unutterable folly of John Wesley. Many people thought William Booth was not quite sane! It has run through all the centuries. Men concentric, who have seen God and a vision of His Kingdom and have been mastered by the passion for that Kingdom, are ever considered beside themselves.

So I would commend to all this passion of Jesus, this worthy passion. To be thought eccentric with Him, to be thought fanatical in matters of religion, is a high compliment as angels watch and listen.

It is a worthy passion this, for it includes all others that are truly noble; all passion of protest against that which is wrong and oppressive, lies within this passion of our Lord for the Kingdom. All passion of endeavor that constructs and builds and toils and suffers, and has no time to eat, is enfolded within this passion of Jesus for the coming of the Kingdom of God.

It will always bring this charge of madness upon those who share it. The world is still self-centered, and in its eyes God-centered men are still the eccentrics of the world. When Paul reached Thessalonica, he had not been there very long before the men of Thessalonica said of him and of his friends, ". . . These that have turned the world upside down are come hither also." It is exactly the same idea. Let me suggest a sermon on the text; ". . . These that have turned the world upside down are come hither also." I will give you the divisions. First, the world is down-side up; second, and therefore, the men who are turning it upside down are turning it right side up; but third, and consequently, the men who are living in the world will think they are turning it upside down. That is the whole business.

Hear me as I say, I hope not censoriously, what the church of God supremely lacks today is this kind of passion. It is not the passion of madness, of frenzy; it is the burning passion that enables the church of God to cooperate with God when the wisdom of the world laughs at it. That is the true passion. We are not quite sure today that these methods of Jesus are the best methods. Are we not a little in danger of being over-busy in conferring about the adaptation of religious thought to the modern mind and the adaptation of religious organizations to modern conditions? I am somewhat tired of modern things, and that because the things of the Christ are ancient and modern. Christ told His disciples that they were to bring forth out of their treasure-house things new and old, and in proportion as we walk with Him we shall be compelled to the foolish things of the world wherewith God confounds their wise things.

That little bit of work you did this afternoon does seem

rather old-fashioned and out of date; that class of children that fidgeted all the while is just a little behind the times, is it not? A thousand times No! That is building for eternity and hastening the coming of the Kingdom of God. That call you made that no one knows about save you and the sick one, the flowers you took, the word of cheer, the tender approach to a soul that asked how it was between that soul and God; all that is Christly work.

I am not undervaluing other methods. God will send some of His workers into the House of Commons, and the more the better. God will send some of His workers on to Parish Councils and Town Councils, and we need them all. But let us not undervalue the foolish, simple, wandering, restless methods; the method that does things as they come and never draws up a program. That is the whole story of the life and ministry of Jesus. He did things as He went, as He passed by, as He went out, as He was by the sea. In the midst of preaching somebody disturbed Him, and He halted His preaching and went after Jairus; and on the way with Jairus a woman touched Him, and He left Jairus on one side to attend to the woman and then went on again. He did the next thing that came, because to those eyes the Kingdom was ever present. That touch of the hand, that glance of the eye, and that tone of the voice, all spoke of it and brought its power nearer. He was content to wait, as He still is waiting, till His enemies be made the footstool of His feet. That will never be done by the clash of arms, or by human cleverness; but by Christ and His comrades, of whom, until the last victory is won, the world will say they are beside themselves. So if we know the wisdom that is from above, we shall sing with Wesley:

> Fools and madmen let us be,
> Yet is our sure trust in Thee.

CHAPTER VIII

THE HEALING OF LIFE

In his strength he strove with God; yea, he had power over the angel, and prevailed; he wept, and made supplication unto him.

HOSEA, 12:3, 4.

THE STORY FROM WHICH OUR TEXT IS TAKEN IS A VERY OLD ONE; it has often been the subject of meditation and that in many applications. Yet it is wonderfully fresh and suggestive, and that because it brings us face to face with some of the elemental things of the soul. I expect I shall be perfectly accurate when I say that the youngest person in this house who heard me read the story had heard it many times before and had read it many times before; yet I do not hesitate also to say that they heard it again tonight with interest. The reason for this is that it makes direct appeal to the deepest things in human life. I repeat that this story of a distant age and of other climes brings us face to face with the elemental things of the soul.

It is the story of a man alone with God in the night, facing the inward and hidden things, keenly conscious of their presence and power. It is the story of a man who desired to be alone with God in the night and had deliberately arranged for such an experience. After having dispatched the droves of cattle in the day to meet his brother Esau, he took his wife and children back again over the Jabbok on to the other side to be away from the danger zone. He had stood there watching them, until they had disappeared into the quietness of the night, and then he had deliberately sought to be alone with God.

On the Divine side, it is the story of how God responded to the intention of this man, of how He stooped down to meet him on his own level, appearing to him and touching him as a Man. That is the story. That is the whole story. That is the marvel of it. A man away from his fellows and alone with his God.

Jacob desired to meet with God that night as we have said; but he did not quite know what that meant, he did not understand what it involved; and he never could have known perfectly what that meant, could not have understood what it involved, had it not been that God respected that desire and responded to the intention; and moreover that He did so by taking the form and fashion of a man and so drawing near to the seeking man.

This story, so old and so familiar then, is arresting and wonderful, among other reasons, because it gives us the account of one of the earliest theophanies, or appearances of God to men in human form. To my own mind there can be no question at all that the Man who drew near to Jacob that night, was none other than the Angel Jehovah, the very Son of God, taking that form at that time in order to draw near to that man, because there was no other way by which he could effectually be reached and mastered.

The story is full of interest also because the transactions between Jacob and Jehovah that night were definite and decisive. They came into touch, nay, into grips with each other. God and the man were set upon a purpose, apparently in conflict, but in reality one. The issue was victory for God and therefore for the man.

This, then, is the story. A man alone with God in the night, desiring to be alone with God, finding himself alone with God, though for a while not knowing that it was God Who had drawn near to him. Presently, when the crimson flush of morning was upon the sky, knowing that he had really been with God as he had desired, this man departed, and limping back to his loved ones, said as he went, ". . . I have seen God face to face, and my life is preserved." That is the wonderful story.

Let us then give ourselves once more to meditation of this familiar, strange, and revealing story. I do not now use that word "meditation" carelessly. I use it quite carefully, remembering the definition of it which I once heard from the lips of Dr. Griffith-Thomas. He said: "Meditation is attention with intention." Let that be the nature of our meditation. We will take time to study the story, not merely because it is an interesting one but in order that we may give attention to some of the things it reveals, intending to submit our lives to a like process and to discover from our meditation some of the true, deep secrets of life, that we may come to a fuller realization of them. I pray that for a little while there may be given to us that grace of detachment which shall enable us to separate from each other and from all lower interests, that so we may be as surely alone with God as Jacob was by the running Jabbok. I know it is difficult, but I know it is possible. It is made more difficult in that I as His messenger stand in some senses between you and Him. Yet may God grant that the shadow of my personality may be entirely blotted out by the light of His conscious presence, and that I may not in any way hinder your coming into close fellowship with Him while we consider the old story once again.

THE HEALING OF LIFE

I suggest that we observe: first, this man's sense of need; second, this man's sense of opportunity as it came to him that night; third, the business of the night between this man and God; finally, this man's sense of realization when the morning broke.

First, then, let us consider his sense of need. Here I am greatly helped by all that to which I have been making reference, our familiarity with the whole story. Jacob that night was face to face with his past. That past was marching back upon him in the form of Esau to confront him. It was twenty years since he had passed by that way. Twenty years before he had left home, then a man of seventy years of age. He had been compelled to hurry away under the shadow and cloud of a great deception. Now he was coming back, and he was realizing the troublesome fact that a man's past is not always behind him. Again and again a man's past swings round before him and marches directly upon him. That is what was happening to Jacob that night. All our language concerning him in this regard is merely the attempted expression of our conceptions of infinite things. These statements are the paradoxes of the spiritual life.

Jacob that night was facing his past. The meanness by which he had taken advantage of his brother's hunger to obtain his birthright; the perchance greater meanness by which he had deceived his father and obtained the blessing of the first-born.

These are the hours that we all know, hours when the past that we cannot undo, though we would like to do so, comes back confronting us again.

In that hour of the night the need of Jacob was not only that occasioned by the fact of that marching upon him of his past; his need was occasioned by the fact that that marching upon him of his past was menacing his future. This man was a hard, astute, bargain-driving, clever man with that material cleverness that succeeds anywhere with material things. Yet on this night, face to face with his past and his future, the underlying deeps of his nature powerfully and persistently asserted themselves. Let us listen to him: ". . . with my staff I passed over this Jordan; and now I am become two bands." That is, translated into modern speech, I started out twenty years ago with no capital, and now I am coming back a wealthy man. Nevertheless, he was troubled, disturbed, afraid. His trouble that night was not occasioned by the thought of his cattle and his property; not principally with the thought that the mother with the children may suffer, though that did trouble him. He was principally troubled by the fear that he might be excluded from the land of his fathers, from the very land which he knew was his in the economy and purpose of God. All the future within the Covenant made with Abraham and Isaac seemed menaced by the past; and, therefore, the man was distraught, troubled, perplexed.

Yet, I am bound to say that I personally do not think that this reveals the deepest need of the man as he himself felt it. The more carefully I ponder the story the more I believe that on this night Jacob was conscious of need more profound than any of these things can possibly measure; that he was conscious that his own life was somehow wrong in itself; that he was hot and restless in the deeper consciousness of the soul. He had been disappointed, he had become embittered. His experiences with Laban had been unsatisfactory in every way. The two bands which he possessed did not give him rest of soul. You may ask me what right I have to imagine that he had any such feeling as he took his way to the place of loneliness with God. I reply that my conviction is based upon what he said in the morning: ". . . I have seen

God face to face, and my life is preserved." That is the language of a man who knew there was disease in his life, that there was something wrong with the central fact of his own being. It was the exclamation of a man who knew fever and restlessness, who knew that ache at the center of his being which no bands could satisfy and to which no material success could minister.

This is the picture of Jacob as I see him at the close of that day. Laban had marched away from him in the morning. Esau was coming to meet him. He had manipulated his possessions so as to appease his brother, for the past of his wrongdoing was confronting him. There was anxiety in his heart about Rachael and the children. But these were not the principal reasons of his trouble. His deepest agony had no relation to Laban, to Esau, or to the wife and children. It was an agony concerning his own soul. Therefore, he did what men constantly do under stress of circumstances; he said, I will stay here a little, alone with God. God is ever the last resort of the soul, self-troubled, restless, consciously diseased. How good a thing it is that even under such conditions He is willing to receive us.

Let us now observe what the story reveals of the sense of opportunity that came to him. There can be no question that to Jacob it was a wonderful day, a strange day, a mystic day. Things happened to him that day that were most strange. He had heard of such things before perhaps in the experience of his father Isaac or of his grandfather Abraham. Indeed, he had also known something of the kind in a dream twenty years before on the very day that he had left his home.

At the beginning of the chapter, two verses tell the strange thing that had happened in the early morning. Laban had left him. The parting had been by no means a pleasant one. Much bargaining had gone on between them. There had been fierce recriminations. Jacob had spoken out at last all the bitter things he had been thinking about Laban. Then there had been the building of the heap of stones and the naming of the place Mizpah; and the covenant of suspicion, the Lord watch between me and thee, the idea being not that of the watching of a shepherd but that of a policeman. Each had practically said to the other, "that heap of stones is a sign that you are not to rob me any more, and that I will not cheat you any more!" So at last Laban had marched away.

Then Jacob saw angels in the early morning. Where they were I cannot tell; what form they took I do not know, but to this man there was given a vision of angels perhaps sweeping across the sky before his astonished eyes. Then he said: "This is God's host!" The sight of them, as we have said, reminded him of the dream of twenty years before. He called the name of that place "Mahanaim," the place of two hosts; Laban's host had gone, but God's host was near. He was conscious of the two hosts. Then the business of the day went forward, but the impression of that morning vision would remain with him until eventide.

Look at him again in the midst of the business of the day, in the midst of the technicalities—while he was arranging the presents for Esau with that cunning which characterized him, sending one drove at a time in the hope that one drove would appease Esau and if one drove would appease Esau, and if one drove would suffice, Jacob was not the man to give two —in the midst of all the astute arrangements, he suddenly broke out into prayer, and this was the way the prayer he prayed commenced: ". . . O God of my father Abraham, and God of my father Isaac. . . ." God was all about him that day, breaking in upon his consciousness in different ways; in the morning by the vision of the host of angels when Laban had left him; in the middle of the day by the remembrance of the religion of his father and his grandfather and of God's relationship to them, a remembrance constraining him to prayer. So, at the end of the day he said, "Now let me stay here and be alone with this God. Let me set past, and future, and this troubled self in right relation with Him."

Then came the surprise. It is only as we read this story quite simply that we catch the true and full force of this. We are not to imagine that Jacob knew immediately that it was the hand of God which was laid upon him. The statement of the story is undoubtedly the statement of Jacob's consciousness; ". . . there wrestled a man with him. . . ." Let us be as realistic about this story as though we were reading it to a little child. This man had stayed behind for the express purpose of being alone with God; and he was surprised and startled because some man suddenly, mysteriously, was with him, coming from no one knew where, and no one knew how; and this stranger put his hand upon him in the night, and Jacob found himself in the strong grip of a man. ". . . there wrestled a man with him. . . ." It is never said that he wrestled with the man. There is a sense, of course, in which he did, but his wrestling was the wrestling of defence against the attack of the stranger. A man had put his hand upon him. Jacob did not know what he meant, what he was going to do, or who he was.

In the presence of this strange experience, Jacob exerted all the force of his strength against the wrestler in the night. Mark the marvel of it, he was successful, so that the man wrestling against him did not overcome him, did not prevail against him. That was the business of the night.

The first matter which impresses me and which we should observe carefully, for its spiritual value is supreme, is that of the tremendous resisting power of Jacob. As a whole man he was invincible and invincible against the hand of God. God could not break in upon this strong will, so long as the man remained a whole man. The whole man was wrong, had been so for years; his central principle of action had been a wrong principle. He had faith in God and had never lost that faith in God. It was the central fact of his mental life. But side by side with it there had been such confidence in himself that his faith had never waited for God. He had ever been trying to help God and so had hindered Him. It was that inner strength of the man which was making for his ultimate ruin and which must be broken down if he was ever to find the real fulfilment of his own life. Yet Jacob in his own strength was that night invincible. There was no way to capture and realize his life save through the overcoming of that strength.

Does this story sound unlikely, contradictory? Let us think once again in the light of our own experience and in the profoundest mystery of our own lives. God ever stands outside human will as is necessary to the perfecting of human life. His one aim is to bring that will to surrender to its own election to His will. There are thousands of men who are resisting God as successfully as Jacob did that night.

At last, as the first flush of the dawn appeared, seeing that He prevailed not against him in conflict with his strength, He adopted another method, that of weakening his strength physically. God's power was limited in the struggle through that night, self-limited, held in restraint, in the first process of the conflict. Now He proceeded along another line, He crippled him.

That method does not always conquer a man, but it does give him a new opportunity. There are men, alas, whom God has crippled with the intention of crowning them, but they have never let Him crown them. That is the alarming, terrific fact that we have to face most solemnly. The last peril is that we may not only resist God while He is attempting to bring us by wrestling into subjection but also when He attempts to break in upon our lives in pain and sorrow and crippling. But Jacob did not fail here. He responded to disabling though he had held out in tremendous and invincible strength against the wrestling of the night. It was when he was crippled, I think as I read the story, that there broke upon him the consciousness that he was having dealings with One Who was not man. He then began to discover that the very thing for which he had remained behind had happened to him, even though he did not know until that moment that it had happened. The hand of the man upon him was the hand of God.

Many a man, when desiring to meet with God, has got into grips with Him, and yet has not recognized the hand upon him as that of God. In the commonplaces of everyday life, oftentimes the very things that batter and bruise, until we halt by the way, are the result of God's hand upon us, and yet we do not recognize it. So it was with Jacob.

When the Man, the Wrestler, at last said, ". . . Let me go, for the day breaketh," Jacob said: ". . . I will not let thee go except thou bless me." That was not said in any strident voice! Hosea tells us the story of that cry. With his strength he strove against God, and God did not win over him in that struggle, neither did he master God therein. Then God crippled him, and at once he prevailed over the Wrestler, not by his strength but by his weakness. He prevailed in the moment when submitting with strong crying and tears, he said: ". . . I will not let thee go, except thou bless me."

Now with close attention let us follow the events. Said the Man to him, ". . . What is thy name? And he said, Jacob." It is more than interesting, it is vital to the story that we remind ourselves of the meaning of this name. We read it and to us it is just a name, but it was a Hebrew word with a very clear meaning. Heel-catcher, supplanter, trickster! That is what Jacob means. Then said the Wrestler to him, ". . . Thy name shall be called no more Jacob, but Israel"; no more trickster but one under the mastery of God. It is of equal importance that we should remember that Israel does not mean prince; the word "prince" has really no connection with the word at all. Thou shalt be called Isra El, one ruled by God. That is what the Wrestler said to him.

Once more let us look at this matter closely. In the moment when Jacob found his strength gone, he became conscious that the touch upon him was not merely the touch of a man but the touch of God; and that he was in the very presence of God. Then he said: ". . . I will not let thee go, except thou bless me." In that "I will not" of weakness, there was almightiness of strength; in that submission to God, he found his way into the place of power. When weakened, he flung himself upon God, claiming His blessing, he was crowned.

Finally, what was the sense of realization that came to him? What did that night really mean to him? We have the answer from his own lips and then from the pen of the chronicler. From his own lips this is the story: ". . . I have seen God face to face, and my life is preserved." Then from the pen of the recorder, this is the answer: "And as he passed over Penuel the sun rose upon him, and he halted upon his thigh."

I do not think that very many words in the nature of application are necessary. The story powerfully conveys its own teaching. As we said at the beginning, we have given ourselves to a reconsideration of this, supremely desiring in the process to have direct and personal dealings with God. The reasons for this desire have brought us into closest sympathy with the theme. For us, also, there is a past that we want to be dealt with; there is a future which is menaced by the past; and deeper than all others, there is the sense within our own souls that we need some healing touch, some infinite and eternal medicine for the soul that will make fever end and bring us new strength and peace. We need healing of life. Is not that the truth concerning ourselves? I will not commit others to that statement if they object, but that exactly represents my own sense of need.

Then be it ours to remember that all this need in the case of Jacob was met in the experience which he described on the declaration he made: ". . . my life is preserved."

Let us begin at the first point, our need as to the past. God puts Himself between a man and his past. We are familiar with the sequel. When the morning broke and Jacob went forward to meet Esau, he found that no present was needed to appease him. God had dealt with Esau. Esau met him with love, and tenderness, and brotherly affection. That sequel is illuminated for us by a quotation from another part of the Bible:

> When a man's way please Jehovah,
> He maketh even his enemies to be at peace with him.

In the moment when we really submit ourselves to Him, He puts Himself between us and all in the past that haunts the soul. It may be, and indeed assuredly must be, that while He puts Himself between us and the past, we shall yet undergo chastisement resulting from the past; but it will be His hand, and it will be only such as is necessary for the making of our lives. All that is possible for us here and now. What in the past is haunting thy soul, O brother mine? I pray that you in this moment let God come between you and your past! He can do it, and He can do it in such a way as to give your conscience perfect peace. God does not deal with the past in the life of a man by some kind of good-natured beneficence which says, "We will say no more about that past!" That is not God's method. It is impossible to him, Who is as surely Light as He is Love. But by atonement, by the mystery of the Cross, by the wonder of the passion; by that which can only have illustration in human history by the Cross of Calvary. God in His pain stands between man and his past gathering into His own being all the sin and its issues and annihilating all in the compassion and passion of His love. That is the only place of rest for a troubled conscience. Nothing less than that can give true peace to the sinful soul. I dare not say that it does not satisfy me for it does. In that sense also, with regard to my past, I am prepared to say, "Thou, O Christ, art all I want."

It is equally true that God stands between us and the future. There are some of us, it may be, who are not especially concerned about the past; we know its failure and shortcoming, but we have trusted His grace, and there is no haunting phantom out of the bygone years that comes to haunt the soul. But the days ahead are threatening us. We see things in the future which are not the result of love and peace but which are threatening our hope, our confidence, and our very life. We are almost afraid to take one step forward, so great is our foreboding of ill. Then let us resolutely dare to put God between ourselves and our future, knowing of a surety that He Who met the man Jacob by the Jabbok that night so long ago and by the correction of his past made his future possible, is the God Who will undertake for all of us who put our trust in Him.

Yet finally and supremely, this personal dealing with God means, if we yield to Him and allow Him the mastery and possession of our lives, that He will deal with the deepest malady of the soul, with that inner heart trouble, that disease, dis-ease, that fever that spoils the life. It is by dealing with that central trouble that He strengthens us for all the future has in store for us.

I thank God that I am able to make that announcement knowing that all about me are those who know the thing is true, for they have found God's healing and so have entered into His peace.

If someone imagines himself or herself to be lonely, let such an one remember that his or her need has already been met in the experience of thousands of trusting souls. There is no temperament that He has not met and satisfied, no peculiar form or fashion of human heart-trouble, soul-malady, spirit-agony, that He has not already healed.

If, then, we will but yield ourselves to Him as He stands confronting us in Christ with the break of the first day that follows the night of our struggle and submission, the sun will rise upon us, and we shall know that having seen Him face to face, our life is healed; and we also shall be able to call the place of our yielding Penuel, the face of God, because it shall be the place where strength weakened becomes strength realized, the place where the old supplanting nature is changed into the victorious life of those who reign in life, because they are ruled by God.

CHAPTER IX

FORGIVENESS

. . . the forgiveness of our sins.
COLOSSIANS 1:14.

THESE WORDS CONSTITUTE A PHRASE OF INTERPRETATION. It stands in this verse in apposition to the word "redemption," and declares its fundamental value. "In Whom we have our redemption, the forgiveness of our sins." Redemption in its finality means far more than forgiveness of sins. In that finality it is complete restoration of the life to fellowship with God. In the fulness of redemption the spirit of man is consciously at peace with God, in righteousness as a condition, and in joy as an experience. In the fulness of redemption, the mind of man apprehends the things of God and finds perfect rest therein. In the ultimate perfection of redemption, the body of humiliation will be fashioned anew and conformed to the body of the glory of the Lord Jesus Christ. But this whole finality is the result of forgiveness. The experiences of fellowship are impossible apart from that of the forgiveness of sins, but let it be added immediately, they are the inevitable result of that experience. Where the forgiveness of sins is truly known, there does immediately result the sense of spiritual peace and mental rest, and the song of the final is already in the heart; so that even if today in these tabernacles we groan, we do so not as without hope and confidence that there shall be the perfecting of our personality ere the work of redemption be completed. All these phases of redemption, spiritual, mental, and physical, follow this fundamental sense of the forgiveness of sins. This, then, is the first wonder and glory of the Cross, for the Cross is the tree to which the Lord bore up our sins that we might be set apart from them, be dead to them, and so live unto righteousness.

> Into the woods my Master went,
> Clean forspent, forspent.
> Into the woods my Master came,
> Forspent with love and shame.
> But the olives they were not blind to Him,
> The little grey leaves were kind to Him:
> The thorn-tree had a mind to Him
> When into the woods He came.
>
> Out of the woods my Master went,
> And He was well content.
> Out of the woods my Master came,
> Content with death and shame.
> When death and shame would woo Him last
> From under the trees they drew Him last;
> 'Twas on a tree they slew Him—last
> When out of the woods He came.

To that tree He bore up our sins, that we being dead to and separated from those sins might live unto righteousness. The first value of the Cross, then, is that of "the forgiveness of our sins."

The apostle's sense of the vital importance of this experience is revealed in this particular passage by two things. It is seen first in the fact that he does thus make it stand for the whole fact of redemption: "In Whom we have our redemption," and as exposition of redemption he is content to write this phrase, "the forgiveness of our sins," knowing very well, none better than he, as all his writings testify, that growing out of that fundamental experience are all the infinite reaches and values of Christian victory and Christian triumph. Here, however, everything begins, and so he puts the gracious first and fundamental part as inclusive of the glorious whole to its finality. "In Whom we have our redemption, the forgiveness of our sins." The apostolic sense of the vital importance of the experience is even more remarkably manifested in the fact that in this relation he reaches the highest level of his teaching as to the One through Whom that redemption is made possible. "In Whom we have our redemption. . . ." We take the phrase, change its emphasis, and make it a question: in Whom have we our redemption, this forgiveness of sins? Clustering about the brief phrase, we find the apostle's highest teaching about the Person of the Lord. Mark the phrases as I take them away from their context, knowing your familiarity with the context, and knowing that you will fill in mentally all that I omit: ". . . the Son of his love . . . the image of the invisible God . . . the firstborn of all creation . . . the firstborn from the dead . . ." the One in Whom all fulness dwells. The stupendous, majestic descriptions lend their dignity, force, and meaning to this: "In whom we have our redemption, . . ." and lend the note of assurance, hope, and confidence to all sin-burdened souls, ". . . the forgiveness of our sins."

If we are to escape the tendency of the age, that of questioning the fact or undervaluing the value of the forgiveness of sins, we must familiarize ourselves with this setting of the thought in relation to the One through Whom the possibility is affirmed. The mystery of forgiveness is commensurate with and must be interpreted by, the mystery of the

One through Whom we have our redemption, the forgiveness of our sins.

First, observe He is no solitary member of the human race but its Root and its Source, ". . . the Son of His love . . . the image of the invisible God. . . ." The One from Whom all things have proceeded is God, Who is love, and the Saviour is the Son of His love in the deepest and most profound sense of the word; in the sense of that mystic relation to Him which is taught from beginning to the end of the New Testament and has been the central belief of the church through two millenniums: He is ". . . the Son of His love . . . the image of the invisible God." So I repeat, this One is not a solitary member of the human race but the One from Whom the whole race has sprung; its Root and Source.

Again, He is no stranger to the race, but Himself its final glory, ". . . the firstborn of all creation." In passing it is necessary that we should remind ourselves that this expression "firstborn" does not mean first in order of time but more probably last in order of time. The "firstborn" is not one who is at the beginning but the ultimate flower and fruitage of the creation. Here the Son of God is seen in that infinite mystery of relationship to the human race which makes Him no stranger to it but Himself the final glory of it; the One toward Whom the whole creation moved by whatever process it went forward, the firstborn, the last, the ultimate glory.

Yet again, and here we touch the inner heart of the matter; He is no stranger to the tragedy of sin but is the One Who was identified with all even unto death; the One Who vanquished all and Who therefore can no longer be described as "firstborn of creation," the final flower and fruit of a process, but "firstborn from the dead" and thus the Originator of a new order and a new race, the One Who moves toward the ultimate realization of the Divine purpose.

Once again, He is no mere heroic dreamer attempting splendid things. There have been many such in the history of the world, but Christ is not to be numbered among them. I repeat, He is not merely a heroic dreamer attempting splendid things, but One Who accomplishes all in the sufficiency of the fulness of Godhead; the One in Whom all fulness dwells; the fulness of originating power, the fulness of capacity for suffering, the fulness of capacity for overcoming all suffering and originating a new and redemptive order. "In Whom we have our redemption, the forgiveness of our sins."

Thus the apostle, unlike so many of his interpreters, makes no attempt to discuss the forgiveness of sins as in the abstract and apart from the Person to Whom the great evangel is immediately related. By these things redemption must always be interpreted, and in their light the possibility of the forgiveness of sins must be considered. As a Christian man, I must decline to enter into any argument or discussion with any man as to whether the forgiveness of sins be possible until that man shall come face to face with this Person. It is a subject transcending all science save theology, and theology, the science of God, is progressive and growing and has never reached its final statement by way of system or exposition. It is inclusively contained within the Divine writings, and its greatness and grandeur are revealed by the fact that through these running centuries, devout and sincere thinkers have differed and have seen only parts of the whole. The catholic church moves on toward the final exposition, but we have not reached it yet, and until we have reached that final science of God we cannot discuss finally the possibility of the forgiveness of sins because it is related to God Himself. In the same way I affirm that this is a truth vaster then all philosophy save that of the wisdom of God. I suppose I shall do no violence to philosophic thought and the history of philosophy if I say that human philosophy has never yet reached the hour when it has been able to admit the possibility of the forgiveness of sins; and that because of its own inability to take in the whole sum of things as that sum of things is contained within God. Behind philosophy there lies theology, and if it be not finally uttered, neither is philosophy finally apprehended, and therefore no man can explain philosophically the mystery of the forgiveness of sins.

We are gathered in spirit around the green hill, around the tree to which Jesus of Nazareth went. Flashing upon it, in the light of these descriptive phrases, we find that He is the Son of the Divine love, the very image of God, the firstborn of creation, the firstborn from the dead, the One in Whom all the fulness of Deity dwells. We are amazed, mystified, and held away, so that we confess that we cannot finally understand; and yet out of the supreme and effulgent glory of the mystery and majesty of the Person, the song that rejoices our heart is this, "In whom we have our redemption, the forgiveness of our sins."

It seems to me, the possibility must be conceded when these things concerning the Person of the One Who claims authority are apprehended. I do not say that the possibility is understood. I do not say it is explained, that man can finally give a definition of the mystery of it as within the Divine economy, but grant this Person, and the possibility may at least be admitted.

From that level let me descend. The possibility of the forgiveness of sins is demonstrated also by the experience of the forgiven. Perhaps this never can be cumulative; perhaps it may be true that we cannot take the forgiveness of this man and the forgiveness of that man and join them together and declare that there is added weight to the argument. There is no aggregate of sin and no aggregate of sorrow; sin is individual, sorrow is individual; we cannot add sin to sin and make a great whole; we cannot add sorrow to sorrow and make a great totality; we must deal with individuals. As in the realm of sin and sorrow, so here also perchance. The experience of one individual, however, is enough to arrest attention and demand consideration. Therefore, I declare that the possibility of the forgiveness of sins is demonstrated by the experience of the forgiven.

What then is that experience of the forgiveness of sins, as an experience? First, it is moral readjustment; second, it is mental transformation; third, it is spiritual emancipation. Having consented to admit that there may be no aggregate of experience, you must bear with me if I speak out of my own experience and become a witness rather than an advocate. What is this sense of the forgiveness of sins which I claim to know and have within my own soul, against which claim you can by no means produce any argument strong enough to render me an unbeliever in that which I myself do know. It is first that of moral readjustment, second, that of mental transformation, and consequently, that of spiritual emancipation. It may be that in the order of the Divine procedure within the soul of man, spiritual emancipation is the first thing, then mental transformation, issuing in moral readjustment. So far as personal experience is concerned, this is the order; moral readjustment, mental transformation, spiritual emancipation.

Moral readjustment. There is an underlying human consciousness of the difference between right and wrong. That consciousness is human. It is not the result of civilization, it is not found alone in any peculiar locality; it exists wherever man is. In that consciousness, so far as we know, man is differentiated from everything beneath him in the scale of beings. I am growingly a believer that we do not know all about the animal creation beneath us and am inclined to believe with St. Francis of Assisi, John Wesley, and others that the animals also have an afterlife. But so far as we know, man stands alone in this matter of the consciousness of the difference between right and wrong. Ask a man for the standard and he may not be able to give it, even though he live in London, but this underlying sense of it is present. There is nothing more full of hope to thinking men than this fact, that this underlying consciousness of humanity always beats true to the revelation of God found in the sacred Scriptures. There comes back to me as I speak an illustration from the Old Testament which I think is very full of light. When Jeremiah was exercising his great ministry in Jerusalem, he said upon one memorable occasion to those people who were rushing headlong to destruction in spite of all his teaching, "Refuse silver shall men call them, because the Lord hath rejected them." I am interested in that word now, not because of its application to the children of Israel, but as the revelation of a persistent fact. Here were people who had had light and opportunity; they had refused the light; then said Jeremiah, "men shall call you refuse silver." That is to say, deep down in the human heart and conscience there is that which recognizes the beauty of holiness, the truth of good, and the right of righteousness. If people of privilege refuse to walk in the light, the people outside watching, name them refuse silver. That is true today. Underlying all our difficulties, our problems, our procedures, and our conflicts, there is this human consciousness, and it is universal; varying in its interpretation, often crude and uneducated, but ever present. Let no Christian soul be deceived, and let no unchristian soul attempt to deceive itself. Man knows the thing that is right and the thing that is wrong.

If I could but reach the deepest of the man who persists in the wrong and persuade from his reluctant soul the absolute truth of the thing he knows, he would tell me that his badness is bad and that goodness is the best. That includes immediately the personal consciousness of sin, of sin committed, of consequent pollution, and of resultant paralysis. I admit men may so harden themselves that the consciousness of sin committed brings no pang to the heart or conscience.

But now let us proceed to think of the man who knowing his own sin, becomes conscious of his pollution, and becomes conscious also of paralysis. To that man hell hardly has any terror. I am growingly suspicious of the morality that results from the fear of hell. I have had to do with men and women—and I have known something of the experience in my own heart—to whom hell would almost be a relief if by any chance they could persuade themselves that its fires would cleanse them from the sense of pollution and filth. It is that sense of pollution in the soul resulting from sin with which forgiveness deals. Involved in that sense of pollution is the terrific, appalling, despairing, agonizing sense of paralysis; "When I would do good evil is present with me." Let us not recite that as though the apostle were a dialectician pressing an argument; he was talking out of his soul, mastered by the consciousness of sin, choked by it, poisoned by it, hindered by it. That is the sense of paralysis which is the heart agony of the sense of pollution. All that is background. All that is the background of Calvary, the ugliness of Golgotha, the terrible tragedy of the green hill.

"The forgiveness of our sins" is first of all the deep, profound sense in the soul, of being delivered from sins, being set apart from them; the relationship between them and the soul, as to pollution and paralysis being broken. I have quoted more than once, though not in the exact words but with slight change, those wonderful words of Peter, "Who His own self bare our sins in His body upon the tree, that we, having died unto sins. . . ." The arresting fact in that verse is that there we have a word translated "died" which never appears anywhere else in the New Testament. It is not the usual word for death. It was a very common word in the Greek classical writers, and it was used for death. But what it really means is simply to be set apart from. That is the sense of forgiveness, the sense that comes to the soul who trusts in Christ; who obeying His call and falling in with His simple condition of repentance and faith, now receives the gift, the setting apart from sin. It is always accompanied by the sense of humbling, the sense of shame, and the sense of sorrow. It is always accompanied by the sense of gratitude and joy and singing. It is a strange, mystic consciousness, Christ-begotten and in no other way begotten; that which every man and woman who has truly trusted in the Lord knows in some measure and which no man or woman finds apart from Him; a mystic sense, no longer as a theory but as a fact—I am forgiven. I repeat, that always brings humbling, and to live a forgiven soul is to live in all humility and in all gladness.

You may discuss this scientifically, philosophically; you may come to the conclusion that science admits no possibility of forgiveness; you may declare that in all your thinking you have never found how this thing can be; and I object to your scientific and philosophic thinking concerning the definite experience of one soul. I know my sins are forgiven. If you will not admit the aggregate, at least stand reverently in the presence of the individual confession.

It is more than a sense of being set apart from one's sins, it is the sense of positive freedom. Witness the new moralities that spring out of this conviction wherever it takes possession of the soul of man. Mark the men who tell you they have been forgiven, men who have been in the grip of every form of evil and bestiality; mark them and see springing out of those lives all beauty and truth, all grace and loveliness; listen to the songs coming up from the souls that were filled with the darkest despair; witness the humility which manifests itself and the new service that begins!

Forgiveness is also mental transformation. There is a sense in which this is gradual, progressive. Peter charged those to whom he wrote to ". . . grow in the grace and knowledge of our Lord and Saviour Jesus Christ." Do not separate those two things. We very often quote that passage partially, "grow in . . . grace." It does not end there; ". . . and in the knowledge of our Lord and Saviour Jesus Christ." Mental transformation is immediate but progressive. We know the Lord and follow on to know the Lord and so grow in knowledge. Through those great letters of the imprisonment, Ephesians, Colossians, Philippians, Philemon, there runs one note of almost agonized prayer on behalf of Paul's children in the faith. What was it he was asking for them? They had faith, and he thanked God for their faith; they had hope, and he rejoiced therein; they had love, and he gloried in it; yet he prayed that they might have full knowledge. This mental transformation is first a new apprehension of God; second, a new apprehension of self; third, a new view of other men. A man forgiven knows God as he never had known Him before. Intellectually, he may have been convinced of His existence and have feared Him with a quite wholesome fear. Following forgiveness, the intellectual becomes emotional, and the fear of Him which was dread of Him, becomes fear lest His heart should be wounded by his sin. A new vision of God and a new understanding of himself, and of his relation to God and to all things in the midst of which he lives, and therefore, a new view of his brother-man; all these follow forgiveness.

A new passion for knowledge and a new devotion to inquiry, the discipleship which will issue in full knowledge; these also result and that progressively.

So finally, forgiveness is spiritual emancipation. The forgiven man is the worshiping man; the forgiven man is the serving man. I have not brought these words idly together; they are closely related, not only in experience, but in revelation. I go back once more for illustration to the mystery of the wilderness temptation of our Lord and to the answer He gave the enemy as he finally assaulted Him, ". . . It is written, Thou shalt worship the Lord thy God, and Him only shalt thou serve." Observe the relationship between the two. The man emancipated spiritually is the man who worships and who serves; no man serves in the full sense of the term, unless his service proceed from worship, and no man worships in the full sense of the term, unless his worship drives him out to service.

The forgiven man is the spiritually emancipated man. He worships, and the first exercise in his worship is praise, while the second is prayer. The first note is praise, not prayer. The new life bestowed upon the forgiven man, the tearing away of the veil between himself and God, and dissipation of the darkness, the sense of God, does not first create within him a desire for something for himself even on the highest levels. He desires first to give to God; there breaks from his heart a song, crude and mean in its expression though it may be, but sacred and holy as a vestal flame in its inner inspiration. I sometimes think the best level of illustration is the simplest. Those who have had to do with souls in the deeper darkness of life, those who perhaps are devoid of all educational and intellectual advantage, have seen new-born souls beginning to worship. Worship is praise, the emancipated spirit, finding the face of God and singing. Our priesthood is first eucharistic. I do not like the word in some senses because I want every child to understand it; but I use it of set purpose for it runs all through the New Testament. What is the eucharist? The thanksgiving! Our priesthood is not first intercessory, it is first a priesthood of thanksgiving. When a man knows his sins forgiven, he finds spiritual emancipation and he begins to praise. Then he comes to a sense of his brother's wrong, and he begins to pray.

Spiritual emancipation means not worship alone, but service, for it means a spirit brought back into right relationship with God and realizing within itself Divine inspiration. The forgiven soul immediately finds fellowship with that in God which makes forgiveness possible. It begins to know something of what it is to fill up that which is behind in the sufferings of Christ, to share His Cross, to be driven out to serve as He served. The Divine inspiration is the Divine compassion, and blessed be God, it is something more; it is the Divine energy. That enables us in all service which the Christ appoints, and the Cross is its true and only way. These are the spiritual emancipations which come as the result of the sense of forgiveness. I am not surprised that when Paul said "In Whom we have our redemption . . ." he covered the ground and exhausted it, calling the first phase of the experience, ". . . the forgiveness of our sins."

Finally, quietly and reverently, we gather back in imagination to Golgotha, to the Cross itself. What is this upon which we look? We look upon the outward symbols. Let us remember that, for that will keep us reverent in the presence of the Cross. We cannot look upon the inner mystery. Here is light too bright for the feebleness of a sinner's sight. Here are matters too profound for the comprehension of finite intelligence. These are symbols, signs. They are signs material, and mental; signs which admit us a little nearer to the heart of infinite mystery.

What are the material signs? The place of a skull, the Roman gibbet, and a Man of matchless tenderness and beauty and sinlessness dying, cruelly murdered.

As He passed through the darkness, words passed His lips giving me symbols in the mental realm of the spiritual things which lie behind. I listen to them, not daring to omit any one of them. "Woman, behold thy son! . . . Behold thy mother!" There are some things I dare not begin to try to interpret! Listen to this, ". . . Father forgive them, for they know not what they do. . . ." Ye men and angels, who is this, what does this mean? Listen to this, ". . . To day shalt thou be with Me in Paradise." Listen to this, ". . . I thirst." Listen to this, ". . . It is finished." Listen to this, ". . . Father into Thy hands I commend My spirit. . . ." How much do we know? The supreme knowledge is that we cannot know. We have been led to the margin of unfathomable things, and most wonderful of them all is that which I have omitted, ". . . My God, My God, why hast Thou forsaken Me?"

"In Whom we have our redemption, the forgiveness of our sins." I come to that tree, and I come a sinful man! Dare I doubt? So help me God, I dare not! I venture; I believe: "My God is reconciled, His pardoning voice I hear." The mystery grows upon my soul as the years run on, but the healing and the peace are more precious today than ever. There, and there alone, let us find our rest.

CHAPTER X

THE RESURRECTION

. . . it was not possible that He should be holden of it.
ACTS 2:24.

SO FAR AS THE RECORDS OF THE NEW TESTAMENT REVEAL, THESE words constitute the first Pentecostal comment upon the fact of the Resurrection. They occur in the second part of the discourse delivered upon the Day of Pentecost by Peter. In the early part of that discourse, he set the things upon which men were looking and which were filling their hearts with astonishment, in relation to the prophetic writings of the Hebrew people. Having done this he commenced, "Ye men of Israel, hear these words . . ."; and then in brief and wonderful sentences, he told the whole story of the mission of Jesus. In this discourse concerning Jesus, there is a main line of argument twice interrupted by parenthetical explanation.

The words of my text constitute the first sentence in the first of these parentheses of exposition. Briefly, the discourse declared that Jesus of Nazareth was a Man, and that He was a Man approved of God unto those among whom He labored by the miracles and wonders which God wrought, approved that is as perfect in His humanity and therefore the instrument of those miracles and wonders and signs. Then the apostle declared that this man was delivered to death by the determinate counsel and foreknowledge of God, and that He died at the hands of men who were without the law, to whom he had been handed over by the men of Israel. Thus he merged two truths concerning the Cross into one great declaration. It was the ultimate in sin, it was the ultimate in grace. The hands of lawless men crucified Him but this within the determinate counsel and foreknowledge of God.

He then proceeded to declare that God raised this Jesus from the dead and had exalted Him to His own right Hand, and that as the result of that exaltation, the Spirit had been poured forth.

The first word of comment, I say, on the fact of the Resurrection, is this word of my text, ". . . it was not possible that He should be holden of it." Its note was that of exultant triumph. Imaginatively one can almost hear Peter saying, ". . . it was not possible that He should be holden of it." He! and as he thus referred to Him, there was within him the memory of the years he had spent in His company, the shame and sorrow of his own denial, the exultant joy of his own restoration, and supremely the sense of the new life and hope that had come to him by the way of the Resurrection. The whole fact of the Person of his Lord, dawning with new meaning upon his soul as the result of that Resurrection, was in his mind as he said, "He!" It was not possible that ". . . He should be holden of it." In the presence of that Resurrection fact, which had changed the man at the very center of his being, he spoke of death almost surely with contempt. "It."

Notice the declaration itself, and broadly first of all. It was a declaration made by this man illuminated by the Spirit, seeing things as he had never seen them; that God raised Jesus because it was necessary that He should do so. We may be very bold at this point and declare that here Peter affirmed that God was bound to raise Jesus from the dead. The character of God was involved, the nature of His law was at stake, the interest of eternal order was implicated. ". . . it was not possible that He should be holden of it." That such an One as He should lie in the power of death irrevocably was impossible. ". . . it was not possible that He should be holden of it." Then, having said so daring and so bold a thing, he halted for argument; and for argument he turned to one of the Psalms with which these men of Israel were so perfectly familiar. Citing from the sixteenth Psalm in our arrangement of the psalter—not exactly as we find the words there but from the Septuagint Version, which is exactly the same in spirit and in truth—he gave these words as constituting his argument for the declaration he made.

> I beheld the Lord always before my face:
> For He is on my right hand, that I should not be moved:
> Therefore my heart was glad, and my tongue rejoiced;
> Moreover my flesh also shall dwell in hope:
> Because Thou wilt not leave my soul in Hades,
> Neither wilt Thou give Thy Holy One to see corruption.
> Thou madest known unto me the ways of life;
> Thou shalt make me full of gladness with Thy countenance.

Then, proceeding, he gave the reason for this interpretation of the Psalm, declaring that when David wrote it, he was a prophet and had been lifted to the high places of vision. Looking down through the ages, he saw the fulfilment of God's Kingdom purposes, not in himself, not in his immediate successors, but in the Messiah, and singing through the ages he heard this song, the song of the Messiah.

In this Psalm then we have a revelation of the things that made the Resurrection necessary. First of all, without entering into a discussion as to the authorship of the psalm or as to its first meaning but accepting this inspired interpretation, let us look for a moment or two at its notes and declarations.

THE RESURRECTION

First observe the exultant joy of the singer.

> My heart was glad, and my tongue rejoiced;
> Moreover my flesh also shall dwell in hope.

And again:

> Thou madest known unto me the ways of life;
> Thou shalt make me full of gladness with Thy countenance.

The reading of the sentence is sufficient to establish the accuracy of the suggestion, that the Psalm is full of exultant joy. Now let us divide these sentences into two parts. First these three:

> My heart was glad.
> My tongue rejoiced.
> My flesh also shall dwell in hope.

Second these:

> Thou madest known unto me the ways of life;
> Thou shalt make me full of gladness with Thy countenance.

Between the two sets of exultant notes, we find Hades, Sheol, the underworld of death and darkness, and so far as humanity was concerned, the underworld of despair; and through fear of which, man had all his lifetime been subject to bondage. The first assurances expressed in the declarations, "My heart was glad, my tongue rejoiced, my flesh shall dwell in hope," were assurances in view of Hades and the dark underworld. The second declarations, "Thou madest known unto me the ways of life, Thou shalt make me full of gladness with Thy countenance," are the result of the realization of the things anticipated. Here is a singer looking toward death who says, "My heart was glad, my tongue rejoiced, my flesh shall dwell in hope, for of this I am assured, Thou wilt not leave my soul in Hades, nor suffer my soul to see corruption." The soul was approaching Hades and the flesh the grave, and yet the singer sings:

> My heart was glad.
> My tongue rejoiced.
> My flesh also shall dwell in hope.

Then presently, without any reference to an historic event, the same voice is sounding on the other side of Hades.

> Thou madest known unto me the ways of life;
> Thou shalt make me full of gladness with Thy countenance.

Now note most carefully that Peter quoted this Psalm on the day of Pentecost as having reference to the Cross and Resurrection. Peter, who had shunned the Cross not for himself but for his Lord, looking back on his Lord's pathway, understood in a moment the attitude of Jesus during the dark days during which He was approaching the Cross; the attitude of mind out of which proceeded such words as these: "Now is My soul troubled"; and such words as these: "My joy I give unto you." Strangely conflicting and apparently contradictory things, which Peter and the rest could not understand, were uttered during that wonderful progress toward Jerusalem which continued in spite of their dissuasions. Luke has chronicled that when He knew the days were well-nigh come that He should be received up, He steadfastly set His Face to go. Peter, in the light of Pentecostal vision, discovered that in the heart of Jesus on all that shadowed pathway there was a song and this was the song:

> My heart was glad, and my tongue rejoiced:
> Moreover my flesh also shall dwell in hope;

and at last Peter had heard spiritually, the song of the Lord upon the other side of Hades and the dark underworld:

Thou madest known unto *me* the ways of life;
Thou shalt make *me* full of gladness with Thy countenance.

Here then is more than the mere recitation of a poem. Here Peter had discovered the deep inner meaning of the death of Jesus and the Resurrection. In this song, he finds the clear declaration of the reason why Christ rose from among the dead.

We have then in the Psalm a revelation of the reason of the singer's joy. First: "I beheld the Lord always before my face." Second: "He is on my right hand, that I should not be moved." "Therefore my heart was glad, and my tongue rejoiced; my flesh shall dwell in hope."

Such an One as set the Lord always before him, such an One as knew God always at his right hand, was able to say, "Thou wilt not leave my soul in Hades, nor suffer Thine Holy One to see corruption." Running through the whole of that Psalm quoted by Peter is a recognition of that which the Bible forever insists upon and which our Christian religion insistently proclaims, the relation between sin and death. Why this hope in the presence of the underworld? Why this hope as approach was made to the deep darkness? "I have set the Lord always before my face. He is on my right hand, that I should not be moved." In that twofold declaration we have the real secret of that which Peter now declared. "It was not possible that He should be holden of it."

In this word of Peter then there is a declaration of our Lord's victory in the realm of sin, and by the citation of this Psalm we are given an analysis of that victory. It was a threefold victory that Jesus won over sin, a victory complete and making the Resurrection necessary.

First, the victory was victory over the possibility of originating evil. "I beheld the Lord always before my face" is the note, not so much of Jesus in His humanity as of Jesus in His relation to God as His Servant. Second, victory over evil as suggested to the soul from without; "For He is on my right hand, that I should not be moved." That is victory within the realm of human life and human nature. Finally, victory over evil as responsibility assumed. For I pray you, that where there is victory as the Servant over the possibility of originating evil and victory as a Man over the assault of evil as from without, there is no place for death in the life of such an One. Yet He descended to death and passed to Hades. In that act, He assumed responsibility;

> He died to atone
> For sins not His own.

Following Him into that underworld of evil and knowing Him as He was revealed by the Spirit and seen in the light of the Resurrection, Peter rose to the height of supreme and final affirmation as he said, ". . . it was not possible that He should be holden of it."

Let us look a little more closely at these things. First, I have declared that here is the affirmation of victory over the possibility of originating evil; "I beheld the Lord always before my face." We gaze with this man Peter upon Jesus of Nazareth, and we see in Him what Peter saw in Him and what those writers saw in Him, a new Creation, a new Being in human history. Man indeed, yet more than Man; God indeed, but God subject instead of Sovereign. We see Him, the One Who being on equality with God did not consider that equality a prize to be snatched at and held for His own enrichment or aggrandizement; the One Who in some unfathomable mystery emptied Himself and took the form of a Servant. There we halt. That self-emptying was His abandonment of the form and activity of sovereignty and the assumption of the form and activity of subservience. I have already done in a passing phrase what I will now do quite definitely. I admit the mystery. I may be wholly wrong, but the growing conviction of my soul is that we never shall account for these things by human philosophies; but the fact is a declared one, that this Son of God, the eternal, immediate Divine manifestation of God to others, Himself did stoop and bend from the form of Sovereignty to that of Service. In that act, an opportunity was created for a new genesis of evil, for in the moment when a will is placed under control, the possibility of disobedience is created.

Let us illustrate here for a moment, not in the realm of our own human life, but in the realm of angelic life as that is revealed to us in the word of truth. In the Epistle of Jude, we find these words: ". . . angels that kept not their own principality, but left their proper habitation, . . ." That leaving of the proper habitation was not the penalty of sin but the act of sin. It was the volitional act whereby these angels exercised will as apart from the control of the Divine and in rebellion against the Divine.

It is impossible to conceive of a servant of God within whom that possibility does not exist. Now, listen to the language of the Psalm; "I have set the Lord always before my face." That is the language of One Who kept His principality by abiding in His habitation; the language of One Who never exercised His will under the constraint of personal desire; the language of One Who never turned His back upon God; "I have set the Lord always before my face." Therefore His heart was glad, therefore His tongue rejoiced, therefore His flesh dwelt in hope! Because He, in the divine economy and in the midst of those movements that came from the will of God, remained the Servant of God. He did not fall from

His first estate by personal volition. There came no act of disobedience and no deflection from the high and awful integrity of unswerving submission to the will of God. That was perfect victory as the Servant of God.

The second phrase leads us a step further and perhaps brings us into more intimate relationship with the things of our own experience. Not only did He say, "I have set Jehovah ever before my face," but this also: "He is on my right hand, that I should not be moved." Quite simply we may declare that the first affirmation means, "I have not moved," while the second declaration is, "I have not been moved." The fall of Lucifer, son of the morning, was the fall of one who moved from his habitation. The fall of Adam was the fall of one who was moved from his habitation as the result of temptation from without. The fall of Satan, so far as that is revealed to us in Holy Scripture, was the fall of a servant in answer not to attacks from without, but to desire from within that turned his face from God. Said Jesus, "I have set the Lord always before My face." The fall of man was different. The sin of man was the response of man to the suggestion of evil that came from without. Now, says this Servant in the great Psalm, "He is on my right hand that I should not be moved." The vision here again is that of the Son of God, but also of the Son of Adam, united to the race. Mark the possibility created when He was born of the Holy Ghost and by the Virgin Mary. He came to stand where man stood at the beginning; not to stand where I stand by relationship to Adam, but to stand where Adam stood before Adam sinned; and therefore in the midst of opposing forces; in the midst of that dark underworld of evil. He came to stand in a place where it was possible to yield. Peter, looking back on the whole life, catches up the music of the Psalm and says the whole story of the Man Jesus is told thus: "He is on my right hand, that I should not be moved." He walked with God and so was upheld. He never exercised will under constraint of suggestion made by others whether high or low, good or evil. He never departed from the side of God, and all the allurements and all the assaults which were presented to His soul and beat against it from without, He mastered because He walked with God. Therefore His heart was glad, His tongue rejoiced, His very flesh dwelt in hope. Therefore, in Him there was neither fear of death nor anticipation of death as for Himself.

So we move to the last phase of this wonderful victory, the most wonderful of all for us men. Why was He glad? Read again the ancient song. He was glad because of the double triumph: "I have set the Lord always before me." "He is on my right hand, that I should not be moved." What was the chief cause of His gladness? Why was He glad because He had thus been victorious? He was glad because of the possibility created by this victory, of yet another victory more wonderful, more profound, more tremendous. He was glad because of the victory in life as creating the possibility of dying vicariously. He was crowned with glory and honor that He might taste death for every man; not because He tasted death for every man, but in order that He might do so. Death had no place in the order of His Being, but because His Being was perfect He was able to die for others. Consequently, there was not only the possibility of dying vicariously for others but of dying victoriously, knowing that when God carried Him into that realm in which He took over responsibility, He could not abandon Him. ". . . Thou wilt not leave my Soul in Hades, . . . Thou wilt not suffer Thy Holy One to see corruption. . . ." Even when the soul is in Hades and the body is in the grave, even when the personality is severed and divided by the mystery of death and is thus found in the land of shadows and the place of corruption, even there God cannot abandon. ". . . Thou wilt not leave my Soul in Hades, . . ." nor ". . . suffer Thy Holy One to see corruption."

Now mark the fact of His dying and the element which we cited before in Peter's inspired declaration. He died by the determinate counsel and foreknowledge of God, therefore He died in fellowship with God. The dying of Jesus was not conflict with God; it was no attempt in the darkness to persuade God to love, but rather cooperation in the darkness with God in order that Love might do His perfect work. Even in His dying He carried forward the double triumph of His living.

What was the first triumph? "I have set Jehovah always before my face. . . ." Cooperation with His will, yielding to it, and never answering the desire of His own soul. Listen to Gethsemane! ". . . not My will but Thine be done!" It is the same triumph in the face of death.

What was the triumph of His human life? The refusal to listen to any voice that suggested that He should depart from the Divine pathway. Listen to His answer to the suggestion that He should shun the Cross. ". . . Get thee behind Me, Satan, . . . for thou mindest not the things of God, but the things of men." That answer was the measure of His devotion. So we see the double victory of His living operating in His dying, for in the mystery of death He is still the Servant of God, originating no evil, and a Man in right relationship with God refusing to listen to the suggestion of evil.

Again, in His dying, we see Him in cooperation with God, assuming responsibility for the sin of the race, and therefore by His dying creating moral values at the disposal of the race. What then is the victory in the case of such an One?

That Hades cannot hold the soul though it possess it, that corruption cannot touch His Body though they lay Him in the grave. We have in this Death and Resurrection of Jesus that in human history which is unique. We cannot account for it by our science, and our philosophies cannot explain it. It was God's interference; God's new mysterious redeeming act; that One died whom Hades could not hold nor corruption touch; and all because of the victory He won over evil in every form. Therefore to Him God made known the ways of life, He was made full of gladness with the countenance of God.

On that Resurrection morning, when He did first reveal Himself to Mary of Magdala and throughout the day to other individual souls and through the forty days of His appearing and disappearing, He was flinging everywhere the sunshine of the gladness of His own heart because of the victory that He had won in His mastery of evil. The risen Lord is Victor over every conceivable form of essential evil, over the possibility of primal genesis from within His own life as the Servant of God. "I have set the Lord always before my face . . ."; over the possibility of evil resulting from the assault that comes from without; "Because He is at my right hand I shall not be moved;" and over evil as responsibility assumed. Resurrection demonstrated that victory; ". . . it was not possible that He should be holden of it." Had death held Him then God had been defeated, or God had been involved. It was not possible that He should be holden of it.

If He be Victor over every conceivable form of essential evil, He is Victor ultimately over all the results of evil, suffering, sorrow, and sinning, as well as sin. How long that ultimate day seems to us in coming! The consciousness of evil remains. We know it, for death and sinning are still with us, and evil lifts its proud head even today threatening goodness. Ah! But my brethren, when that consciousness of evil threatens to oppress the heart overmuch, let us ever condition it by this fact of His victory over evil at its heart and center, knowing that we are taking part in an administrative warfare. The central battle has been fought and won.

If He rose not, then we are of all men most pitiable, for we have seen a vision and indulged a hope which is false. But not with the gloomy foreboding of any such suggestion do we end this meditation, but as men and women who remind our heart amid the travail and the toil that He is risen, and that because it was not possible that He should be holden of death.

CHAPTER XI

THE WAY OF RIGHTEOUSNESS

. . . thus it becometh us to fulfil all righteousness.
MATTHEW 3:15.

THESE ARE THE FIRST RECORDED WORDS OF JESUS AFTER HE HAD come to man's estate. We have in the Gospel of Luke a record of what He said as a boy twelve years of age, Wist ye not that I must be in the things of My Father (my Father's house)." That was a truly remarkable utterance characterized by all naturalness and simplicity, the naturalness and simplicity of a boy undefiled, artless, and sincere. They were words in which He revealed, even at that time, a sense of relationship that was mystic and peculiar, for there can be no doubt that His reference was to God as He said, "My Father's house" or "the things of My Father." Even then, also, there was a sense of responsibility resting upon Him, ". . . I must be in (My Father's house)." In that "must," moreover, there was revelation not of responsibility alone, but of response thereto. In that word the boy uttered the deepest thing of His heart, the central inspiration of the life that was opening full of beauty and full of promise, "Wist ye not that I must be in the things of My Father (My Father's house)."

Between that hour and this of His baptism, eighteen years had passed, during which once again, according to St. Luke,

He had ". . . advanced in wisdom and stature, and in favour with God and men." There had been definite growth and development; mentally, in wisdom, physically in stature, spiritually, in grace with God and men. The double favor ". . . with God and men" was the outcome of the double fellowship of those eighteen years. Through them all He had lived with God and with men; in a close, perpetual fellowship with His Father and naturally with the people of Nazareth, not aloof from them but mixing in all their life.

As He approached thirty years of age, a strange and wonderful thing happened in Judæa. A voice was heard which was unmistakably the voice of a prophet crying in the wilderness,

. . . Make ye ready the way of the Lord;
Make His paths straight.

It was a voice so prevailing that men crowded out to the wilderness to hear him, were swept by his fierce invective and his stern denunciation, and multitudes of them bent and bowed themselves in repentance. Among those who heard the voice was the Carpenter of Nazareth, and hearing it He answered it; "Then cometh Jesus from Galilee to the Jordan unto John. . . ." At this point in the narrative we have a statement which is a very arresting one. When this man from Nazareth presented Himself to the stern, hard, ascetic, magnificent prophet of the desert for baptism, John hesitated, and said to Him, ". . . I have need to be baptised of Thee, and comest Thou to me?" There is nothing really arresting in that, nothing very startling in it if we read it with our knowledge of Jesus; but if we remember that at the moment when John said it, he did not know Who Jesus was, then it became arresting, startling, suggestive. John himself distinctly declared later that he only knew that this Jesus was indeed the One Whose coming he had been predicting when he saw the

Holy Spirit descending upon Him. When Jesus presented Himself, John had not yet seen that sign and so did not know Him as the Messiah. It may be that in their earlier boyhood days they had met and played together, but there had been long years of separation. John had retired in early life to the desert and there in loneliness, in meditation, brooding over the sins of his people, he had prepared for the stern ministry to which he was being called. Jesus had remained in Nazareth. Looking into His eyes he said, ". . . I have need to be baptised of Thee, and comest Thou to me?" The explanation is not far to seek. John stands supreme in all the long and illustrious line of Hebrew prophets; brief, stern, and severe, he had so entered into fellowship with the righteousness and holiness of God that when he looked into the eyes of the Galilean peasant that day, he saw light that he had seen in no other eyes, purity which he had seen nowhere else, and without at all knowing Who He was, he recognized that here was One separated from the multitude in His purity, and he said, ". . . I have need to be baptised of Thee, and comest Thou to me?"

In that connection Jesus uttered the first words of His ministry that have been recorded, and in the uttering of them He struck the keynote of the whole of that ministry, unveiling in a flash the whole truth concerning it. With gentleness to John He said persuadingly, ". . . Suffer it now, . . ." and then added, ". . . for thus it becometh us to fulfil all righteousness."

These words were introductory to His mission. They came out of a quiet mind, full heart, and fixed will. They were the utterance of One Whose mind had grown in wisdom, Whose heart had grown in grace, Whose will had been constantly yielded to the will of His Father. He clearly saw His mission and understood its deepest meaning and in quiet simplicity in this act He dedicated Himself to it.

In the words He uttered, we have first a revelation of the ultimate toward which His face was set; that ultimate is in this connection expressed in the word "righteousness"; ". . . thus it becometh us to fulfil all righteousness." Second, in the declaration we have a revelation of the work that was devolving upon Him and upon all those who were already in association with Him, John being among the number, as were the men of the past and those who ultimately come into association with Him, His disciples, and His church; ". . . to fulfil all righteousness." In the first suggestive word, "Thus," so pregnant with meaning yet so simple that we may hurry over it, He revealed the method by which His work was to be accomplished and the ultimate order of righteousness established.

Let us then follow these three lines of thought, considering first, the suggestion of these words of Jesus concerning the ultimate order, "righteousness"; considering second, the work which He revealed as His work and the work of all associated with Him, ". . . to fulfil all righteousness"; dwelling last upon the method revealed, ". . . thus it becometh us to fulfil all righteousness."

The keynote of our meditation is struck in the word "righteousness." Our difficulty is immediately created, as it is so constantly, by our familiarity with the word. It is one of the commonplace words of the Christian church, one of the great words which is no longer confined to the Christian church but has passed out and is perpetually being used by men of the world. What does it mean? We have sometimes said that by a shortening of the word we may gain access to the heart of the intention, rightness; and by still further shortening it we may come nearer to the simple statement of its profoundest meaning, right. Yet we are not finally helped by that. What is righteousness? Righteousness is found absolutely in God and in God alone. Turning back to the Old Testament Scriptures where the word so often occurs, we find one great illuminative passage in which the word itself does not occur but in which the whole fact is so poetically and forcefully set forth that nothing can be added to it. In the Book of Deuteronomy, we have the song which Moses wrote at the close of his life and taught to the people that they might sing it. It is found in the thirty-second chapter of the book;

> For I will proclaim the name of the Lord:
> Ascribe ye greatness unto our God.
> The Rock, His work is perfect;
> For all His ways are judgment:
> A God of faithfulness and without iniquity,
> Just and right is He.

An inclusive and final definition of righteousness lies within that stanza of the great song of Moses. This righteousness is absolute in God, and the measure in which man understands righteousness is the measure in which he knows God. All the Divine attributes are needed for the exposition of the righteousness of God. Righteousness is a greater word than holiness. Righteousness is the positive of which holiness is the negative. The babe in its mother's arms is righteous but not yet holy; righteous in that it is perfectly related to God until the touch of another shall spoil it; needing no priestly magic to make it a Christian. Holiness is the negative virtue which results from the exercise of the positive condition of rightness. In God both truth and grace are included in righteousness. In Him righteousness is not a hard, ethical condition, integrity alone. In Him righteousness has at its heart love and grace, tenderness and compassion. He ". . . will by no means clear the guilty, . . ." but He will die in the stead of the guilty, cancel sin and so render the guilty guiltless. Righteousness is absolute in God.

What then is righteousness in man? I want to answer the question individually, socially, and in regard to things. Righteousness in man individually is adjustment to God, thinking with God, feeling with God, willing with God. That means not merely what man is in himself, but all his attitudes and relationships to his fellowmen and to things. In man righteousness is adjustment to God. Righteousness is not the rendering of homage to God on a day, in a place, in an attitude. Righteousness is an adjustment of the whole life to God, every day, in every place, in all conditions, and in all attitudes. Whereas it is true that we cannot put God on the same list with our material possessions, it is also appallingly true, tragically true, that many people put their material possessions where God ought to be. Although it seems almost a frivolous thing to say, the frivolity is tragic, it is nevertheless true, there are men and women who are entirely adjusted to their houses, automobiles and bank accounts. They think in the realm of these things, they feel under the impulse of these things, they will under the mastery of these things. The tragedy of the business! That is all background and negative to our meditation. The thing that stands in the foreground and is the positive end of our meditation is that righteousness in a man is life adjusted in all things to God.

In social life, righteousness is the proper articulation of the lives so adjusted. Socially, righteousness is that relation between man and man which is the outcome of the adjustment of individual lives to God. The motive of relationship and the method of relationship result from the adjustment of life to God and its right relationship with Him. We imagine too often that we are in right relationship with God and then proceed in our relationships with our fellow men as though there were no connection between the two. Yet there is always connection between the two. A man whose relationship with his fellow man is wrong at any point is a man whose relationship with God is wrong in spite of his song, his creed, and his profession. To be adjusted to God in all truth is to be true, and the man who is true cannot lie to his fellow man. To be adjusted to God in grace is to be gracious, and the man who is gracious cannot be mastered by malice in his dealing with his fellow man.

Once again what is righteousness as to things? What do I mean by things? Just things! Houses, cars, bank accounts, trees, fields, birds, beasts, minerals, mountains, valleys, subtle and hidden forces not yet discovered, things already discovered such as electricity, anything, everything. What has righteousness to do with them? What does righteousness mean in regard to them? It means the discovery of things as to their being and as to their true purpose in the Divine economy. There is nothing inherently evil that God has created. What then, is the matter with the world? Men not adjusted to God, men not articulated as within that great adjustment have not discovered the forces that they need; or having discovered them, do not know their true purpose and are misusing them. The ultimate Kingdom of God in this world will not be a kingdom from which are banished all the things that we see and touch. It will be a kingdom in which man has discovered them and their true meaning, and one in which man will no longer lay hold upon some subtle potent thing that has its purpose in the universe and use it for a kingdom in which things we call poisons will be relegated to their proper place, made use of, since all are gifts of God. Righteousness with regard to things means also the development of the thing discovered. An imperfect flower in your garden is proof of the lack of righteousness somewhere. Arrested development is proof of lack of righteousness. The opposite is true. Righteousness means that the flower found for the first time in the forest, under the touch of man in right relationship with God and in cooperation with his brother man will become beautiful with a beauty of which we never dreamed but which was potential in the flower when first man found it. The discovery and development of all the great and gracious, sweet and wonderful secrets of old mother-earth.

Finally, righteousness as to things means that they are used and not abused, that they are made the servants of humanity and not the masters of men; like the very Sabbath of God, they are made for man and not man for them.

In the presence of the great word we dream wondrous dreams, and no dream we dream approaches the glory of the reality of righteousness. Do you wonder that the New Testament writer upon one occasion made use of the words ". . . the fruits of righteousness. . . ." Righteousness blossoms into beauty and produces fruits. Righteousness is a word full of beauty, and we, alas too often, have made it merely hard, mechanical, ethical. It is bursting with life. It describes man coming to the fulfilment of his manhood because his face is lifted to the throne of God. It describes humanity finding the true social order because human life is articulated as the result of the adjustment of the individual to God. It describes the earth, blushing with beauty, laughing with flowers, becoming more glorious in its light and more full of ease and delight in its being. It is God's great word, a word in which He sings out to men if they but have ears to hear it, the exceeding beauty of His own being, the exceeding joy of His own heart, the characteristic grace of His purpose for the people whom He has made.

If righteousness is absolute in God, and relatively in

man is man's adjustment and articulation, what is righteousness resultantly? "For the kingdom of God is not eating and drinking, but righteousness and peace and joy in the Holy Ghost," righteousness first, then resultantly peace, and finally, joy. What then according to the suggestion of that declaration are the results of righteousness? First peace. ". . . thus it becometh us to fulfil all righteousness" said Jesus, in a world which at the moment was hushed and subdued by an appalling peace. Jesus was born when war had ceased and ceased by the agony of the surfeit of itself. The pax Romanum was upon the world for the world was worn out with struggle. The temple of Janus had been closed for a generation and there was peace, appalling peace. Jesus said: ". . . it becometh us to fulfil all righteousness." Out of the righteousness which He saw and toward which He set His face, there springs peace, not the pax Romanum but the pax Dei. The peace of God is not weariness, tiredness, inability to fight. It is rather full activity of life in rhythmic power without friction, without weariness. ". . . the Lord . . . fainteth not neither is weary." The peace of God grows out of righteousness. Humanity will never find that peace save by the way of righteousness. Out of that peace will come joy and joy is satisfaction, delight, rapture! That is God's ultimate for humanity.

We seem to have wandered very far, but we have come nearer than ever perhaps to the Man Who stood on the banks of the Jordan as He said, ". . . thus it becometh us to fulfil all righteousness." These were the visions of His eyes, these the ideals of His mind, this the golden goal toward which He set His face. Now note His description of His work; ". . . to fulfil all righteousness." There is in that phrase the recognition of righteousness as possible. Righteousness in the thinking of Jesus was not a counsel of perfection, a forlorn hope.

It was possible, first, because man can be adjusted to God. There is that in God and in man which makes such adjustment possible. The deepest truth of man's nature is that he is created for that adjustment. As Augustine put it long ago, "God has so fashioned the human heart that it never can find rest until it rest in Him." To take the great statement and put it in another form is to declare that it is possible for man to be adjusted to God. He is made for that, not for houses, cars, and credit at the bank, but for God. God has that in Himself which is kith and kin of humanity; He made humanity in His own likeness and image. Having made humanity, it is not merely true that humanity can only rest in Him, it is equally true that He can never rest save as humanity finds rest in Him. If you challenge that, I remind you of the words of Jesus when they criticized Him for breaking Sabbath, ". . . My Father worketh hitherto and I work." God and Christ can never rest until humanity is at rest. Jesus realized, moreover, that man can be articulated, that it is not impossible. I will borrow a figure of speech from an old prophet: it is not impossible for the lion to dwell with the lamb; it is not impossible that men of differing and diverse temperaments and races should come into realization of that unity which does not destroy their distinction. Under the illumination of the teaching of Christ and in the light of His principles and purpose, man discovers—mark the paradox but follow me—the value of difference necessary to total agreement; differences in form and fashion, in thought and outlook. Thank God there are differences! Yet differences is an ugly word; there are diversities, that is a little better. But let us borrow a literary word, diereses, that is differences which merge and mix with each other and make harmony. That is God's ultimate for humanity. That means differences not only as to types, temperaments, and races, but as to thought, and that within the Christian church first of all. As the years run on, a man comes to respect with profounder respect than he did, the opinion from which he radically differs. He comes to see that a man who stands for a doctrine of the church which is sacerdotal may himself be as true as the man who stands against him. Perchance in some sweet morning, when life's fitful fever is over, we shall laugh together as sons of God over the things in the presence of which *today* we quarrel and rend the body of Christ. It is for this larger outlook that Christ came, this harmony which is not monotony.

The word of Jesus recognized, moreover, that righteousness is already operative. To fulfil is not to create, but to cooperate, and set free, and enable it to complete itself. I believe with John that ". . . the whole world lieth in the evil one"; but I also believe that that which lieth in the evil one is potential with righteousness. As the evil one holds the world in his embrace, he holds that in his embrace which he cannot forever hold. I believe with all my heart

> That cannot end worst which begun best
> Though a wide compass first be fetched.

Of course there was also recognition of righteousness as hindered, held back. That is the supreme thought and therefore it needs no argument.

So we come to our last thought. The word "thus" suggested the method. What did He mean by "thus"? He meant that from which John shrank. From what, then, did John shrink that day when he looked at Jesus? I believe John had welcomed eagerly all who really came in repentance for baptism, but when Jesus came he said, ". . . I have need to be baptised of Thee, and comest Thou to me?" He shrank from the idea that the sinless should confess sin. Jesus confessed sin when He went to that baptism. He shrank from the idea that the righteous should repent. When Jesus went to that baptism, He repented. He shrank from the idea that the free with the freedom of purity should seek remission of sins. When Jesus stooped to baptism, He sought remission of sin within His own soul. John looking into the eyes of Jesus said, It is wrong, this cannot be! Thou art sinless, "I have need to be baptised of Thee, and comest Thou to me?" How can the sinless confess sin? How can the righteous repent for sin? How can the free ask for remission? Jesus said, ". . . thus it becometh us to fulfil all righteousness." By the very things from which thou art shrinking, righteousness will be fulfilled. Righteousness will be fulfilled by the Sinless bearing sin, by the Righteous repenting for sin on behalf of others, by the Free seeking to be bound in order to break the bonds and set at liberty those that are bound. Never let us read this story and forget those meanings of the baptism of John; it was baptism unto the remission of sins by way of repentance. John, or his disciples, plunged beneath the waters of the Jordan all that came owning their sin, declaring their repentance, and seeking remission. When Jesus was baptized, He confessed sin, He repented for sin, He sought remission.

Whose sin? Not His own, but yours and mine. When John saw Him again, it was after the quietness of the night, after he had seen the descending Spirit, and there had come to him the overwhelming conviction that his hands had plunged beneath the waters of symbolic baptism the Christ of God, the Messiah. On the day after, John looked at Him and said, "Behold, the Lamb of God, that taketh away the sin of the world."

Now carefully observe our Lord's use of the plural pronoun: ". . . it becometh us." The word was spoken to John, "It becometh us," it becometh Me, as well as thee; it becometh thee as well as Me; it becometh us. It is as though He had said: "John, I will show thee the way. Thy mission has been a Divine mission. Thou hast been the herald of My coming, thou hast proclaimed Me as coming with a fire and a fan! Lo, I come; but '. . . thus it becometh us to fulfil all righteousness.'" Righteousness will never be fulfilled by the voice that denounces sin; righteousness will never be fulfilled by the voice that thunders against it! All of which is necessary but such ministry will never fulfil it. There is only one way, it is the way of the Cross, it is the way of fellowship with humanity in its sin, repentance for its sin, and the bearing away of its sin.

He gathered into this "us" all the men of the past who had trodden the sorrowful way. There was a day when Moses said something that revealed the deepest in him more wonderfully than anything he said before or after. It was the day when in the presence of God, he said of the sinning people: ". . . this people have sinned a great sin, and have made them gods of gold; Yet, now, if Thou wilt forgive their sin; and if not, blot me, I pray Thee, out of Thy book!" That is the way by which the people were lifted and saved. There was a later day when another man wrote: "I say the truth in Christ, I lie not, my conscience bearing witness with me in the Holy Ghost . . . I could wish that I myself were anathema from Christ for my brethren's sake, my kinsmen according to the flesh." That is the way the Kingdom is coming. Thus it becometh us to fulfil all righteousness; by standing with the sinner, and confessing the sinner's sin; by sharing the burden of it, repenting for it, going down to death if need be for the saving of the sinner. ". . . thus it becometh us to fulfil all righteousness."

For us the wondrous facts and forces are centralized in Him. He is the Righteousness of God, the Revealer of the beauty of righteousness, adjusted to the will of God. He in the articulation of Himself with others will set up the Kingdom of God. He is the One Who fulfils all righteousness.

At last John in mystic vision heard Him speak and this is what He said, "I am the Alpha and the Omega, . . . the beginning and the end" of the new heaven and the new earth wherein dwelleth righteousness. He is the strength of our fellowship in the method. I cannot take up that Cross and share the burden of sin and repent and suffer with the sinner save as it is true of me that the love of Christ constraineth me and that the life of Christ masters me. Where these things are so, we shall enter into fellowship with the suffering by which, and by which alone, the Kingdom is to come.

CHAPTER XII

JEHOVAH OF HOSTS—THE GOD OF JACOB

Jehovah of hosts is with us; the God of Jacob is our refuge.

PSALM 46:7; 11.

IN THE HISTORY OF THE HUMAN RACE NOTHING HAS EVER BEEN done for its help or uplifting save through the principle of faith. Doubt is always destructive. Faith is forever constructive. That is to state the principle in the widest and broadest possible way. I am not now speaking only of the faith of the Christian, though, of course, it is to that I am proposing to come. It is true in every walk of life and every department of thought that the man of faith builds. The man who lacks faith breaks down.

This being granted, I submit that the particular quality of faith which has done most for the uplifting of humanity is that of faith in the living and eternal God. Faith that believes in the existence of God, and believes, moreover, in the Divine interest in human affairs, is the faith which has most helped the race.

The fact of God as the foundation of faith is our theme. I am speaking to Christian workers, to those upon whom the burden and the toil that makes His Kingdom come is resting, to those who sometimes amid the conflict are weary and almost discouraged. I am perfectly sure that it is the occasional experience of anyone doing real work for God. If we know what it is to get underneath even the edge of the world's agony with the imperial, lonely Christ, then we know what it is to have days of darkness, hours of questionings, problems, trials, temptation, and difficulties in Christian service.

Yet notwithstanding all such hours, and occasions, and questionings, an undercurrent of conviction exists in the heart of every member of the Christian community; it is one of unswerving and unabated confidence in God. He is the rock foundation upon which we build—the strong rock upon which faith fastens while we toil and suffer and serve all the while confident of the ultimate victory.

If I remind you of these things, it is because I think sometimes amid the toil we should stop and be conscious of the rock. The rock is always there, but perhaps the consciousness of some trembling child of God will be stronger for pausing to think of it.

These old Hebrew singers and seers had a very keen consciousness of the fact, though, perchance, they did not understand the nature and character of God as we do. They had to wait for the full shining of light in the Person of Jesus. This Psalm begins with the announcement in a single word of all the truth that it afterwards unfolded. God—and the psalmist has said everything when he has said God.

Yet, essential light is always such that we cannot look at it. We have not yet been able to gaze upon pure light. Light must be analyzed to enable us to appreciate it, to understand it. The pure light is the final fact, but the light must be broken up in order that we may apprehend it. After the psalmist has uttered the word which is all conclusive, he proceeds to say things about it until he comes to the seventh verse in the heart of the Psalm, until he comes to the closing sentences of the

Psalm, and in these two verses he breaks up for us the essential light. "Jehovah of hosts is with us; the God of Jacob is our refuge." All I want to do is to consider this breaking up of the essential truth concerning God upon which our faith has fastened and must fasten if we are to continue to be workers together with Him and for Him.

Will you follow me, then, along two lines of meditation? First, a consideration of the twofold truth about God which my text suggests, and second, the twofold statement the psalmist makes based upon the twofold fact. The twofold fact concerning God—He is Jehovah of hosts, He is the God of Jacob. The twofold declaration he makes about this God; first, "He is with us"; second, He is "our refuge."

First, then, the twofold declaration concerning God: "The Lord of hosts . . . the God of Jacob."

"The Lord of hosts," or, as the American Revision has given it to us, "Jehovah of Hosts." The name by which he knew the Deity as self-existent and eternal. Other names of God which have come to us from the Hebrew people are preceded by qualifying words but never so with Jehovah. The Hebrew never wrote this name fully. It was the unpronounceable name, the incommunicable name, the name that stood lonely in majesty as the sign and symbol of the infinite things of God which no man could perfectly comprehend and therefore no man perfectly explain. Jehovah was the name which most forcefully gave expression to the facts concerning God which were beyond human comprehension —His absoluteness, without beginning, without end, without counsel taken, without forethought—for there was no thought before him—Jevoah.

If we are wise, we stand with the Jew in the presence of the name and confess our ignorance while we bow in reverential worship. Jehovah speaks of the continuousness of

God, the self-determining power of the Most High, and His inward sufficiency, so that there is nothing beyond His consciousness. It is the greatest of all the words into which the fact of God is compressed in such a way as to announce forevermore to men that it cannot be expressed so that the mind of finite man can ever understand it.

The psalmist comes very near qualifying the word, for he adds "of hosts." Not that the word "of hosts" really qualifies "Jehovah," for, rather, the word "Jehovah" qualifies the "of hosts."

"Hosts." How is that word used in the Bible? It is employed in the Old Testament Scriptures and in the New Testament in different ways. It is used first with regard to the stars. We read in Genesis, "And the heavens and the earth were finished, and all the host of them" (2:1). In the prophecy of Isaiah, "Lift up your eyes on high, and see Who hath created these, that bringeth out their host by number; He calleth them all by name; by the greatness of His might, and for that He is strong in power, not one is lacking" (40:26).

The same term is also used of the angels. ". . . I saw the Lord sitting on His throne, and all the host of heaven standing by Him on His right hand and on His left" (I Kings 22:19); and in the song that sounded o'er Bethlehem's plains after the angel's solo, it is recorded, ". . . there was . . . a multitude of the heavenly host praising God . . ." (Luke 2:13).

In the Book of Exodus the word is applied to the children of Israel. They are spoken of as the host of God. Thus it is used of the stars in the heavens, of the unfallen intelligences that people the world beyond our vision and knowledge, and of the companies of men that march across the earth and dwell upon its surface, of stars and seraphim and saints, host of stars, hosts of angels, hosts of saints. I believe in my text it is used of all these.

This phrase, "Jehovah of hosts," teaches us that Jehovah is absolute, sufficient, and superior. It declares to us that God is the Lord of the heavens and all their inhabitants. As one has beautifully expressed it, "The universe of matter and the world of mind were not only created, but are marshaled and ordered by God." We are now looking upon one side only of the Divine nature and being, thinking of Him as the One Who knows all hosts and marshals and controls them by His own power, and we are reminded of the wisdom of God and of the might and majesty of the Most High—"Jehovah of hosts. . . ."

Turn to the other half of the declaration concerning God. "The God of Jacob. . . ." If we were not so familiar with this text, we should be startled by the very daring of bringing together two such descriptions of God as we have within its compass. "Jehovah of hosts, . . ." and in a moment, by a rapid change of terms, we are given another revelation of God, which I do not hesitate to say is far more startling than the former, especially when considered in the light thereof. "The Lord of hosts, . . ." and then suddenly, "the God of Jacob. . . ." "The Lord of hosts, . . ." and as the phrase passes our lips we are amid the eternal expanse, the unfallen intelligences, the vision of any one of which would blind us were it granted to us at this moment. And suddenly, almost without warning, we move from the stellar spaces on to the earth. The stars grow dim until they are seen but as flecks and points of glory upon the darkling brow of night; the angels pass from our vision; and we are on one small planet, amid the hosts of heaven, in one small country upon that planet, looking into the face of one lonely man—Jacob. The psalmist says that the God Who is the God of all the hosts is the God of that man as surely and positively interested in that one speck of thinking life as in all the unfallen intelligences of the upper spaces; as surely and as positively committed to that man as to all the order of the infinite universe.

We have not yet reached the height and the depth of the mystery. We have not yet reached the word that is most startling of all in this consideration. Notice carefully what the psalmist says: "The God of Jacob. . . ." I think we should not have been quite so startled if the psalmist had said the God of Israel. He says, "the God of Jacob. . . ." I know only one man who is meaner than Jacob and that is Laban. The only comfort I ever got out of Jacob is that he was one too many for Laban. Of all men for astute, hard-driving meanness recommend me to Jacob. But God is "the God of Jacob. . . ." Oh, my soul, here find thy comfort! I do not know whether it helps you, but it helps me. He is the God of Jacob, mean as Jacob was. This is the thing on which my faith fastens. "The Lord of hosts, . . ." yes; but "the God of Jacob! . . ." But was that man such a man as I? The longer I live the more astonished I am that God ever loved me at all. The longer I live the more astonished I am at that infinite grace which found me and loves me and keeps me. The meanness that lurks within, the possibilities of evil that I have discovered make me ask, "Will God look at me?" He is "the God of Jacob." He was his God and loved him notwithstanding all his meanness, enwrapped him with provision, led him, told him where to rest his head, and when he had laid that head upon the stone, linked heaven and earth with a symbolic ladder to teach him His care for him even while he was Jacob. Infinite in His majesty, "The Lord of hosts . . ."; infinite in His mercy, "the God of Jacob. . . ." Stupendous is His power, upholding all things by the word thereof, "the Lord of hosts . . ."; sublime in His pity, "the God of Jacob. . . ."

This revelation moves me more than any other. The very distance of the other fact enables me to assume an erect posture in the presence of it. "The Lord of hosts . . ."—and I hear the music and rhythm of the eternal order amid stars and angels. "The God of Jacob . . ."—I thought He was far away, I hoped I might, perchance, see the glistening of His dazzling robe of glory among the everlasting spaces. But He is not far away, He is with Jacob! It is not only in immensity but in littleness that God is great. Mark the condescension of this figure of speech; note the beauty of it. Notwithstanding the failure and wreckage of this life, despite the fact that it is anything but what God meant it to be, that in its foolish attempts to create its own destiny and carve its own fortune it has led itself into the region where character is blighted and spoiled by the dwarfing influences of vain ambition, yet the inspiring word comes to me—"the God of Jacob. . . ." He has created man, and man has broken all His laws; but He is his God still and broods over him tenderly, his folly notwithstanding.

Let us consider what the psalmist says concerning these facts. First, then, the declaration, "The Lord of hosts is with us. . . ." May I make application of the truth by reminding you again what this phrase "of hosts" means? He is the God of the stars, the God of the angels, the God of men in multitudes and companies. The God of all these hosts is with us, and for our making, for the making of Jacob, He will press all hosts into service if necessary. "But," you say, "this is imagination. Do you mean to suggest that this God, Who is the God of the individual, of Jacob, will use the stars for our making?" I desire to tell you nothing that is not within the covers of the Bible. I have no commission to speculate or philosophize. I have a commission to preach the Word. Let me read some Old Testament words:

> The kings came and fought,
> Then fought the kings of Canaan,
> In Taanach, by the waters of Megiddo;
> They took no gain of money.
> They fought from heaven,
> The stars in their courses fought against Sisera.
> The river Kishon swept them away,
> That ancient river, the river Kishon. . . .

And then we are not surprised that the writer of the historic fact in poetic language addresses his soul thus: " . . . Oh, my soul, march on with strength." "The Lord of hosts is with us. . . ." The God of the stars is committed to me, and, if there be necessity for it, the very stars in their courses shall fight for me against the foes that hinder me as I climb upward toward the home of God. He will command the whole universe for the making of a soul. Do you doubt me there? Then let me remind you that for the purchase of my soul and yours, for its reconciliation and redemption, He gave in one supreme gift that which was infinitely superior to all the stars—the One by Whose word they were made, and in Whose might they have consisted through the ages. He gave Him for the remaking of my broken, maimed, spoiled life. The stars, the hosts of God if need be, will be pressed into the service of the making of the saint, and into the service of the saint as he goes forth in toil for God.

But what of angels? Need I tarry to say anything about angels? I fear I must. This is a very Sadducean age. I am never quite sure whether there are more Sadducees or Pharisees in the world today. I do not mean in the accidentals of past manifestations but in the essentials. The Pharisee was the ritualist in his age. The Sadducee was the rationalist, and if you want to know the essentials, you can find it in one brief description in your New Testament. ". . . the Sadducees say that there is no resurrection, neither angel, nor spirit. . . ." And there are a great many Sadducees abroad today. They smile and they say, "You do not really believe this story that angels help us." I believe angels help us. I still believe with the psalmist that "The angel of the Lord encampeth round about them that fear Him. . . ." I still believe with the New Testament writer, "Are they not all ministering spirits, sent forth to do service for the sake of them that shall inherit salvation?" Poetry, do you say? I know it is poetic statement, but it is fact that makes the poetry. I believe that what Jesus said once was true. I do not quite understand it, but I am sure it is true. Jesus said, "See that ye despise not one of these little ones; for I say unto you that in heaven their angels do always behold the face of My Father which is in heaven." I tell you honestly that I do not perfectly understand it. But there are certain things in it I am sure of. "My Father in heaven," the "little ones," and "their angels." How the angel beholds the face of the Father, or how the beholding of the angel saves the child I do not quite know; but I am sure of the Father and sure of the children, and sure of the angels. And men and women, I beseech you, doubt this Sadducean age that questions the ministry of the spirit and the ministries of the angels, and believe me, if we could see things as they are now, the Lord of hosts has His hosts of angels guarding the children, watching our way, preparing as we go.

Angels? The prophet Elisha was shut up in the city, and his servant was terribly anxious, and he said to him, "Master, what shall we do?" And the prophet said to God, "Lord, . . . open his eyes. . . ."

> And lo! to faith's enlightened sight
> All the mountain flamed with light.

Jesus faced His passion, and when a blundering disciple smote His enemy with an old sword, He said: ". . . Put up again thy sword. . . . Thinkest thou that I cannot beseech My Father, and He shall even now send Me more than twelve legions of angels?"

But what about the hosts of men? Is Jehovah indeed with hosts of men? Yes, and not only is He Jehovah of hosts concerning the companies of His saints; Jehovah is the Lord of all hosts and of all the hosts of men. He is the Lord of all the armies in the world. Let no man misunderstand me for a moment. Let me say to you bluntly what is in my deepest soul. I hate all war as I hate hell, and I believe you can never justify it by Christian standards under any circumstances whatever. But if men will fight, God is the God of battles. He does not inspire the battle, but He governs its goings, and remember this, that no army ever marches across any path of this earth but in the check of His strong hand. It may be a little difficult sometimes to understand what God is doing. I suppose there have been moments in the lives of all of us who know anything of what it is to love and serve Him when we have grumbled with Carlyle, "Yes, God is in His heaven, but doing nothing." He is always doing something.

You say, "What has this to do with me?" He will compel the march of men to contribute to the making of men. He will press into the service of turning Jacob into Israel whole armies as they come and go. Hosts of stars, hosts of angels, hosts of men, and the Lord of all of them is with us.

Oh, take heart, my brothers, my sisters! Is the burden pressing heavily, is the toil almost too great to be borne? Do you stand upon the brink of great enterprises, afraid because of the vested interests, because of the hosts of wickedness?

I bring you a message full of heart, hope, and courage. God, by His Spirit, sing it as an anthem in your heart. "The Lord of hosts is with us, . . ." and while its music thrills my soul I dare go back to battle and suffering and to the defeat of half an hour because I know at last the victory will be won, and the Lord of hosts cannot be defeated.

A final word about the other fact—". . . the God of Jacob is our refuge." What did He do for Jacob? Think of his history. See at what infinite pains God was to make something out of him. Oh, the patience of God! oh, the waiting! oh, the forces pressed into the making of a man! oh, the opened heavens and the ascending and descending angels! oh, the glimpse of hosts He gave him one day! He called the name of one place Mahanaim which means the place of hosts. He said, "With my staff I passed over this Jordan, and now I am become two companies." Jacob, you have to learn that none of them are your own, that the Lord of hosts possesses every last skin of your cattle, and there are other hosts besides. There is Esau's host. He is coming to meet you with armed men. Jacob, you have yet to learn that a man may march against you with armed men all to no purpose if God is on your side; It was in that day that he saw God's host. What he saw, who shall tell? The host of God passed him, and he said, "Mahanaim," it is the place of hosts.

And he went down over the Jabbok, and God met with him and crippled him to make him. It was a wonderful night, only do not let us misinterpret it. I beseech you, do not talk as though Jacob wrestled with God and overcame Him. It is not true. Do not recite Jacob's words in the wrong tone. You know perfectly well that you may say correct words so that the tone gives a lie to the meaning of the words you recite. Do not imagine he said, ". . . I will not let Thee go except Thou bless me." If you want to know all go to the prophecy of Hosea. It is declared he was heard when with strong crying and tears, he said, ". . . I will not let Thee go except Thou bless me." It was a voice choked with sorrow, the voice of a man being beaten, being crippled in the last agony of despair as he went down beneath the pressure of that mysterious hand. He won when he was beaten; he triumphed when he yielded; and God never let him alone until that night by crippling him He broke him.

And the day broke, and the people over the Jabbok saw him coming back again. Let us go and meet him. "Jacob, where have you been?" "Do not call me Jacob. My name is not Jacob. I was Jacob, a mere supplanter; but I am Israel, God-governed. Do not call me Jacob any more." I think I would have said, "Man, tell me, what is the matter? When I saw you last night, dividing up those bands to mollify Esau, you were erect, but now you are lame." "That limp will follow me to the end. It is the patent of my nobility; it is evidence of the fact that God has won at last." ". . . the God of Jacob is our refuge."

Oh, man, conscious of your own weakness! oh, brother, conscious of the evil within you, which baffles, beats and spoils you, ". . . the God of Jacob is our refuge." When the only pillow we have is a stone—a hard, unkind, unsympathetic stone—then will He open His heaven, so that His hosts may teach us that they with us are more than they that be against us; and if the God of Jacob be our refuge He will put His hands upon us, and, it may be, wound us, but the wounding is only for the deeper healing; it may be, cripple us, but the crippling is only for the stronger work that lies beyond; it may be, shatter all our cherished dreams, smiting the light of the mirage into nothingness; but it is in order that He may light the truer light and give to us the very nature of the sons of God.

I do not think any of us become Israels until we have been at the Jabbok. We never get to power until His hands have been upon us, and sometimes today as in the dim and distant past, God has to put the scar on the flesh and crippling on the life before He can do very much with us. Oh, dear heart, tried as by fire, sing while the fire burns, sing while the pain is hot. If you are trusting Him, He breaks to make, He cripples to crown. Then by God's grace we are going on; we are not thinking of resigning; we are not going to give this fight up, or anything up, except sin. "The Lord of hosts, . . ." marshaling all for our making, ". . . is with us; the God of Jacob, . . ." patient and strong and purposeful, ". . . is our refuge." We will follow, we will trust, we will fight—God helping us.

". . . the God of Jacob is our refuge." Another word will convey the true meaning of this. The God of Jacob is "our high place"; "The name of the Lord is a strong tower, The righteous runneth into it and is set on high (and is safe). Such is the real word: The God of Jacob is "our high place." What means it? We have come down from immensity to localized position, from hosts to individuality, from the magnificent outlook of the Divine movements to personal life. And what is the promise about the God of Jacob? That He will be our "high place"; that we may be set in Him above circumstances, above enemies, above self, and so we look to the future with all confidence and security, because "The Lord of hosts is with us; the God of Jacob is our refuge."

If this announcement engender within us confidence, rest, assurance, it must also produce consecration. If looking on at our work with its light and its possibilities of sorrow and joy, we are confident and glad and the tone of our voice has in it the ring of the triumphant hosanna, if we are confident by reason of these words, then let it be remembered they must also produce consecration.

How will the fact of the Divine presence be manifested to the world? By the effect it produces upon us. So, while we take our joy and comfort out of the blessed thought that "the Lord of hosts is with us, . . ." we must not forget that the eyes of men are fixed upon us to discover Him of Whom we speak, and they will not see Him in shining glory; but if "the Lord of hosts is with us," and "the God of Jacob is our refuge," in the quiet calm of our spirit, in the tenderness of our love, in the straightness of our dealings with each other, in all the growing beauty of our lives, men will see that the Lord of hosts—of order, of precision, and magnificence—and the God of Jacob—of love, of care, and sympathy—is with us. Ours is the blessing, but ours is also the responsibility. Let us remember that the effects produced will be in proportion to our realization of the Divine presence, and our realization of the Divine presence will be in proportion to our yielding of ourselves to the will that is known, to the word that is spoken, that doing the will we may know the doctrine and may pass from glory into glory, the light and beauty of the Divine shining evermore upon our faces, and in our lives, that others, too, may come to see the glory of the Lord of hosts, the patience of the God of Jacob.

CHAPTER XIII

THE TRAGEDY OF LIFE WITHOUT FAITH

I had fainted, unless I had believed to see the goodness of the Lord in the land of the living.

PSALM 27:13.

THE PSALM FROM WHICH OUR TEXT IS TAKEN IS A SONG OF CONflicting emotions, in which victory is on the side of the nobler. As we listen to the singer we discover the opposing forces at war within the soul. Faith opposes itself to fear, joy strenuously contends with sorrow, songs resolutely lift themselves for the silencing of sighing.

The fear, the sorrow, the sighing are patent. Note the questions at the commencement of the psalm which even though they be prefaced by affirmations of faith, reveal the assault of fear, ". . . Whom shall I fear?" ". . . Of whom shall I be afraid?" Observe the tumult of circumstances as revealed in the phrases that run like a dirge through the psalm; evil doers came to seek to eat up my flesh; mine adversaries and my foes. An host against me; war against me! The day of trouble! Mine enemies round about me! My father and my mother have forsaken me. Mine enemies, mine adversaries, false witnesses, such as breathe out cruelty! There can be no escape from the sense of the tumult and trouble in the midst of which the singer lived.

Nevertheless, the Psalm in its entirety has not made this impression upon the heart of man. It is pre-eminently a Psalm of faith, of joy, of song. Note the affirmations with which it opens. "The Lord is my light and my salvation . . . the Lord is the strength of my life"—or even better, more accurately—"the Lord is the (stronghold) of my life." Observe the affirmations answering the questions. My heart will not be afraid! I will be confident! Mine head shall be lifted up! I will sing, yea, I will sing!

Then observe, after the opening stanzas of praise, the prayer that breaks from the heart of the singer, and notice how through the brief prayer there throbs the note of perfect confidence mastering that of overwhelming pain!

Hear, O Lord, when I cry with my voice:
Have mercy also upon me, and answer me.
When Thou saidst, Seek ye My face; my heart said unto Thee;
Thy face, Lord, will I seek.
Hide not Thy face far from me;
Put not Thy servant away in anger:
Thou hast been my help;
Leave me not , neither forsake me, O God of my salvation.
When my father and my mother forsake me,
Then the Lord will take me up.
Teach me Thy way, O Lord;
And lead me in a plain path,
Because of mine enemies.
Deliver me not over unto the will of mine enemies . . .
For false witnesses are risen up against me, and such as breathe
   out cruelty.

Finally consider the last stanza of the Psalm, marking well its appeal;

Wait on the Lord:

Be of good courage, and He shall strengthen thine heart: and let
thy heart take courage;
Wait, I say, on the Lord.

The spiritual experience revealed in this song is one which, I venture to affirm, we all most earnestly desire. The tumult of sorrow we know. Is the triumph possible? Is it possible to know triumph in the midst of such tumultuous circumstances of grief? We wonder, we question, we doubt. Our sorrows are so subtle, our pain is so poignant, our difficulties are so complex, our circumstances are so peculiar.

Well, let us consider the reason of this singer's triumph. It is, of course, declared in the opening affirmations—

The Lord is my light and my salvation; . . .
The Lord is the stronghold (strength) of my life. . . .

It is illustrated in many subsequent statements which I have already quoted. From the standpoint of the soul's experience, the secret is most forcefully revealed in the words of my text. "*I had fainted*, unless I had believed to see the goodness of the Lord in the land of the living."

A critical examination of the text seems at first destructive of its simplest meaning. You will observe that in the Revised Version and the Authorized, the first three words are italicized; "*I had fainted* . . ." In Miles Coverdale's translation, that wonderful version that has been, thank God, preserved for us in the *Book of Common Prayer*, the phrase has yet more of emphasis, "I should utterly have fainted, unless I had believed to see the goodness of the Lord in the land of the living." There also, the whole of the words are italicized. These words constitute an exegetical gloss, introduced by the translators to fill up some gap, some hiatus, to complete the sense of the text. As a matter of fact we must omit them, if we are to be careful in our consideration of the text.

What have we left? ". . . Unless I had believed to see the goodness of the Lord in the land of the living." When we yet further examine the text, we find that the word "unless" is not found in some manuscripts; neither is it found in the Septuagint, in the Syriac, or in the Vulgate. In the manuscripts in which the word is found, in the Massoretic Text, it is dotted over and beneath, which suggests that it is a spurious word.

As to the first words, "*I had fainted,*" we certainly must omit them. The word "unless," I am not prepared to omit. The absence of it from some manuscripts is not conclusive evidence. As old Hengstenberg suggests with quaint humor, the Massorites evidently lost their feet at this point. The sense of the passage demands the word. The statement without it is incongruous, following as it does immediately after the words, ". . . false witnesses are risen up against me, and such as breathe out cruelty." When the word is retained the whole text becomes a gasp, an exclamation! It is an imperfect sentence, indeed, no sentence at all, but a cry which is almost a groan. It is completed by a revealing hiatus, an eloquent silence. ". . . Unless I had believed to see the goodness of the Lord in the land of the living!" Then the translators attempted to fill this gap, and inserted the words, "I had fainted," or "I had utterly fainted." I can understand why they put them in. They were trying to write what the man was thinking. He did not do so. He left the blank, suggesting a something that could not be expressed. "I had fainted!" Nay, verily, that is altogether too weak. The horror was greater than that. There are moments in which the soul cannot faint. That is the sense of my text. This man who sings so finely, whose music marches to major strains, all the while mastering the minor, pauses and reveals the deep secret of that major music in this half-finished exclamation: ". . . Unless I had believed to see the goodness of the Lord in the land of the living." The horror is too profound for words; the terror is too terrible for utterance. It is nameless.

This, then, is a brief word of wonderful unveiling of the soul's consciousness of some lonely singer in the long ago, perchance David, more probably Hezekiah, I know not—but of some soul who had been looking out upon life. Poetically referring to the thing upon which he looked by the phrase, "The land of the living," a phrase describing the earth as he saw it, the dwelling place of men; he said: "Unless I had seen more than the land of the living, unless I had believed to see the goodness of the Lord there—!"

Leaving from this moment the peculiarly personal notes of the psalm, let us consider the essential thoughts of the text along two lines, first, the land of the living as it appears in itself; second, the land of the living as it appears in the light which is here described as the goodness of the Lord.

First then, the land of the living as it appears in itself. We must introduce this line of meditation by reminding ourselves of the viewpoint. It is not that of childhood. Childhood never sees the land of the living as this man saw it. Childhood, thank God, is beneficently sheltered and cannot see the things that some of us see so clearly and so tragically today. No child looks tragically upon life. Oh God! must I not amend that to say no child ought to do so! I fear there are some children who do, but it is not the natural viewpoint of the child.

Once again, it is not the natural viewpoint of youth. As Browning sang, "Youth sees but half." Youth is only intended to see half. It has not yet seen life in its entirety.

This is the viewpoint of that which, for lack of a better term, I may describe as maturity, the viewpoint of the man or the woman who has been compelled to face all the facts of life, who has passed through childhood's years with their sweetness and their softness, their laughter and their fun, who has gone beyond the golden age of youth, who has seen the colors fade upon the eastern sky and has tramped under the grey or under the blazing heat.

What, then, are the experiences of such? The land of the living is to them the place of weakness. There comes to us inevitably sooner or later this overwhelming sense of inability. We look back over the pathway we have traveled. We look at the things we have done, and looking back, we note how imperfect they all have been. We look carefully at the things we are doing today, and the sense of imperfection is even more appalling in the presence of immediate service than when we look at that which has been rendered. Then, ah, then, we look on, and there are so many things to be done which we shall never do, intentions that will never be fulfilled, work that has to be dropped and left and cannot be carried out. Not that the work does not need doing, not that the intention was not glorious, not that the vision was untrue, but that we are unable to do it. The appalling sense of inability, incompetence, weakness!

The land of the living is the place of disappointment. The sense of disillusionment comes inevitably to the human soul. We become disappointed with ourselves; we become disappointed in others. We become disappointed in the matter of our hopes and our aspirations. Many of them are not realized; and those we do realize, are they ever what we thought they would be? Are we ever satisfied? Is it not so, that when we have climbed the mountain height upon which we set our eyes and towards which we have striven strenuously, we are disappointed because there stretches away beyond us other mountain heights shutting us in, and we have

THE TRAGEDY OF LIFE WITHOUT FAITH 181

not reached the level we thought we should have reached when that mountain height was climbed.

The land of the living is the place of mystery. Oh! this tangle of human life; the injustice of things; the perplexing problems that fret the soul; the thousand questions that perpetually force themselves out of the agony of life and find no answer. By mystery are we hemmed in; we do not know; we cannot explain; and the sense grows upon us with the passing of the years.

The land of the living is the place of sin. I use the word resolutely. Employ any other term that may better help you. However much we may argue concerning it, and whatever philosophy we may employ to attempt to explain it, there is this appalling consciousness of that which is wrong, out of joint, and not out of joint merely, but diseased withal. The terrific sense of the presence of the poison, of its power, and its pollution.

Again, and let this be the last word in the dark and dreary outlook, the land of the living is the place of death. Death, indiscriminating, ruthless, ghastly! Do you tell me that you have lost your hatred of death? Then you are abnormal, and your abnormality is not the abnormality of health but of disease! Death is ghastly, death is hateful! Death that touches the little child in its sweetness, and the child is gone! Death, that strikes down the standard-bearer at the head of the army and leaves a gap that cannot be filled! Death, that by some accident or catastrophe sweeps upon the soldiers of the Cross and the servants of sin alike and engulfs them together so that the place that knew them knows them no more.

Unless there is something more to say than all that, what a tragedy life is, what a horror! The land of the living, this life in the midst of which we find ourselves, without

God, what does it mean? No final wisdom or knowledge; no adequate strength to deal with things; no authority that moves right onward toward a goal; no possibility of restoration. I do not wonder that this singer gasped out, ". . . Unless I had believed! . . ."

But the gasp was but an interlude in a song. Let us then look again at the land of the living as it appears in the light of the goodness of the Lord. Immediately we are halted by a phrase that suggests a truth, ". . . the goodness of the Lord!" The truth suggested by the phrase is that of the Lord of goodness, the biblical conception of God, the conception of God which inspired this song, the conception which inspired all the songs of this great Psalter. Shining through the whole of them in their unveiling of the human soul is the light of the God of revelation, the God of the Bible.

Goodness is one of the richest words in our vocabulary if we will but interpret it by the teaching of the biblical revelation. A greater word than holiness is this, a finer word than righteousness, including both, but having other qualities, which suffuse them with light and tenderness and mercy. The Hebrew word here so translated means radical and fundamental rightness, but it was a word that was used and translated by other words, beauty, gladness, prosperity. The Lord of goodness is the Lord of all that is right, all that is beautiful, all that is glad, and all that makes for the true prosperity of human life. He is the Lord of goodness, for He is the fountain head from which all these things proceed and the means by which these things become real in the experience of the race.

What light does this fact of God fling upon this strange, weird, life of ours? How does it help us? In what sense does belief in this God turn the sighing into the song, the fear into faith, the sorrow into joy? What are the things that make the triumph note of a song like this that thrills with pain?

I affirm in the first place that in the light of this revelation we come to understand that life is related to Him, and therefore that it is greater than all its experiences; creating their possibilities, but refusing to be exhausted in them. There is a saying of Jesus which we quote perpetually, and never perhaps without seeing some new light in it. "And this is age-abiding life"—that is life which is the life of the age, which cannot be destroyed in an age, or exhausted in an age, which runs through the whole of them, and touches them, and changes them, but is not changed by them—"to know Thee, the only true God. . . ." Now mark what this means in the case of human life. In the light of this revelation I come to the profound consciousness that my life is greater than all its experiences.

Life itself, whatever mystery it may have to face, whatever pain it may have to endure, whatever darkness it may have to go through, whatever agony it may have to bear, whatever sins it may have to mourn, life is vast. It is a Divine creation, and it is thus to this very God of goodness. Therefore, all these experiences of life, being related to Him, take on a new meaning, have a new value, have a new suggestiveness.

I have said that the land of the living is the place of weakness, that we become conscious of inability. In the light of this revelation of man's relationship to God, we discover that the sense of inability is a suggestion of possibility. I cannot do these things, and yet they are things that are to be done and can be done. The fact that I have seen the vision of them is in itself worthwhile. Human life will be measured presently and ultimately not by what it has achieved, but by what it set itself out to achieve, which, if it but be related to God, it will achieve in spite of all the darkness and the apparent disappointment of the present hour. That I know my own weakness is a sign of my own power. That I know there are things I do not know is a sign of my capacity to know the things I do not know. When a man says, "I cannot know the Infinite," in that acknowledgment he confesses that he knows it. He cannot include all the facts that are within it within his present consciousness. But to recognize the Infinite is in some sense to know it. That is at once a demonstration of relationship to God and a result of relationship to God. It would be a dark day indeed for the race if men became satisfied with the things that they have done and the things they are doing and imagined that when they had done their piece of work, all work had forever been completed. It is this very sense of inability which becomes the inspiration of endeavor for it rises out of a sense of possibility.

Again, the experience of the land of the living as a place of disappointment is after all but a demonstration of high possibilities to the man who has seen the face of God and rejoiced in the light. Noble disappointment is a demonstration of the splendor of things seen although never realized. Art thou disappointed with thyself tonight? Then know this, that if thou hast seen a vision of thyself which is finer and higher, in the seeing there was value. The goodness of the Lord in the land of the living is that which makes a man, broken and disappointed with himself, look up into the Face of Deity and resolutely and daringly say, "Thou wilt perfect that which concerneth me. If you take that away from me, then I despair in the midst of life. But leave me that, and,

> With spirit elate,
> The mire and the fog I press through,

THE TRAGEDY OF LIFE WITHOUT FAITH

> For heaven shines under the cloud
> Of the day that is after to-morrow."

If the land of the living be the place of mystery, to the man who has seen the goodness of the Lord in the land of the living or who believes to see the goodness of the Lord in the land of the living, the very fact of mystery is but the expression of profounder things, greater and more glorious. In the twilight of the Jewish Dispensation, the great founder, the lawgiver, uttered words that are to us today fresh and wonderful because of their immediate value; "The secret things" are the things that fill the soul with fear, the things of that realm of mystery which lies about us in life; the problems that confront us; the questions we ask and no answer comes; the secret things! Well, what of them? "They belong to the Lord, and the revealed things are for us and for our children." When we believe to see the goodness of the Lord in the land of the living, we know that there are no secret things from Him, that what we know not, He knows, that what amazes us never amazes Him, that the things for which we find no solution lie naked and open to His vision. Then if there are things which assault us and we cannot understand why they are permitted, the fact that they are permitted no longer troubles us, for He has permitted them, and He can make no mistake. The whole problem of evil lies there illuminated, and there and there alone the heart can find its rest.

The land of the living is the land of sin. The consciousness of sin is born of the conviction of holiness. Apart from the conviction of holiness there is no consciousness of sin. Then let us remember that in the full biblical revelation of God, at the very heart and center of the awful holiness that appals us, there burns and flames the infinite compassion which becomes passion and acts there-through for the saving of sinning souls. Woe is me, I am a sinner! Unless I believe to see the goodness of the Lord in the land of the living! But believing that and seeing that and knowing God, then even my sin shall not make me afraid!

And what of death? Our protest against death is the protest of life, and our horror of death is the horror of health. When once we see the goodness of the Lord in the land of the living, we discover that death is not in His original intention for humanity. The scientists may tell us it is but the fulfilment of the natural order. We affirm that it is the carrying out of an unnatural condition resulting from human sin, that there should not have been any place for death had there been no failure and no sin. The goodness of the Lord in the land of the living transfigures the sackcloth and declares that through death there is the life, and beyond death there is a resurrection. If you take these things away from me, then death is still a horror so terrible that the only relief from it is in itself. I am not surprised that men who lose the Face of God end their lives, ". . . unless I had believed to see the goodness of the Lord in the land of the living!" Without that light, life is not worthwhile; life is a tragedy. Blot out this God from the heavens, deny me the Deity of the Face that shines in human tenderness for the unveiling of the Divine, take this God of the Bible away from me, then life is some hideous mockery and sport of demons. Unless! Oh! the horror of it, the nameless horror of it! Fainted? Nay, the soul becomes too quick and alive, with very agony and despair, challenge and revolt, hot anger and rebellion, ever to faint. Rebellion against what? Against the tragedy, the weakness, the disappointment, the mystery, the sin, and the death, the whole dark outlook!

Ah! but we have believed to see the goodness of the Lord

in the land of the living; we have believed because we have seen the goodness of the Lord in the land of the living, and we believe still to see the goodness of the Lord in the land of the living. We believe that all the things which in themselves fill the soul with fear are held in the grip and grasp of the Great Father of an infinite grace.

At last there will be some explanation of all the pain and the mystery and the disappointment.

What then is to be the true attitude of the soul? Let the psalmist tell us as he ends his song.

". . . Wait on the Lord." Or as the American version has it, ". . . Wait for the Lord. Be strong, and let thine heart take courage. Yea, wait thou for the Lord."

Those who have seen the Face of God are those who have seen it in the Face of Jesus. This is the ultimate in the biblical revelation. Through all the Old Testament we have prophecies, hopes, gleams of light, rosy flecks of a dawn yet to be. Would we view God's brightest glory? we must look in Jesu's Face! To the soul who has seen the Face of God in the Face of Jesus, faith is forever against fear, joy lays hold upon sorrow, and songs rise up against sighing.

What then is the condition? Wait! There is nothing more difficult to do. It is much easier to work for God than to wait for God. To dare in active service is a far less wearisome thing than to wait, and yet by waiting the victory comes as well as the vision.

Moses, nurtured in the Court of Pharaoh, came to an hour when there was born within him a passion to deliver. What was his mistake? The mistake of imagining that in the hour when that passion was born, he was able to do the thing he desired to do. He had to wait for forty years. He always had to wait. In the hour of the wondrous deliverance, when by plague and judgment God set His people free, Moses did no other than wait. It is by waiting upon the Lord that the victory will be won. His goodness will be seen in the land of the living in proportion as His people wait upon Him.

I repeat as I finish, that this outlook is not that of childhood, and the final message is not for the child; the outlook is not that of youth, and the final message is not for youth.

The outlook is that of the men and women who have looked at life, looked at it all, and who if they have had nothing other to look at than life, have gasped with horror and been faint with fear! If such have believed to see the goodness of the Lord, then He teaches them this lesson, that in their waiting, they give Him His opportunity to work. He worketh for him that waiteth for Him.

CHAPTER XIV

THE JUSTIFICATION OF THE SINNER

God's Difficulty—God's Solution

... that He might Himself be just, and the Justifier of him that hath faith in Jesus.
ROMANS 3:26.

THE MEASURE IN WHICH WE APPREHEND THE MEANING OF THE words of the text is the measure in which they challenge our belief. In the earlier part of the letter we find the teaching of the writer as to the attitude of God towards human sin. I content myself with one quotation; "For the wrath of God is revealed from heaven against all ungodliness and unrighteousness of men, who hold down the truth in unrighteousness." The terrible conclusion of the writer as to the condition of the human race, a conclusion which he declared by quotation from one of the ancient psalms, is found in such words as these:

There is none righteous, no, not one;
There is none that understandeth,
There is none that seeketh after God;
They have all turned aside, they are together become unprofitable;
There is none that doeth good, no, not so much as one:
Their throat is an open sepulchre;
With their tongue they have used deceit:

The poison of asps is under their lips:
Whose mouth is full of cursing and bitterness:
Their feet are swift to shed blood;
Destruction and misery are in their ways;
And the way of peace have they not known:
There is no fear of God before their eyes.

By this writer, who first makes clear the attitude of God towards sin and then concludes the whole race as under sin, we are told that this God can be true to Himself in character and yet clear the members of this race from the guilt and penalty of sin.

If we take the declaration without due consideration of the conditions, we shall deny its accuracy. We shall declare that it is impossible for God to be just, that is, true to Himself in nature and character, and justify the ungodly, that is, liberate them from the responsibility or penalty and guilt of sin and treat them as just men. In our courts of law, justice and mercy can never act together. I am not arguing that there never should be clemency in the courts of law. I am not arguing that it may not be well in certain circumstances to extend mercy toward guilty people. I do declare, however, that in the exercise of mercy, there is the violation of justice. It may be that some man arraigned in an earthly court committed an act of wrong under extenuating circumstances that call for clemency and the court so acts towards him. That is not a violation of justice, for it is just that he should be pardoned, as when some man steals a loaf of bread for starving wife and children.

In the Hebrew economy, in the instructions to judges, this matter was most carefully stated, "If there be a controversy between men, and they come unto judgment, and the judges judge them; then they shall justify the righteous, and condemn the wicked." How then can God justify the wicked? How can God be just to Himself, and the Justifier of sinning men? The wonder is great, but the fact is gracious.

Let us consider this matter not theoretically merely, but in order to apply the truth to our own souls' need. Let us try to understand God's difficulty, and then let us consider so far as we may, knowing ere we begin that the light may be too bright for the feebleness of a sinner's sight, and that such a profound matter can be perfectly apprehended—God's solution of His own difficulty.

God's difficulty; to be Just and the Justifier of the sinner. God's solution of his own difficulty; God may "... be just and the Justifier of him that hath faith in Jesus."

We commence by reminding ourselves of the separation between man and God. We recognize at once the intimate relationship between man and God; that all men are offspring of God; that the deepest thing in human nature is not the fresh-life of which we have had our fathers after the flesh, but the spirit-life in which every man is offspring of Deity. In this recognition we are coming face to face with the nature of the separation of which we are to speak.

Passing quickly over the solemn ground, we remind ourselves of two things; the holiness of God and the depravity of man. The holiness of God is the supreme revelation of the biblical writings. It is, moreover, to all those who have eyes to see intelligently, the supreme revelation of creation. This is the apostolic argument in the earlier part of the letter. Paul declared that the Gentiles, the men without the particular revelation which had been granted to the Hebrew people, were nevertheless not without revelation for in nature the wisdom and power of God are clearly revealed. In those things also, we have a revelation of the holiness of God. Let us disabuse our minds of any preconceived notion of what holiness may be: not that our interpretations have been at fault, but that sometimes they have been altogether too partial. The holiness of God is demonstrated by all His works. In the Book of Psalms it will be found that those singers of the ancient times—wonderful singers expressing all the emotions of the human soul in the presence of God—constantly celebrated ". . . the wondrous works of God." The phrase runs through the psalter. The perfection of God is manifested in creation, is seen in form and color, is heard in sound, is detected by all the senses of men. The perfection of God is revealed in all the processes of creation: in those crises and upheavals which fill the soul of man again and again with fear and dread but which in the last result are ever seen to move on toward something yet grander and more beautiful. No man has thought carefully in the presence of the wonderful evolutionary method of God in the created order—which, by the way, is only one method and does not account for everything—without having been impressed by the wonder of it all; the slow-moving processes ever onward and ever perfect in themselves and yet ever growing into more wondrous perfection, and then the clash, the upheaval and the new glory. God's creation uttereth forth His praise. "The whole earth is filled with the glory of God"; and perfection is holiness demonstrated through creation.

The holiness of God is demonstrated also in the perfection of His government; His government of the world in wisdom, in truth, in justice, and in power. These things are not always seen at near range. In many an hour of darkness and conflict we tremble and are afraid. Therein we foolishly judge Him by the limitation of our vision. If we wait but for a generation, and then look back to things that puzzled us, we always see that God has been over-ruling, out of all the chaos creating cosmos, out of disorder establishing order, in the graphic language of the ancient psalm, making ". . . the wrath of man to praise Him, and the remainder girding upon His thigh as a sword"—thus holding it in reserve. All this is but demonstration of the holiness of God.

To state the whole fact, again quoting from the ancient psalms, "As for God, His way is perfect. . . ." Nothing imperfect is tolerated by Him. The autumnal fires destroy the effete beneficently to make way for new life and new beauty. These autumnal fires in nature are but the sacramental symbol of the fact of the Divine presence in which the whole creation ever exists. Scientists have described these fires by the technical term "eremacausis," which means quietly burning. These slowly-burning fires are ever purging nature's floor, and they constitute a fitting symbol of that presence of God everywhere that became clear to the vision of the ancient prophet when he said, ". . . who among us can dwell with the devouring fire? Who among us can dwell with everlasting burnings?" All those who have looked upon human life clearly, carefully, and intelligently, and with spiritual perception, have seen that all our cities, all our nations, all our empires, are within His fire, which surely, ultimately destroys the effete, purifies the strong, and leads forward toward the ultimate consummation of absolute perfection. God's holiness is attested everywhere.

It is supremely declared in the biblical revelation. In the divers portions of the past, the supreme message is that of the holiness of God. In all the songs Divinely inspired, in all the prophecies Divinely taught, in the whole system of the law, the one monotonous message is this, "I, the Lord Thy God, am holy." All these divers portions of the past, however, are as nothing when put into comparison with the simple and yet sublimely complete message that He gave to men in the Person of His Son.

If there be one truth supremely manifest in nature, supremely declared in revelation, it is that of the holiness of God; that holiness that has no place for ultimate imperfection, that holiness that can only be satisfied with perfection in any and every realm, material, mental and moral. The unveiling of God in the Word, in all nature, and in all history, is the revelation of supreme holiness.

We turn from that thought, and we think of man. I will not again read the indictment of the apostle in this context. I only ask you to have it in mind. If inclined to challenge it at any point, I pray you before you pass your verdict, consider it with great care. Having myself done so, I declare that I am convinced that the picture is a true one.

Think of the depravity of human nature as it is revealed in unexpected ways. Man's depravity as revealed in the imperfection of his works even at their highest and their best. There is no true artist but will tell you that the finest creation of his mind and genius is failure. In the realm of art, we are in the realm of creation more peculiarly than in any other realm; yet art has always failed, and in its passionate desire for perfection it sometimes becomes grotesque and foolish. We smile today at some of the manifestations, but they are tragic manifestations of human failure. Futurism is a very modern revelation of man's failure, as well as of man's inherent capacity for creation and passionate desire for expression.

Man's failure is revealed also in his government. That I am not proposing to argue at any length. I take the widest outlook, I survey the centuries and declare that man has never yet governed perfectly. We have made our boast in our ability to govern, and at this moment are faced with a tragic situation in which the supreme, appalling revelation is incapacity for government so that lawlessness is permitted unchecked.

THE JUSTIFICATION OF THE SINNER

Humanity's failure is revealed as surely in the imperfection of its words and these again at the highest and best. Humanity's attempts at interpretation of the poets and the philosophers all fail, so that each succeeding generation comes up with a sigh and finds disappointment in the things that have been said and attempts interpretation once more and again fails.

Take the narrower outlook. Humanity spoils everything it touches of its own life. Business at this hour is full of things of defilement. I am not saying that no man in business is upright. I am not foolish enough to say such a thing; but I am saying that he finds it extremely difficult to be prosperous and upright at the same time. Commercial life is permeated with things of iniquity and evil.

Man spoils his own pleasures with evil. Things perfectly innocent and proper are defiled as man touches them. Tell me what there can be of evil in the racing of two horses mounted by men who almost seem part of them so perfect is their understanding of them? Yet, no reputable man cares to have his name associated with the turf! What can there be inherently evil in cards with pictures of kings and queens and knaves on them? They were invented to amuse a mad king! Yet they have been polluted and fair lives are being damned and ruined by gambling with them. These are rough and ready illustrations, but they are illustrations. Man touches religion itself, and it is degraded and so spoiled and made the means for the manifestation of an evil spirit in protested defense of itself. There is nothing more terrible than that in the whole history of religion that men defend the truth of God in a temper that is born in the pit.

If these are the general facts of the separation between God and man, think within a narrower circle of man's fear of God, man's dread of God, and man's dislike of God. Has man a dread, a fear, a dislike of God? There are thousands of homes characterized by all that is refined in the more modern sense of the word where the very name of God and religion are taboo. Men do not want to talk about God. I protest that it ought to be the most joyous thing in all the world to talk about God, that men should find their chief delight in talking together about Him. Those who really know our God delight to speak of Him, and there is nothing narrow in the speech and nothing mean in the conversation. It is broad with the breadth of His own beneficence and beauty and glory and glad with the happiness of the happy God. Yet men are afraid and will not talk of God but turn their back upon God because of an underlying consciousness of wrong and distance from Him. The reason of man's fear of God is not in God, it is in man. The men who have known God best have had the least slavish fear of Him and have exulted in their conversation concerning Him and their relation to Him. In the light of the Divine requirements as they have been revealed in the Scriptures of Truth—"And what doth the Lord require of thee, but to do justly, and to love mercy, and to walk humbly with thy God"—what is there that makes men anxious not to have dealings with Him? Nothing other than that they have not done justly, have not loved mercy, and have not walked humbly with Him.

That God can justify sinning men and still be just Himself seems to us impossible. Let us remember that on the Divine side the difficulty is created by the desire of God. If God were other than He is, were God other than Love, His passion for perfection might be vindicated by my destruction. He might blot out the evil thing, sweep away the failing race. But listen to one or two very old and very familiar words, perhaps with a slightly altered emphasis; ". . .

Adam, . . . Where are thou? Do you read that as though God were occupied in the work of a policeman? Then you blaspheme. That is not the cry of a policeman; it is the wail of a father. He did not want information as to the geographical location of a man who was hiding; that idea is absurd! The cry was the revelation of the spiritual agony of God in the presence of human sin. Listen to another of these words. It is the language of the broken-hearted prophet Hosea who learned God's pain by the tragedy in his own home, and it expresses that pain of God in presence of Israel's sin; "How shall I give thee up, Ephraim?" In the New Testament the whole truth is declared; "God so loved the world . . ."! That is the supreme fact; love craving for fellowship; God desiring the fellowship of His children; God wounded in His own heart, in His own being, and suffering in the presence of human sin.

Out of that love arises the difficulty of God. His desire is to justify the sinner, to make a way for His banished ones to return, to find a way back for Adam, to restore Ephraim to His original intention, to bring the world to Himself in spite of sin and wandering. That is the Divine desire, the Divine passion. How can He do it? God cannot exercise one attribute at the expense of another. He cannot deny justice when He acts in mercy. He cannot forget the requirements of law when love would operate.

Yet the difficulty is not merely in that God must vindicate law. The difficulty is deeper. He must vindicate law because of the nature of the law that He must vindicate. His law for man was love-inspired and so absolutely perfect that, being broken, results follow which are destructive of such as break it. Punishment is not additional to sin, it is inherent in sin. What a man soweth that he reaps. The harvest of broken law is not the harvest of anger, it is a harvest that grows out of man's own sinning.

Speaking within the limitation of the human outlook, therein is the supreme difficulty. The principle of law can be vindicated by the annihilation of the sinning man; but because law is inspired by love, and love is set upon the perfection of that man, and because the thing the man has done has within itself the elements of man's destruction, the love that inspires law must insist upon the law, while yet it feels out after the man. How can that law be met which has sprung from love, and how can that man be restored? How can this God of perfection be true to Himself and take sinning men back to Himself on the level of the righteous?

There is only one way. He must make them righteous. He must put righteousness at their disposal by some process so that it really becomes theirs, mastering them and dealing with all that which has resulted from their sin, restoring them to His holiness, upon the basis of some power that overcomes sin. Nothing short of that can satisfy the requirement of this God Whose desire is that of the restoration of man.

Again I ask, "How can this be done?" Nicodemus was not so great a fool as some people seem to think. I am weary of hearing men talk about him as though he were a flippant fool, an intellectual idiot! Nicodemus was a tremendous man, and our Lord dealt with him so. When he said, ". . . How can a man be born when he is old?" he was not trifling, but asking the most agonizing question a human soul can ever ask. When I have arrived at manhood, how am I to undo the past years and their influences. I am molded, fashioned; how am I to escape from myself? How can I begin again. It is one of the most terrific questions that was ever addressed to God in Christ. ". . . How can a man be born when he is old?" How can he have that justification that takes hold of

THE JUSTIFICATION OF THE SINNER

the inner fact of his failing manhood and deals with it? That is the question.

The gospel we preach is not simple; it is profound. We do not ask you to receive the pity of God as though He would excuse you and admit you presently to heaven in spite of what you are. God cannot deal with men like that; has not done so and will not do so! He must justify and still be just! He cannot justify, unless He remains just. There is the problem and the difficulty.

Hear then God's solution of the problem; ". . . He might be just and the Justifier of him that hath faith in Jesus." At this point I call a halt of most serious importance and significance apart from which we shall be all astray within five minutes. We must first note Who this Jesus is, to Whom reference is made. Because I am dealing with Paul's teaching and argument, I go back to Paul's definition. His letter opens with it. He was filled with the consciousness of this supreme fact of the Person Who in Himself is of the very essence of the gospel.

"Paul, a bond servant of Jesus Christ, called to be an apostle, separated unto the gospel of God, which He promised afore by His prophets in the holy scriptures, concerning his Son, who was born of the seed of David according to the flesh, who was declared to be the Son of God with power, according to the spirit of holiness, by the resurrection of the dead; even Jesus Christ our Lord."

It is necessary that we go back to that passage to know Who this Person is. There is a racial aspect of humanity from which no individual escapes. This Person, born into this flesh, Who identified Himself with the race, was in essential spirit the Son of God. He came to dwell in flesh that had been the very instrument of sin. The Person toward Whom our faith is directed is not mere man of our humanity. He is

Man of our humanity, but He is also One Whom we cannot dismiss by calling Him Jesus of Nazareth; we must also name Him Son of the Highest. We cannot account for Him wholly within the terms of our humanity; we must include within our thinking His relationship to Deity. That relationship is essential so that when we look at the Son we see, to borrow a phrase from another of the letters of the New Testament, ". . . God was in Christ reconciling the world unto Himself. . . ." Therefore, upon all He said I must place the measurement of the Divine wisdom; upon all He did I must place the measurement of the Divine power. From the narrowed focus of His human life, I must look out into all the immensity of the Divine. When I see Him at work and listen to His speech, I know I am observing God and listening to God. His tears are the tears of God. His sighs are the sighs of God. His pain is the pain of God. This One Who was contracted to a span for human observation, brought down into human limitation for human outlook, is One in Whom all the fulness of the godhead dwelleth bodily. We shall never understand our redemption until we get this outlook upon the Redeemer. If you tell me Jesus was a Man Who persuaded God to love me, you are uttering that which is almost blasphemy. Jesus is God persuading me back to the love of God and enabling me to answer the persuading. Jesus is the name employed in the text; the sweetest, simplest, human name; employed in order that my frail finite mind may fasten and fix itself upon Someone Whom in measure I can understand, and having done so may find that I have been admitted into the spaciousness of all the eternal Deity.

Paul says that in Him ". . . a righteousness of God hath been manifested, . . ." which means infinitely more than that God's righteousness is revealed in Him. The manifestation of righteousness in Jesus is the putting of righteousness

THE JUSTIFICATION OF THE SINNER

at my disposal, not clothing me in it, but communicating it to me so that it becomes the inspiration of my life. This is done ". . . through the redemption that is in Christ Jesus. . . ." The exposition of that term "redemption" is found in the words "a propitiation . . . by His blood." The word "propitiation" suggests something that covers the guilty person so that the results of sin do not fall upon the guilty head. "By His blood" brings us back to the tragic, awful symbol of the very pain and passion of God. Here is the Cross. Therein I learn what I cannot explain, that He bare my sins in His own body on the tree. How, I cannot tell! I could have explained it had it been the activity of man for I also am a man. When I discover that behind the revelation of the Man there is the activity of the God who out of love enunciated law and now out of love doth suffer the consequent penalty of broken law, then I feel that the Rock to which I come will hide me, for God will not violate His own holiness, and even though I cannot explain the method by which He justifies me, I know that seeing He has taken my burden, I may take from Him with humility the gift of pardon which His grace extends.

The way of appropriation is that of faith. The only unpardonable sin is to reject the offer of His grace. The only sin that hath no forgiveness is the rejection of the operation of the Spirit Whose office it is to reveal the things of Christ and place at our disposal all the grace He came to bring me. That unpardonable sin cannot be committed in an hour or a moment. It is not one act. It is persistent, definite, final refusal of Christ. There is no other sin that hath no forgiveness.

The Sabbath day is nearly done. We have been trying to face supreme things. The supreme things of life are those of relation to God. Does that need any arguing? I think not. In view of His holiness then let us ask, "Where do we stand?" To those who are conscious of wrong, of sin, of failure, and consequent lack of fellowship with Him, we bring now the message of the gospel. It is that God places at our disposal righteousness through Christ His own Son, places at our disposal righteousness which is the outcome of the redemption provided through propitiation. He has taken our place as to all the result of our sin and gives us His place as the result of that very suffering.

What shall we do? Shall we not trust Him? Shall we now come to Him saying:

> Nothing in our hands we bring,
> Simply to thy cross we cling.

In such trust we shall have that justification which He bestows while still just to Himself, and enter into the eternal peace.

CHAPTER XV

THE SUPREME INSPIRATION OF FAITH

Remember Jesus Christ, risen from the dead. . . .
II TIMOTHY 2:8.

THIS IS AN HOUR PECULIARLY TRYING TO THE YOUNG PEOPLE of our church. The child, thank God, has no consciousness either of the suffering of the hour or of the problems by which we are confronted. It is wonderful how God fashions the heart and does not allow a little child to apprehend agony until it is strong enough to face and bear it. A sweet little girl this week said to her uncle when he came into the house, "How many Germans have you killed?" He, wise man, understanding the child-heart, said, "Not more than twelve!" She hugged him and kissed him! Dear child-heart, knowing nothing of the agony, knowing nothing of the problems. God help us to guard our children from understanding.

In all probability, those who are older have had to face these very problems before in some other guise, and they are affected, chiefly, by the tragedy of the suffering.

To the young, that is, to those who believe and who think, this is a critical hour. The problems they are called upon to face concern the goodness of God and the government of God. Believing and thinking young life is compelled today irresistibly and in spite of desire to ask whether God can be good, whether God is really governing at all. How can belief in the goodness and government of God be reconciled with all that is going on in Europe today? That is peculiarly the problem of believing and thinking young life. The difficulty is created because the facts remain too well authenticated to be doubted. The fact of the goodness of God and the fact of the government of God as well as the appalling facts of the suffering and wrong of the hour are certain.

I have selected this text because it reveals a principle of life and action, steadying, inspiring, strengthening. It does not solve problems. Indeed, it brings some of them yet more acutely to mind. It does, however, remind us of a fact in history, stupendous, mysterious, assuring, which makes it possible for us to wait for the hour of solution in the sure confidence that there are explanations. How it does this I think we shall see as we proceed.

First, let us give ourselves quite simply to the text itself without any further reference now to the problems of the hour. To these we will return briefly in conclusion.

These words are found in the last writing of Paul preserved for us. When he wrote them, he was in prison and facing death. He was charged with crime; mark the significance of his own words, ". . . in bonds as a malefactor." What the charge was specifically we are not told. Different conjectures have been made; that he was arrested and imprisoned on a charge of sedition, on a charge of having complicity in the burning of Rome, on a charge of treason. Most probably it was this latter charge of treason which was preferred against him on the ground of his preaching of the Kingdom of God and the Kingship of Jesus. In Thessalonica they charged him with acting ". . . contrary to the decrees of Caesar, saying that there is another King, *one* Jesus." His trial had two stages. The first was over when he wrote this letter. In it he had been deserted. Listen to his pathetic words, "At my first defence no one took my part, but all forsook me. . . ." He seems to have expected some delay before the second stage of the trial for he urged Timothy to hasten to him bringing Mark with him. He charged him also to bring a cloak, a suggestive revelation of his physical suffering in the chilliness of the dungeon, and also some precious parchments. The probability is that there was not the delay he expected and that Timothy never again saw him alive. Mark it well, in those days of loneliness, in the grip of a hostile worldpower, forsaken by his friends, suffering the chill of the dungeon, and anticipating the end, he wrote, "Remember Jesus Christ, risen from the dead, of the seed of David. . . ."

Timothy almost certainly received this letter in Ephesus. The first letter was sent to him there, and the probability is that he remained there having the care of the churches. Tradition has it that he was martyred in Ephesus. Ephesus was the capital of Pro-Consular Asia. It was the child of Athens with its culture, and Asiatic paganism; a strange mixture. It was the center of the worship of Artemis or Diana, and it was also a commercial center. Wealthy, superstitious and corrupt, it was a place of grave peril to the infant church. The man in oversight of that church held a position of peculiar responsibility and subtle peril. The struggle against almost overwhelming odds must have been fierce, and to that man in those circumstances these words came: "Remember Jesus Christ, risen from the dead, of the seed of David. . . ."

It was the charge of an old man in the darkest hour when all the reward of fidelity to Christ seemed to be the dungeon and death. It was a charge to a young man called upon to live and exercise his Christian service in a city where the forces opposed were mighty, subtle, and apparently overwhelming;

"Remember Jesus Christ, risen from the dead, of the seed of David. . . ."

Let us, then, consider these words in the simplest way; observing in turn, first, the meaning of the injunction; second, the reason of its giving; and third, how it may be practiced and what is the value of such practice.

"Remember Jesus Christ, risen from the dead. . . ." In the Authorized Version the text reads thus: "Remember that Jesus Christ of the seed of David was raised from the dead. . . ." When we put the two versions together, we recognize the fact that they both say the same thing in different ways. The Authorized Version is strictly accurate in interpretation in that it fixes attention upon the main thought of the apostle. The main thought of the apostle here was that Jesus Christ rose from among the dead. The Authorized Version is faulty in that it deflects attention too much from the Person. It need not do so; when once we have begun to think, it will not do so; but the first sense of the soul in a natural reading of the text in the Authorized Version is to have the attention fixed only upon the Resurrection. That is the ultimate value, but it is not all the value. The Revised Version rendering is far more literal and direct, and I venture to say far more helpful and accurate.

There are two possible mistakes that we may make in the reading of our text. We may over-emphasize the abstract idea of resurrection, as though all the apostle charged Timothy to remember was the Resurrection. We may over-emphasize the fact of the Person, making Jesus Christ supreme apart from the fact of the Resurrection.

There is a twofold thought here; first, remember the actual Man, and remember that He was an actual Man. Mark the balance of the apostolic writing for there is great care evidenced in it; "Remember Jesus Christ, risen from the dead. . . ." That is the central thing, there the light is focused, from there it flashes, but that there might be no mistake, he added, ". . . of the seed of David." Let me miss out the central thought—to which I am bound to come back. "Remember Jesus the Messiah . . . of the seed of David." Immediately we are brought back to recognition of Christ's actual, positive humanity. He was ". . . of the seed of David"; a Man descended from and related to humanity and knowing all human experience.

We must keep this fact central to our thinking of Him. ". . . risen from the dead. . . ." Necessarily that involves the actuality of His death. It has been asserted that He never really died but swooned and was resuscitated. The actual Man of our humanity did most actually die, but we are to remember Him as risen from the dead, not "raised from the dead," but "risen from the dead." The apostle was fixing attention not upon the act but upon the fact. Paul said in effect: "Let your last thought about Jesus Christ, and your perpetual remembrance of Him, fasten Him upon your mind as alive, though having been dead." That is Paul's more logical way of saying that which John said more poetically, quoting the words of Jesus as he heard them in the Isle washed by the sea, ". . . I am the first and the last, and the living one; and I was dead, and behold, I am alive for evermore." "Remember Jesus Christ, risen from the dead, of the seed of David. . . ."

Having realized the importance of the central note of the injunction, we may fasten our attention upon the Person. Necessarily we think of more than the Resurrection, but in the process of remembering Jesus Christ, we shall qualify everything by the final fact of the Resurrection. So let us think of Him, of His Person, of His teaching, of His Cross.

Think of His Person. John the Apostle of love said concerning Jesus: ". . . we beheld His glory, glory as of the only begotten from the Father, full of grace and truth." "Remember Jesus Christ . . ."; and in so doing we think of incarnate grace and truth. There are no better words than these, and if for a moment I borrow other words, it is only that we may catch some of the splendors focused within them. "Remember Jesus Christ . . ." and remembering the Person of Jesus Christ, we remember sweetness and strength; light and love; justice and compassion; righteousness and mercy; the merging in a personality of those qualities and quantities which sometimes seem to be in antagonism but when perfectly blended are seen to present the true man. "Remember Jesus Christ. . . ." Yes, but He was murdered; those hands that were ever doing good were nailed to the Cross; those feet that were ever hurrying upon errands of mercy were transfixed with brutal and bloody nails; He was mauled, spit upon, done to death! I remember Him! Then remember Him risen! Grace and truth cannot be finally crucified, it must rise again. All the high things that make humanity beautiful cannot forever be laid in the dust spattered with blood. "Remember Jesus Christ, risen from the dead. . . ."

Remember Him again in order to listen to His teaching. How shall I summarize the teaching of Jesus? I will do it by the use of three words; righteousness, peace, joy. I wonder if I have put them in the right order. It is the apostolic order, yet listen to the teaching of Jesus; remember the keynote of His great Manifesto, the first note. Presently, as you read that Manifesto through, you hear the deep and awful tones of stern denunciation, and you hear again and again the infinite music of perfect tenderness, each marvelous strain blending and merging into the ultimate and final harmony; but the first note of the Sermon on the Mount is "Happy!" "Blessed" as we read it, but it is far more accurately, "Happy!" Before He is through with that great ethical enunciation, He will

THE SUPREME INSPIRATION OF FAITH

make you shake and tremble and shiver with fear if you are a man at all. He will probe the innermost recesses of your soul and bring to bear upon the secret things of your life the white light of the eternal throne; but the keynote is "Happy." That is the ultimate purpose, but happiness must be based upon righteousness. So He went about teaching.

Have you ever taken time in your busy lives to write out for yourselves all the words of Jesus? When you do it some day—and it is a good exercise, only do not in God's name buy that red-letter Testament to do it by, that is laziness —get a small practice book; you will not want more, the recorded words of Jesus will not fill an ordinary practice book. Having thus written them, read them through, forgetting the context just for once and the occasion on which they were spoken. Read them again and again. Ponder them and you will find three notes running through them: righteousness, peace, joy. Yes, but they silenced Him; they buffetted the mouth that had uttered the words; they murdered Him so that the dear, sweet lips could say nothing else. "Remember Jesus Christ, risen from the dead . . ."! You may for a while silence the voice, but you cannot silence the Word of the living God. After the drear, deep, dense darkness of those days and nights in which the world and heaven were without Christ, His body in the grave, His spirit descending to Hades, behold Him risen! Now He will speak not with one human mouth, but with twelve, with five hundred, with ten thousand, until today the speech of the risen Son of God is being proclaimed by all the sacramental host who are born again of His Holy Spirit. "Remember Jesus Christ, risen from the dead. . . ."

When I remember His Person, I see Him murdered. When I remember His teaching, I find His voice silenced, so that the central, awful, appalling thing I remember is the

Cross. Dare to look at it, dare to face it! Here is one perfect example of humanity, of beauty, of strength, of tenderness, of compassion, of clarity of intellect, of marvel of emotion, of balance of volition; dead at the hands of lawless men. Where is God? You have never seen the Cross if you have never been driven to ask that question. When modern philosophers take the Resurrection away from me and leave me only the Cross of such a Man as this, they leave me an infidel in revolt against God, declining therefore to believe that there is a God, or if there is, that He is good. The Cross alone is the place where all hope goes out in hellish darkness, and all faith is eclipsed forever. You tell me the Cross is vulgar! So it is and with a vulgarity too terrific for words. The vulgarity that mauls and puts to death the most beautiful things the world has ever seen. The Cross; oh the brutality, the scandal of it!

"Remember Jesus Christ, risen . . ."! Then I must look at the Cross again; I must think about the Cross again; I must find some other explanation for it. Now I find that if He was slain by the hands of lawless men, encompassing the men in their lawlessness was the ". . . determinate counsel and foreknowledge of God . . ." and the very things I was made to doubt in the presence of the Cross—His government and His goodness—flame out with new meaning. Here is the government of God. Here is the goodness of God. This is a mystery for which you will find no solution in your heart, which the wise men of the world never understood nor do they today. It is the mystery of God, Whose highest exercise of government and authority is put forth for the saving and making again of the men who smote Him in the face and trampled Him underfoot.

Let us now go further and inquire why Paul charged Timothy to "Remember Jesus Christ, risen. . . ." Timothy had been ordained to a life and service which were extremely

THE SUPREME INSPIRATION OF FAITH

difficult. There are two notes in this letter which are of supreme importance. The first is: "Be not ashamed of me, and be not ashamed of the gospel." The other is: "Suffer hardship."

Be not ashamed. By that first charge we are imaginatively in Ephesus, cultured Ephesus, and there Timothy was to preach a crucified and risen Christ. It was not easy, or popular. Christ crucified to the Greek was foolishness, and the shame of the Cross was in front of the young evangelist. The apostle knew it, he also had felt it, the shame of the gospel!

"Suffer hardship." The word has in it the actual thought of privation and suffering, pain and agony. Because he had to exercise a ministry and live a life in which these notes were necessary, the apostle said to him, "Remember Jesus Christ, risen. . . ."

Paul used three illustrations in this connection; those of the soldier, the athlete, the husbandman. "No soldier on service entangleth himself in the affairs of this life . . . if also a man contend in the games, he is not crowned, except he have contended lawfully . . . the husbandman that laboureth. . . ."

This is no mere piece of rhetoric; mark the suggestive selection. First the soldier, whose sphere of service is conspicuous, heroic, magnificent; then suddenly, the athlete, who walk in life was one of discipline and training in order to crowning; finally, the husbandman, the notes of whose work are patience and obscurity. The soldier, conspicuous, dashing, daring; the athlete, carefully training himself, contesting for crowns and reward; the husbandman quietly going on from day to day with regular duties. Note the different emphases. The soldier, called to conflict in order to win the approval of him who enrolled him; that is an ancient method of saying a soldier serving king, fatherland, and country. The athlete, contending for the crowning that shall be just and true and honorable. The husbandman, toiling for the fruits without which the soldier and the athlete are no use.

Once again, look at these illustrations, in order to come to the supreme thing that was in the apostolic mind. All this has been incidental; there is a unifying principle, something that is common to each of these illustrations. You may express it in the old way—no cross, no crown; no pains, no gains. It is true of the soldier, of the athlete, and of the husbandman. Did you ever understand this verse so well as you understand it today? "No soldier on service entangleth himself in the affairs of this life . . ."! That does not mean that the soldier will not waste time playing; it means that nearer and dearer to the soldier is the call of duty, than mother, wife, sweetheart, child. No cross, no crown! No pains, no gains! The athlete must contend lawfully. Again it is the same principle. No cross, no crown! No pains, no gains! No sloughing off of things unnecessary, no restraint put upon the forces of the physical and mental life; then no crowning, no garland, no winning! Most wonderful of all, and I do not say that carelessly, the husbandman laboreth. We must read into that word laboreth all its full significance. The Greek word means the toil which reduces strength, the toil that brings fatigue, the work that brings the weariness which is the touch of death. That man away back in the country today who ploughs and watches is laboring; putting down into dear old mother earth his own vitality and strength, and if he does not, then there will be no reaping of the harvest and no golden fruitage.

Those are the illustrations. Paul said in effect to Timothy, the young evangelist called to the Christian service and ministry: "You are called to a service and ministry so difficult that you will need the quality of the soldier with its touch of heroism, the severance of every tie that binds to this life; the quality of the athlete, the careful training which refuses the things that hinder and contends lawfully; the toil, the labor, the fatigue of the husbandman." Who is sufficient for these things? Where is there sufficient inspiration to enable a man so to serve, so to live? "Remember Jesus Christ, risen from the dead. . . ."

So we pass to the final word, the injunction itself. We have now reached the point where we are very likely to say, "How can we remember Jesus Christ risen?" The word remembrance is very accurate and beautiful, yet unless we are careful we may miss its meaning. Strictly the word does not mean remembrance, recollection; it means fixity, having in mind, keeping it there. The memory is not being referred to as something which works spasmodically, but as a faculty of the soul which is to be charged forevermore with this wonderful image of the risen Christ. How can that be? Bear in mind the memory is not moral, it is not immoral, it is non-moral. Memory has no relation to the right or wrong of a thing. You tell me it is more easy to remember an evil thing than a good thing. No, it is not. That is your fault. The result of the low level on which you have trained your mind! There is no such thing as a cultured memory. Neither is memory automatic, self-acting. As Professor James once said, "Never forget, memory does not act by itself. If I say to you, Remember; you will say, What? Memory will be of no use until I tell you what to remember." It is well to have these things in mind, for by doing so we shall get rid of a good deal of false thinking about memory.

The exercise of memory is scientific, philosophic, pragmatic. It is scientific. The basis of memory is knowledge. You cannot remember anything you do not know. It is philosophic. The activity of memory is thought. You have to think upon the thing you know, to set your mind on it. Finally, it is pragmatic, that is practical. There must be application of the thing you know or memory will become atrophied, paralized. I will take three other words. The activity of memory may be defined thus: association, imagination, inspiration. We must know Jesus Christ risen from the dead. That is the basis of association. Then we must think upon Jesus Christ risen from the dead and that imaginatively and not merely logically, allowing our imagination to work and have full play. Finally, let association interpreted by imagination become inspiration. That is to remember Jesus Christ.

Mark the value of that exercise. I go back quite hurriedly to the things I have suggested. In the difficult, unpopular, severe service, "Remember Jesus Christ risen. . . ." Put it in another way, I will borrow from another New Testament writing probably by the same man: ". . . consider Him that hath endured such gainsaying of sinners against Himself . . . Who for the joy that was set before Him endured the cross, despising shame, and hath sat down at the right hand of the throne of God." Is your service difficult, must you endure hardness? Consider Him Who endured the Cross, the ultimate hardness. Is your service difficult, must you be careful not to be ashamed? Consider Him Who despised shame. Never forget the rest, ". . . and sat down at the right hand of the throne of God." "Remember Jesus Christ, risen . . ."!

"Remember Jesus Christ risen . . ." in the hour of darkness and mystery. Goodness and truth are violated, they are trampled in the streets; goodness and truth are wronged in reeking tube and iron shard and smoking cathedral; "Remember Jesus Christ risen, . . ." and be perfectly sure that goodness and truth are not buried beneath the ruins of Rheims, but that they will rise again and their victories will be mightier for the baptism of blackness and blood. Righteousness, peace, joy, are destroyed. "Remember Jesus Christ risen, . . ." and know that righteousness marches to its last throne trampling down the hosts of wickedness, and that peace finds its final realization as death is slain in death, and hell in hell laid low, and that joy will come at last even though it finds its way to the ultimate anthem through sighing and groaning and tears.

Where is God? "Remember Jesus Christ risen. . . ." Why does God permit war today? "Remember Jesus Christ risen . . ."! Why did God permit the Cross? In that Cross His government and goodness were challenged. In that Cross His government and goodness were vindicated. "Remember Jesus Christ risen . . ."! But Christianity has failed; all its precepts are trampled in the dust! What then? "Remember Jesus Christ risen. . . ." Did He fail? Through suffering and weakness and all that made Him contemptible, He won His victory. That is the story to the end.

I would say to every Christian man today who enlists in his country's service and boldly faces death: "Remember Jesus Christ risen . . ."!

I would say to every Christian man today who remains at home true to duty's call, in some cases a more difficult thing to do than to go to the front: "Brother, 'Remember Jesus Christ risen. . . .'"

But there is no comfort in this for those who fool in such an hour as this. To the men who are neither going to the front nor doing anything at home there is no comfort. Remember it was Jesus Christ who rose—not Judas, not Herod, not Pilate, not Caiaphas! It is a curious thing that when I searched my New Testament to find some man in the days of Jesus who was a dilletant, fooling, I could not find one. When Jesus passes by in any guise or garb, He forces superlativeness, and there is no man in all the story who was fooling! Men today who do not see that the day of the Lord is at hand and drop into line somewhere ready to suffer and die, for them there is no comfort in this.

But to the man, the woman, who faces the problem, the distress, the darkness, and then buckles on the armor and goes by way of the Cross; I say to such: "Remember Jesus Christ risen. . . ."

CHAPTER XVI

CHRIST JESUS, THE LORD

For we preach . . . Christ Jesus as Lord. . . .
II CORINTHIANS 4:5.

THERE IS NO HUMAN INTEREST WITH WHICH CHRISTIANITY DOES not deal. It comes in love with light and life to the whole circumference of things. It speaks with authority concerning all the facts of the material and moral universe.

As to the material, Christianity first halts men on the threshold of investigation and conditions their attitude through all the processes by affirming God in the language in which the Book of the Christian opens, "In the beginning God . . ."; it also declares that His glory is the consummation of purpose in the material realm.

In the moral realm, Christianity declares the eternal principles which are the standards of creed, and therefore of character, and ultimately therefore of conduct.

These imperial values of Christianity in the abstract are the direct issue of the supernal royalty of Christ. The it in Christianity is the result of the Him. Christianity is Christ crowned.

Christianity is the religion of a Book of which Christ is the one Subject. Christianity is the religion of this world, and because of this world Christ is at once the Source, the Sustainer, and the Goal. Christianity is the realization of truth in the material, moral, and spiritual realms, and Christ Himself is Truth. It follows as a necessary sequence that for the creation of Christian conditions in life, personal, social, national or racial, there must be submission to Christ. Therefore, the message of the Christian pulpit, of the Christian church, is that indicated by the words of my text, "For we preach . . . Christ Jesus as Lord. . . ."

To that theme I invite your attention, and I shall ask you to follow me along three lines of consideration; first, of the person of this Lord Christ Jesus; second, of His purpose; finally of His power.

What, then, is the Person of the Lord as presented in the New Testament? The apostle speaks of Him here as Jesus. Who is Jesus, according to the gospel narratives? I am not now going to argue for the truth of the things affirmed. I simply desire to state them.

Jesus of Nazareth was directly created by God through the agency of the Holy Spirit. Just as the first man according to the account of Scripture was created from the material, so was the second Man; only, instead of the dust of the ground, the seed of the woman was made the basis of the Divine creation. He came into human history a Man of humanity and yet distinct from it; not by the will of man nor by the act of man, but by the will and act of God; peculiar, different in that creation, and yet identified with humanity in all the essentials of human nature. This is the Man to Whom Paul is referring when he says, ". . . we preach . . . Christ Jesus as Lord. . . ."

I go back again to the gospel stories, and as I carefully observe Him in the doings and teachings of His human life there are certain things which impress me.

The first is that He was a Man whose life was perfectly

adjusted toward God and therefore perfectly adjusted toward His fellow men. He always spoke of God with reverence, and yet with almost amazing familiarity; spoke of Him as His Father, made incidental references to Him which showed that in His conception God was touching all life at every point. Flowers; your Father clothes them. Sparrows; your Father is with them when they die. Children; their angels do always behold the face of the Father in heaven. All through His speech we find Him recognizing God; familiar with God; seeing God everywhere. All these beatitudes of this ethical manifesto may be woven into a perfect chaplet, the first resting place of which is on the brow of the Man Who uttered them. And this is conspicuously true of the one which says, "Blessed are the pure in heart, for they shall see God." He was a Man always in the presence of God, always conscious of Him, seeing Him everywhere, and that without a trace of fear in His heart.

Therefore He was a Man Whose life was perfectly adjusted toward His fellow men, in righteousness, in truth, in simplicity, in strength, in sympathy.

The Man presented to our vision in the New Testament was also a Man perfectly balanced within Himself, a Man in Whom there was nothing grotesque. Any man who develops one side of his nature at the expense of all the rest is grotesque. In Christ I see Man perfectly balanced with all essential qualities developed. I would like to take time to defend that statement, especially with regard to the physical. I differ entirely from the conceptions of most of the great artists concerning Jesus Christ. Have you ever seen a picture of Christ that satisfied you? I never have. The majority of artists have presented Him as weak, anemic. Hoffmann satisfies me most. Yet I would add to his portrait a physical Christ of greater beauty. It may be objected that the Scriptures say, ". . .

when we see Him there is no beauty that we should desire Him." That does not mean that He was devoid of beauty, but rather that men were so blind that they could not see it. Moreover, the thought of the prophet there was surely spiritual rather than material. Still another declares His face was more marred than any other. Yes, but have you never seen a beautiful face marred with lines of sorrow and suffering? I believe that in His physical life, Jesus was a Man of great and perfect dignity of beauty.

Turning to the mental side, we cannot but be astonished by the dignity and grandeur of His mental conceptions. Take an illustration on a low level. Clever men constantly endeavored to entrap Him in His talk. Do we ever find Him entrapped? I am overwhelmed again and again, not by His adroitness as though He were subtle and cunning, but by the transparency of His mental method with men, until at last it is written, ". . . no man after that durst ask Him any question."

If I turn to the spiritual, no argument is needed. His conceptions of God, of the eternal ages, of man's spiritual nature; His interpretation of all the things of the eternities are final. No man has gone one single inch beyond His thinking about God and eternity.

While He was thus perfect in each side of His manhood, He was most perfectly balanced and perfectly fulfilled the functions of human life. No ascetic was He. The men of His own age said He was a gluttonous man and a winebibber. So freely did He mix with men in the ordinary affairs of everyday life that the religious teachers of His age imagined that He was an utterly irreligious man. Yet as we look at Him, we see a Man; King of the race, perfect in His Manhood.

Whatever your difficulties may be concerning the doctrines of the Catholic church, I challenge you at this point;

find me a man in all history or in imaginative literature who begins to compare with Him. If He never lived, the men who dreamed Him were the greatest dreamers the world has ever seen. They have presented to us One Who in the ideal His life presents, holds enthraled the honest admiration of all men in this and every age.

This, however, is not the final thing the Scriptures say of Him. They declare Him to be the Son of God, not as other men are the sons of God, but in a peculiar and mystic relationship which is revealed to us in the writings of this same man Paul as in none of the other writings of the New Testament. In the Philippian letter when declaring how He came into human observation, Paul says that originally He was in the form of God; that He did not count that high, exalted method of manifestation a prize to be snatched at for self-enrichment, and then that He took the form of a servant. In reading that passage we must keep the mind fixed carefully on the one Person referred to from beginning to end. There is no change of nature suggested in the process described. It is the same Person Who, being in the form of God, came into human observation by taking another form—not another nature but another method of manifestation, a method adapted to human comprehension, and was made in fashion as a man. Therefore, when I look at the Man of Nazareth in the light of New Testament teaching, I see not only perfect humanity, but veiled Deity; the Son of God incorporated in human life as never before; able to act with God for men for specific purpose.

What does the New Testament say concerning the office of this Person? First, that He came for revelation of God through a channel within the possibility of human comprehension. He came in order that men might look upon One of their own kind and so see God Whom they had never seen.

I think it well to make this distinction. By incarnation God did not come nearer to men. He came into observation. God has always been near man.

There are men today who know God. There are also men who do not know God. God is no nearer to the man who knows Him than to the man who knows Him not. It is true of all men and women that in God they live and move and have their being.

Go back to the palace of King Belshazzar, and see him carousing with his lords, violating all the laws of decency. Now watch the mystic handwriting upon the wall, and hear the charge against him, ". . . the God in whose hand thy breath is, . . . hast thou not glorified." Belchazzar's breath, foul with obscenity, in the hand of God! No man gets away from God. In God every man lives and moves and has his being, yet men today have no knowledge of Him, no consciousness of Him. In Christ, God came out of His hiding place that men might see Him. In our thinking of God, we may build up our conception upon the basis of that perfect humanity. Throw out the lines into eternity, and they include all the truth about God. The tears of Jesus are the revelations of the agony of God. The tender touch of Jesus is that by which man knows how gentle God can be. The stern severity of the words that scorched like fire as they fell from the lips of Jesus unveil God's holiness and His wrath abiding upon sin. The wooing, winsome words in which He called to weary and heavy laden men were the very speech of God calling men back to His bosom, back to His heart. He came for revelation.

He came for more. He came according to the teaching of the New Testament for redemption; redemption wrought through His identification with sinning men to the last issue of their sin. I know how incomplete that statement is, yet ponder it well. I listen to that strangest, profoundest word that fell from the lips of Jesus as He was dying on Calvary, ". . . my God, my God, why hast thou forsaken me?" I am always afraid to begin to interpret the meaning of those words. The very question they ask suggests mystery even in the mind of the dying One, and who am I that I should try to unveil the hidden mystery? Yet, listening to the words, they forevermore suggest to me the ultimate issue of sin. It was the language of sin in its last experience. It was the language of sorrow at its profoundest depth. It was a word which expressed the most unutterable experience that ever comes into human life, the experience of an unexplained mystery of silence. He was identified with man in his sin to its last issue. In the transaction of the Cross He so dealt with sin that I come to that Cross, and while men are discussing the atonement, I know that my sins are not merely pardoned, but canceled, made not to be. In the presence of that Cross I find that heart's-ease, notwithstanding sin, which I can find nowhere else.

So that this Man upon Whom we look, perfect in His humanity, mystic in His Deity, flaming in His revelation of God; in deep, dense darkness that I can never fathom, so wrought that this poor, broken heart, buffeted by reason of its sin finds healing and rest.

That is the Person presented in these gospel stories; presented finally in the full dignity of this great and wonderful description, the Lord Jesus Christ. Of Him the apostle says: ". . . we preach Christ Jesus as Lord. . . ." Lord by the victory of life and death; Lord by the appointment of God; Lord by the administration of the Holy Spirit.

Let me now pass to a brief word as to the purpose of our Lord Jesus Christ according to the teaching of Scripture.

What was the passion of Jesus Christ? I am not now referring to the ultimate mystery of that passion baptism whereby He redeemed men. What was the master-passion or the master-motive of the life of Jesus? That is not an easy question. I sometimes think we find the difficulty of it if we ask it about ourselves. What is our master-motive? There is one in every human life. We give as reasons for the things we do things which are not *the* reasons for the things we do. We give second or third causes for the things we do as final. They are not. If we could get back to the underlying conception of life that masters us, we should have the true answer.

What was the underlying conception of Jesus, the motive of everything, the master-passion of His life? I answer the inquiry in one brief phrase, the Kingdom of God. To some that may seem a very insufficient answer. The reason is that we have taken the phrase the Kingdom of God and materialized it until we imagine it only refers to the establishment of a beneficent order in the world. The phrase is greater than that. To say the Kingdom of God is to say everything. To say that the master-passion, the motive of the life of Jesus was the Kingdom of God is to touch the deepest, profoundest thing in all His life. We might be inclined to say that the motive of His life is best stated in His own words, ". . . the Son of Man came to seek and to save that which was lost." That, however, was not the deepest thing. He was full of compassion for men, but there is a profounder depth. The deepest thing in His life was expressed in prophetic language long before He came in flesh, and this is it: ". . . I am come to do thy will, O God." He emphasized it in the prayer He taught His disciples. He said, ". . . when ye pray, say Our Father which art in heaven, Hallowed by Thy name. Thy Kingdom come. Thy will be done, as in heaven, so on earth." He came not so much to save men as for the glory of God. We are all in danger in these days of laying the emphasis elsewhere. No one will imagine I am undervaluing His compassion. But that ministry which culminated in the Cross was for the glory of God and the establishment of His Kingdom; for the vindication of God's character in the world and the universe in answer to the slander which lies at the heart of evil. The Devil came into human life by slander; ". . . hath God said . . . ?" and there lurked in the question the suggestion that God was withholding something good from humanity. Jesus Christ came to give the lie to that lie; to reconcile to God all things in earth and in heaven. Not merely this little planet of ours, but the whole universe was involved and touched by the ministry and passion of this King of the race.

The master-passion of Christ, then, was that of the Kingdom of God. His motive in all that He does for me is that I should be in that Kingdom, submitted to it, realizing it, manifesting it. That is His passion for the world at large. It is His motive in all His ministry in the wide universe of God. That is a great declaration in the writings of Paul in which He speaks of the day when ". . . he shall deliver up the kingdom to God." For that day He came, He lived, He toiled, He suffered, He died, He rose, and He waits in patience, and at last He will see of the travail of His soul and be satisfied; not merely when He has redeemed humanity, but when He delivers the Kingdom to His Father. The master-passion of all the life and ministry of Jesus is that of the Kingdom of God.

While that is the ultimate purpose, notice, still within the thought of purpose, His method so far as we are concerned. I do not think that can be better stated than in the line of the hymn:

> He is my Prophet, Priest, and King.

Take these three words, and think of all they suggest.

The work of the prophet is that of declaration, proclamation, revelation. So He began proclaiming, declaring, revealing, and He said enough. Obey His words in your life, and your life is in the Kingdom of God. Obey His words in civic and national life, and they alike conform to the Kingdom of God.

Never forget that even in these days when men are denying certain facts concerning Him, denying the supernatural facts which we believe lie at the heart of our religion concerning this Lord Christ, they are still claiming that the Sermon on the Mount is a perfect law of life. It was His proclamation of the Kingdom of God. That marvelous and awe-inspiring ethic was His prophetic forthtelling to the world of the will of God. He was a Prophet proclaiming.

He was also a Priest. If the word "prophet" suggest proclamation, the word "priest" suggests propitiation. Again we have a word which we need to use very reverently. It proclaims His work in redemption. As I affirmed concerning His prophetic work that He said enough, so I affirm concerning His priestly work that He did enough. There is nothing to be done beyond that which He has done. I do not want to argue it. If I did and were to test the declaration by the witnesses, thank God, they are here. I could call witnesses to the truth of it. He breaks the power of canceled sin and sets the prisoner free. The thing that mastered me, gripped me, poisoned me, the thing I could not escape from, He has overcome, and it is underneath my feet. I have been made master of the very forces which mastered me. He has provided redemption, plenteous redemption. He not only said enough, He did enough.

Finally, He is King. That is administration, realization. Men say He is not crowned. Let there be no sigh when you say it. Hear the ancient prophetic word, "He shall not fail nor be discouraged, till He have set judgment in the earth; and the isles shall wait for His law." "We see not yet all things put under Him. . . . But we see Jesus. . . ." To see Jesus is to be perfectly sure that His work as King will be brought to ultimate victory because of His work as Prophet and as Priest.

What, according to Scripture, is His program? The day of grace, the day of judgment following it, and then the establishment of government and the handing of the Kingdom to His Father. The day of grace is that in which we live. There is a day of judgment coming. I do not mean a day of twenty-four hours, an assize. I mean a method of judgment in the world for the establishment of His Kingdom. We half-quote a great many passages of Scripture. Do you remember when Jesus was reading in the synagogue from the prophecy of Isaiah concerning His own ministry, where He stopped? He read these significant words: ". . . to proclaim the acceptable year of the Lord. . . ." and He closed the Book. Reverently, let me open the Book again at the verse where He closed it. What do I find? After the words "the acceptable year of the Lord" there is a comma, and then ". . . the day of vengeance of our God. . . ." As surely as He came to proclaim the acceptable year of the Lord, He will come to proclaim the day of vengeance of our God. How long the day of judgment will last, none can tell. It will in all probability be brief, for judgment is ever His strange act. But it must come. I have no greater comfort than to believe that. It is for that day of judgment I as often pray as for any tender, merciful deliverance of the saints. What this world supremely needs is the rod of iron, which is not a rod of cruelty but an inflexible rod of strict and absolute justice. He is coming so to reign. I at least cannot lose the vision of the coming reign when I think of this King. It is in His program. It is not the last method. There are other methods, other dispensations stretching away beyond. It is not for us to waste time speculating. Our duty is to fulfil our present responsibility which is that of preaching the gospel of His grace, for the gathering of His own, and for the preparation of the world for that larger establishment of the Kingdom that lies beyond.

Finally, as we have tried to glance at the Person and to consider the purpose, let me in a last word speak of the power of this Lord Christ. What is the nature of the power of the King? First it is spiritual in essence, dealing fundamentally with the deepest facts of the human life, and second, it is regenerative in operation.

Spiritual in essence. They wanted to make Him King while He was upon the earth on the basis of material supply, but He would have none of it. He fed the multitudes, and they desired to take Him by force and make Him King, but He hurried His disciples away across the sea, and Himself climbed the mountain. He will never be made King on that basis. There are men today who would make Him King if He would find them work, and give them food, and supply all their material needs. He will do all that when they come into the Kingdom, but He does not begin there. He begins not with the incidental of the flesh but with the essential of the spirit. He comes to set up God's Kingdom not by force of arms, by policy or cunning, by bribery or corruption, but by dealing with the spiritual center of life, by bringing the being back into right relation with God.

On the basis of the remade, reborn spirit of man, He reconstructs everything else. So He has proceeded through the centuries, and we count His method slow. The slowness of God is due to the longsuffering of God. It is also on account of the fact that He must begin with the spiritual fact at the center. So He begins with me. It is sometimes argued as to whether heredity or environment is the stronger force. I am perfectly in sympathy with the view that environment is a far stronger force than heredity, but environment is not enough. Put a man in an environment, and you may lift him just a little higher. It is very valuable, but you cannot remake the man by environment, and unless you begin with something in the man that is essential he will degrade the new environment into which you put him. Jesus Christ is a King Who begins with the essential fact. He is not going to be made your King by bribing you with bread and work. He claims the allegiance of the spiritual essence of your being, and when He gets it, then, according to His own great word, ". . . seek ye first His kingdom . . . and all these things shall be added unto you." He has never yet failed in His promise. He begins at the center with the spiritual life. There are men who have lost consciousness of their own spiritual nature, men who have no vision of God, and who say, "Let us eat and drink, for tomorrow we die." He comes to such lives, to such spiritual natures as have lost consciousness of God and of themselves, and what is His first business? To quicken them. ". . . you hath He quickened, . . ." That is the first thing. He brings a man to the consciousness of God and of his own spiritual life. In the same moment and upon that basis, He begins the great work of reconstruction. Regeneration means the destruction of the destroying forces and the reconstruction of the essential nature of man. So Christ comes to carry out this work. That is the nature of His work.

Again, what is the extent of His work? It is limitless and it is limited. It is limitless as it proceeds from the spiritual to the material. There is no point that it does not touch. The remade man in his spiritual life is a man who is rendered capable of the reconstruction of his mental life. The remade man in spiritual life is a man capable of reconstruction in his own physical life. He will also go into the wilderness and make it blossom as the rose; He will go into the midst of groaning creation and heal it.

Christ begins in the center, and from that regenerated center, the forces of renewal pass out through all the life. Remade spiritually, renewed mentally, with all the forces of your physical life under the control of the Spirit, your home will become a different home, the neighborhood in which you live will feel the influence of your life. Waves of influence proceeding from reconstructed spirituality will pass out through the whole world.

In what sense is He limited? As to the nature of the effect He produces in the life of men. I do not say He is limited in the production of effect, but that He is limited in the nature of the effect He produces. You cannot come face to face with the Lord Christ and be the same afterward. You can, however, decide what the nature of the effect He produces is going to be upon your life. You come face to face with Christ and with His claim, and then you make your choice, and on that choice depends the nature of the effect He produces. His gospel is a savor of life unto life or of death unto death.

Even if you have seen nothing in Him save the life of ideal beauty, then what are you going to do with it? To accept it is to follow Him and to be remade by His power. To refuse is to choose the low and to be degraded. Christ is limited by our choice, our decision, our will.

Let my last word be this about His power. His power is inevitable. It is beneficent if we so choose; it is destructive if we so choose. ". . . we preach . . . Christ Jesus as Lord. . . ." We preach Him not as One Who lived and died and passed away but as the living One. The mystic touch of His hand is still upon our hearts. We are conscious of our nearness to God, to the great Revealer, the great Redeemer.

Let us crown the Person of the Lord and so know His power working in our lives, and from henceforth share His purpose and by falling into line we march with Him toward the goal of the ages, the establishment of the Kingdom of God.

I pray those of you who have known Him longest join with me and crown Him anew and so anew receive His power and as never before be one with Him in the passion of His heart to see the Kingdom established.

And you who never yet have crowned Him, now, in the silence, without sign or sound or symbol, do this and you shall know His power, and cooperate in His purpose.

CHAPTER XVII

CHRIST AND SINNERS—IDENTIFIED AND SEPARATE

... He was reckoned with transgressors: ...
LUKE 22:37.

... separated from sinners. ...
HEB. 7:26.

THESE TWO STATEMENTS CONCERNING CHRIST ARE NOT CONtradictory; they are complementary. To understand them correctly is to see that one is the necessary outcome of the other in the case of the Person, the imperial Person, concerning Whom they were both written. To appreciate their unity is to discover the very heart of the great gospel of the grace of God. The first words were spoken by the Lord Himself. He was making quotation from the ancient prophecy claiming the fulfilment of the prediction in Himself. The last words from the letter to the Hebrews constitute a statement made by one who was showing the superiority of the Priesthood of Jesus over all priesthoods which had preceded. The first statement "... He was reckoned with transgressors ..." refers ultimately to His death. The second statement refers finally to His indestructible life. The first statement finds its fulness of meaning in the Cross. The second statement has

CHRIST AND SINNERS—IDENTIFIED AND SEPARATE 233

its ultimate demonstration of truth in the Resurrection and the Ascension and the session in glory of the self-same One Who was crucified. Taken together, they reveal the method by which Jesus Christ became the Saviour of men. ". . . reckoned with transgressors, . . ." but ". . . separated from sinners. . . ."

I think perhaps the truth may thus be stated. Christ's separation from sinners in identification with them, made possible their separation from sin in identification with Him. ". . . reckoned with transgressors, . . ." He came into their midst but was always by infinite distances separated from them; but by the identification with them of the separated One, He made possible their separation from sin as He brings them into new and living identification with Himself.

Now, because that seems to me to be the very heart of the gospel of the grace of God for weary and sinning souls, let us reverently consider it. First, we will take these statements as declaring the truth about Him, Who was at once ". . . reckoned with transgressors . . ." and yet ". . . separated from sinners. . . ." Then, we will consider them as revealing the relation creating the salvation which is at the disposal of man. Finally, we shall see that these two statements not merely indicate something true more than nineteen hundred years ago, but true here and now as they reveal the perpetual method of Jesus with men, that of identification with sinners in separation from them, that by such means He may bring them into separation from the thing that blights and spoils and ruins, by living identification with Himself.

First, then, let us take these two statements quite separately. ". . . He was reckoned with transgressors. . . ." He was ". . . separated from sinners. . . ."

"He was reckoned with transgressors . . ." in His place in the world. He was reckoned with transgressors in His own choice of companionships. And in the economy of the grace of God, He was reckoned with sinners even unto death.

". . . He was reckoned with transgressors . . ." in His place in the world. Born of a woman, He so entered into the very life of man, coming into the currents of that life in personal and close and intimate identification. To use the very graphic phrase of a New Testament writer, He "took hold" upon our human nature, made it part of Himself, made Himself part of it.

Then even by the outward sign and symbol of human process of the Roman taxing and the imperial counting, He was reckoned, counted among sinners. There went out a decree from Caesar that all the world should be taxed. In the process of the Roman taxing and the imperial counting. He was in the world, one more added to the number of the Roman census, another life added to the great whole. He was one of the crowd, so small and insignificant that none knew of Him, or would have known of Him apart from heavenly revelation of His coming in songs of angels to the waiting shepherds and the shining of a star to men who sincerely gazed out into the heavens and attempted to unlock their great and profound secrets. Apart from these supernatural signs, He was One amongst the rest, reckoned amongst them. It is very wonderful how Jesus Christ has sanctified all life, even the taking of a census. There is no phase of human life, if we have eyes to see and ears to hear and hearts to understand, but that the sanctifying touch of Jesus is upon it. It is such a prosaic thing, this taking of a census! Think on the morning when you write your name down that He ". . . was reckoned among transgressors, . . ." conformed to the economy of man, part of the great bulk of sinning, suffering, sorrowing souls; reckoned among sinners, even in the commonplace of His placing in the world.

He was reckoned among sinners strangely and wonderfully enough in the choice of His companions. Think of those boyhood days at Nazareth! Remember that He was reckoned among the children in Nazareth, and never believe the picture that shows you the boy Jesus with a halo. All such pictures misinterpret Him. He wore no halo other than the sweet halo of a disposition strong and gentle, heroic and tender. They loved Him in Nazareth. Until He began to preach, Nazareth never tried to fling Him from the brow of the hill into the valley. I read that He "increased . . . in favour with God and man"; He was one of them, just one of the children of Nazareth. They said later, "Is not this . . . the son of Joseph . . .?" It was a mistake, but they were to be excused, for ". . . He was reckoned among transgressors, . . ." one of themselves all the way through. One of themselves also, presently, when passing from youth into manhood, He worked for His living as a carpenter. There is infinite music in that statement to all who toil for their living. He was one of us, working, toiling, tempted, trusting; reckoned amongst us, reckoned amongst us by heaven's decree of infinite love, reckoned amongst us by earth's observation, reckoned amongst us by hell's attacks; one of us, ". . . reckoned with transgressors. . . ."

But, presently, He left Nazareth, left the carpenter's shop, left the quietness and the seclusion and came into public life. Now, let us see His friends. Who are the men who were His companions and gathered about Him? Let me be careful here to use only the statements of Scripture. Who were the people that He received unto Himself? It is very difficult to translate the word. We talk today in certain sections of society of "receiving." What is it to receive, according to the word here, according to its real meaning? We may read it, "He receiveth sinners to Himself"; that is, He takes them to His heart, He takes them to His secret love, He takes them to His confidence. That is the thing that startled and appalled the whited sepulchers who pretended to be teaching God's law and God's Kingdom. He received sinners; sat down at the table and ate with them. He was the friend of publicans and sinners.

Let me tell you what so eminent a scholar as Dr. Bruce once said about this. Speaking to Mr. Samuel Chadwick, he said, "You know, Chadwick, that word 'friend' is not good enough; it does not really catch the meaning of the word behind it." Mr. Chadwick looked at him and said, "What would you put there?" "Well," he said, "the face of the matter is, the only word that catches it is the word the boys use—'chum.'" He is the chum of publicans and sinners. I tell you who said that as you might object to it if I said it. He so lived and acted that these men who stood for righteousness—the righteousness of scribes and Pharisees—said, "That man is the companion, the chum, the intimate friend of publicans and sinners."

". . . He was reckoned with sinners . . ." by His own deliberate choice. Oh, if we did but know Him, how surprised we would be! If we did but understand this radiant Son of God, how startled we should be if we watched Him! The scribes and Pharisees would have been more astonished if they had known Him better. Imperial mentally, He might have been the chosen companion of the savants of His time. Imperial artistically, He might have taught painters how to express in colors the visions which they saw. He might have whispered symphonies to waiting musicians as He has been doing ever since. But He passed the learned and the great and found the sinners and made friends of them. ". . . He was reckoned with transgressors. . . ."

What did this identification with sinners finally mean?

First, by way of incarnation He was reckoned in the human census as one of a crowd. Then by chosen companionships, so that He became the butt and scorn of the unrighteous and blind teachers by whom He was surrounded. We never understand all that means until we see Him at last on the rough Roman gibbet. With whom was He there? With political prisoners? No! With those guilty of first-class misdemeanors—what a curious phrase that is, as though there could be a first-class criminal!—No! Numbered with whom, then? Oh, my masters, would God we could see it, with robbers, thieves, or to take the wholly expressive word of our translation, "malefactors," evil-doers, numbered with them, in the midst of them, by His own choice! Listen to the gibe of the men in front of the Cross, to the cruel, devilish, cynical, self-satisfied sneer, "He saved others, Himself He cannot save. . . ." Oh, how they lied! He could have saved Himself. He could have come down from the Cross. He could have called for ten legions of angels who would have swept the unholy mob that mocked Him into hell.

Yet, again, He could not, Why not? Because He had chosen to be ". . . reckoned with transgressors, . . ." and in His dying there was a sacramental symbolism in those hands outstretched between two men—the refuse of humanity, malefactors. He was reckoned with transgressors!

But He was ". . . separated from sinners, . . ." first in His character, therefore in His conduct, and finally, beyond the brutality of the Cross, in the marvel of the Resurrection.

". . . separated from sinners . . ." first of all in His character. When He was coming into the world, in one of the wonderful New Testament songs concerning Him, it was said that God had visited and redeemed His people in order that they should serve God in holiness and righteousness before Him all their days. Mark those two words, "holiness and righteousness"—not two things but two manifestations of the same quality and quantity and fact. What is holiness? Rightness of character. What is righteousness? Rightness of conduct. Holiness refers to the inward, righteousness to the outward. Holiness is something internal. Righteousness is something external. They belong to each other. Apart from holiness there is no righteousness; apart from righteousness there is no holiness. That is to say, if a man sing to me of his holiness and I see no rightness in conduct, I deny the holiness he claims. These two things are always together, and we have perfectly learned their meaning in human history from this Man.

In these facts He was separated from sinners—reckoned with them but always separated from them. Separated in that character of holiness, separated from them because He was a Man of true conceptions, of pure desires. These are the two things that underlie all life: the conception which is intellectual, the desire which is emotional. These are the things that create the volitional, drive the will, and help it to make its choices. If I can only find out what your conception of anything is, if I can only find out what your desire is, then I know which way you will choose. That is the revelation of your character. I can only learn it as I wait for the activity. I trace back from the external activity to the internal character, and there in the making of the character I have the conception, the desire, the choosing. That has been the trouble in my life, has it not in yours? My conceptions have been false, my thought of things has been wrong. I wish I could put this into one sentence. Every sin committed externally is the outcome of a sin committed internally. Whatever I do that is wrong in conduct is due to the fact that I am wrong in my underlying conception of things.

But this Man sat down at the table with men of impure

conceptions, of untrue thinking, and He was of true thinking and pure conception. He saw everything in its true relationship to everything else. There was nothing distorted in His outlook, nothing out of place. True in His thinking, in His conception, and pure therefore in all His desires and so separated infinite distances from the men whom He made His friends, from the men among whom He sat and with whom He ate. Reckoned amongst them for He sat with them at the board; separated from them by the distance between high heaven and deep hell.

Thus He was not only apart in character, which is holiness, but also in conduct, which is righteousness. Never deceiving, never oppressing, never taking advantage of weakness. I will not argue it. We know it.

But my text having all that as supposition, yet in absolute fact, makes a statement that goes infinitely beyond all. Now for one moment let us look at the context. "For such a high priest became us, holy, . . ." that is the first thing; ". . . guileless, . . ." that is, without deceit, without crookedness; ". . . undefiled, . . ." that is, not taking into His character any defilement by which He was surrounded in other people. Now, hear this, and mark the continuity, ". . . separated from sinners, and made higher than the heavens." What, then, is the real meaning of this passage, ". . . separated from sinners . . ."? Not separate, but separated. The final thought is of the Resurrection. He Who had been reckoned among transgressors unto death, and yet had been separated from transgressors in all His life, was at last separated from sinners by the act of God, when He took Him out of the midst of them, out of the grave into which they had put Him, separated Him from them and made Him higher than the heavens. That is the final fact in Christ's separation from sinners.

The Resurrection of Jesus in some senses is the severest, the profoundest condemnation of the sinner. In some senses, when God raised Jesus, He said to the listening race, "this is the Man of My choice. This is the Man Who satisfies My heart. This is the Man Who has accomplished My purpose. This is the Man I choose to come back to Me out of death. I separate Him from sinners and make Him higher than the Heavens."

Reckoned with transgressors by the stoop of the incarnation, by the reckoning of human governments, by the choice of His own free will in friendship, by the mystery of His passion in the economy of God. Separated from sinners in the purity of His character, in the rectitude of His conduct, and therefore in the splendor of His crowning.

And now, I pray you notice how these two things create the gospel. The gospel at once smites me with condemnation and heals me with salvation. The gospel makes me know my sin as the law by Moses never did. The gospel frees me from sin as the law by Moses never could. This paradox and contradiction of the great Evangel only has its explanation as we see that both these things are true concerning Jesus. Because of His separation from sinners He was powerful; because of His identification with sinners He brought that power into touch with the sinner; and wherever the sinner consents to unification with Him, He communicates to the sinner the power which is His by separation from the sinner.

Separation is the cause of power. Identification is the contact of power. Unification is the communication of power.

Separation is the cause of power. We must come down from the Son of God who is infinite—and consider finite things if we would understand. Tennyson sang about Sir Galahad:

His strength was as the strength of ten,
Because his heart was pure.

Look through that little window of poetry and imagination and see this tremendous truth flaming in letters of fire. Purity from sin is that which creates power to help men beaten by sin. Look at it in your own life. If you want to help a sinning man, the measure of your ability to help him is the measure in which you do not sin yourself. We know perfectly well it is utterly useless for us to say, "Be pure," to a man if there be impurity in our own heart. Fathers—God Almighty say it to me!—it is no use telling your boy to be pure if you are impure. Power to make other people pure consists in personal purity. Now we are all agreed. Separate from sinners so that no taint of impurity was on Him, blessed, holy, perfect Man of Nazareth, and in that purity which man misinterpreted and hated lay the power by which He lifts men. Said the Pharisees, "This Man receiveth sinners. . . ." Now, do let us be fair, even to Pharisees, though it is very hard. What did they mean? They meant, "You cannot touch pitch without being defiled." They meant, "If this Man is going to make a friend of sinners, He Himself will become a sinner." The Pharisees were quite right, they were perfectly correct, if I had been the one they were talking about, or you. If I make a companion of sinning men, I shall be contaminated. Young man, you have just come up to the great city. You have been a month in the city. Tell me, who are your friends. If your friends are impure, for God's sake and your soul's sake, quit them now. They will make you impure.

But there is a difference in this Man. Why is it if I make a friend of sinners, I shall become contaminated? Because in me there is sin, there is that to which sin appeals; there is corruption calling to corruption and answering back to corruption. But in Jesus purity was not negative. It was positive, and so it was power, and when He took a poor, wretched sinner to His heart, and sat and ate with him, instead of the defilement of the sinner spoiling Him, the virtue of His purity lifted the sinner. ". . . reckoned with transgressors, . . ." but, Hallelujah!—separated from them! In that infinite separation of His purity lay the dynamic by which He was able by contact to lift the man who was impure.

That leads to the next thing. If He had not been ". . . reckoned with transgressors . . . ," His separation from them could never have saved them. His purity cannot save a man until He identifies Himself with that man. You may be pure as the snow, and if you stay on the mountain top where pure snows are, you will never make pure some loathsome thing that lies in the valley. You may be pure, but if you shut yourself up within convent walls and never touch the sinning masses without, you cannot help to make them pure. The greatest saint is not the person who cultivates his or her own life within such convent walls by severe austerity. The greatest saint is the slum sister in the Salvation Army who puts her sweet womanhood against the surging sorrows of her fallen sisters. Where did we learn this lesson? From the Man separated by the distance of the infinite snows, Who came down and lived among sinning men, made friends of them—yes, I will say it, made chums of them. He took them to His heart in an embrace of tenderness and brotherhood and so helped them to feel the tides of His purity and to sob out upon His dear and wounded heart the sorrows of all their sin. ". . . reckoned with, . . ." and therefore by such contact able to bring the power of His purity into touch with men.

Yet He could only finish that great work which He

CHRIST AND SINNERS—IDENTIFIED AND SEPARATE 243

began in life by dying. How far must He go with me if He is to correct my impurity by His purity? He must go all the way. He must go on and on until in His soul He fulfils the prophetic word that was always so mysterious, ". . . the pains of hell gat hold upon Me. . . ." May God have mercy on us if we lose sight of that Cross and its deepest meaning. Oh, brutal Cross of Calvary, oh, hateful Cross; but it is my Cross—that is the place of my sin. This selfish heart of mine ought to be transfixed with wounds. These evil hands of mine ought to be nailed there. These unholy feet of mine, swift to run in the ways of evil, ought to be there.

> In my place condemned He stood,
> Sealed my pardon with His blood,
> Hallelujah! What a Saviour!

"Reckoned" with me there when the pains of hell enwrapped the soul, and the darkness of the hiding of the face of God broke upon the spirit; reckoned with me there! That is the mystery of salvation, and because of that, if I come to that Cross, and coming to it say,

> Rock of Ages, cleft for me,
> Let me hide myself in Thee!
> Let the water and the blood,
> From Thy riven side which flowed,
> Be of sin the double cure;
> Save me from its guilt and power,

then by such reckoning with me in the power of His infinite separation from me, He takes my guilt and gives me His purity; or in the far finer and more majestic and wonderful language of Scripture, ". . . He was made to be sin on our behalf: that we might become the righteousness of God in Him."

The last thing I want to say is this—that was not merely

His method historically; it is His method now; it is His method here. Then what? He received sinners, He ate with sinners, He was the friend of sinners, He was without sin. And tonight, what? Are you a sinner? I will leave the whole congregation now, except the man who says, "Yes." I have no gospel if you say, "No." I am not here except to preach to the people who are sinners, because I have been ordained by the One Who said, ". . . I came not to call the righteous but sinners." I have no message for the righteous man. Are you a sinner? Is the burden of it on your soul? Is the filth of it on your character? Is the poison of it in your blood? God help you, my brother! Did you creep in here tonight thankful that nobody knew all about you? Are you sitting somewhere in the midst of these people, a leper, and conscious of it? He is by your side. If there should happen to be in this house a hundred righteous people who need no repentance, He is not with them, He is with you. These are not distant things that have passed. these are present living realities. He is down there by the man who is an outcast from his own self-respect, by the side of the man abhorring himself, loathing himself, and yet sinning.

He is calling to you. Oh, He is unlike you, absolutely unlike you, pure as the white light in which God dwells. Oh yes, you say, "I am afraid of the white light." My brother, the white light in which God dwells is the red, passionate love of His heart, and if the light of God enwrap you until you are afraid as it burns to save, the Man is with you tonight—this Man, Christ, God-Man, mysterious and wonderful, calls to you, but He is unlike you.

Now, what will you do? Will you turn from all His pure presence reproves, and will you yield to all His pure presence approves? That is the final question. You know your sin as you have never known it before. Will you turn from it?

To what shall I turn?
To Him.
To what in Him?
To His purity. Will you choose it?
Ah me, but that is the one thing I cannot do!
Behold Him again,

> In His feet and hands are wound-prints,
> And His side;

and know this, that as you turn from the impurity His separateness reproves to the purity that separateness approves; because He was ". . . reckoned with transgressors, . . ." because He still is near to every sinning heart, by the mystery of His death He will blot out your transgressions like a thick cloud, He will cleanse your inner life of the very forces that have ruined it, and He will make you like Himself.

Will you let Him? More marvelous, more mysterious, more overwhelming than anything else is this final fact to which we ever have to come. He stands and waits and asks, and you can say "No!" I beseech you as though God did beseech you. I pray you in Christ's stead, ". . . be ye reconciled to God," and be reconciled to God by yielding your life to Christ, Who was ". . . reckoned with transgressors . . . , ". . . separated from sinners . . . ," and therefore is the supreme and perfect Saviour of sinning men.

CHAPTER XVIII

THINGS SHAKEN—THINGS NOT SHAKEN

And this word, Yet once more, signifieth the removing of those things that are shaken, as of things that have been made, that those things which are not shaken may remain.

HEBREWS 12:27.

THE FIRST VALUE OF THESE WORDS IS THAT THEY CONSTITUTE A Christian interpretation of a phrase in a Hebrew prophecy. Their final value is that they reveal a perpetual method of God in His dealing with men.

As to the first of these. The prophet Haggai was looking back to God's shaking of the world by the giving of the Law, and he was looking on to the shaking of the world by the coming of Christ. The writer of the letter to the Hebrews had exactly the same double outlook. The letter was written to Hebrews who were filled with fear because the Hebrew economy was being shaken to its foundations by the Christian faith, and the writer reminded them of what their own prophet Haggai had said. By the giving of the moral law the whole world had been shaken with a shaking symbolized by the Mount which burned with fire. Then he reminded them that the shaking in the midst of which they lived, and of which they were tremendously afraid, was in fulfilment of the prophecy. God was indeed shaking; shaking the order of things that He Himself had made, but the purpose of that shaking was that things which can be shaken should be removed so that things which cannot be shaken should be seen to abide. The final value of this word, then, is that of its interpretation of this shaking. It is a revelation of a method of God. This method of God was recognized by all these old prophetic writers and as surely by the New Testament writers. Ezekiel thus gave expression to a Divine determination and so revealed the same Divine method; "I will overturn, overturn, overturn it: . . . until He come Whose right it is; and I will give it Him," the Whole fact was expressed by Paul in his Corinthian letter when speaking of God's anointed and appointed King, His own well-beloved Son, He said of Him: ". . . He must reign, till He hath put all His enemies under His feet." Not: He must wait, but He must reign. The word marks executive activity.

In these words, then, we have faith's outlook upon convulsion and upheaval. The facts of convulsion and upheaval are perpetually patent to all men, and they are variously described. We speak of change, we speak of revolution, we speak of calamity, we speak of catastrophe, or we sometimes use that so expressive expression, the deluge. I say these facts of upheaval, of convulsion, of shaking, are patent to all men. Faith sees all this, and faith feels all this, but faith sees far more. Faith is a volitional activity of the soul of man in response to a Divine revelation. It goes without saying that knowledge must precede faith. There must be some truth upon which faith can fasten. Knowledge makes its appeal to the intellect, and faith, not able to prove, ventures. The beginning is always with God. Whether the first approach of God to the soul of man is of value, depends entirely upon the soul's response to that approach. When response is made to the first gleam of light, the soul finds itself admitted to the shining way which broadens to the perfect day, and so it comes to clear vision. This is the history of all prophetic interpretation of the ways of God with men. The words of our text reveal the distinction between the outlook of the man of faith upon the circumstances in the midst of which we are living and the outlook of the man who is merely the man of sight. Faith watches change and revolution, and calamity and catastrophe, yea, observes the sweeping deluge, and then says: God is shaking. The Lord sitteth King upon the water floods.

Let us, then, consider the conception in itself and attempt to make a present application of it.

I have said that here we have the vision of faith in the day of upheaval. What is that vision? It is, first of all, a vision of the fact that it is God Who is shaking the order in the midst of which we live. It is, second, a vision of the reason why God is shaking that order. Thrones are trembling, empires are rocking, battles are raging, and all men know that. But faith knows more. Observe the absolute accuracy of the prophetic word; notice the modern element in the writing:

> ... I will overthrow the throne of kingdoms; and I will destroy the strength of the kingdoms of the nations; and I will overthrow the chariots, and those that ride in them; and the horses and their riders shall come down, every one by the sword of his brother.

That is the story of the things in the midst of which we are living, and that is how faith looks at it. Faith declares that it is God Who is shaking. Faith is conscious also, as men are conscious everywhere, of spiritual and moral disturbances. Ideals are shattered, laws have failed to fulfil their function, and policies everywhere have broken down. All men know these things, but faith, looking at the disorder, observing it, acutely conscious of it, yet climbing the height, says: God is shattering our ideals to teach us the vanity of them; God is so dealing with humanity that it bursts the bounds of laws and so learns the inadequacy of laws which it is able to make for itself; God is breaking down our policies and laughing at their folly in order that we may learn their futility.

So we come to the second fact which faith sees, and it is of supreme importance. Faith sees the Divine purpose in the shaking. God's shaking is for the destruction of the transient, whether it be good or bad. It is for the destruction of everything that is evil. God's shaking of things in a terrific hour of judgment like this, is His breaking of the bruised reed, His quenching of the smoking flax. I have of set purpose quoted those pictorial words of Scripture. We generally use them, and in some senses with perfect justification, as indicating the fact of God's patience. He will not break the bruised reed; He will not quench the smoking flax. That is true in so far as it goes. It reveals one method of the Divine activity.

But to make this the final meaning of these words is to be false to their intention. The declaration is that He will not break the bruised reed, He will not quench the smoking flax until He send forth judgment unto victory. When He sends forth judgment unto victory, He does break the bruised reed, and He does quench the smoking flax. The bruised reed and the smoking flax are not the emblems of frail humanity striving towards goodness. What is a bruised reed? Weakness weakened. What is smoking flax? That which has within it the element of its own destruction. God leaves the bruised reed in all its boastfulness and leaves the smoking flax to smoulder in its own fire until He send forth judgment unto victory. Then He breaks the one, and quenches the other.

God today has been sending forth judgment unto victory. He is breaking bruised reeds, and He is quenching smoking flax. He is working for the destruction of evil things and for the destruction of good things if they are outworn, because they may become hindrances though at one time they were helps. "Lest one good custom should corrupt the world," God will break through and destroy the custom. That is the atmosphere of the text. God shook the mountains in Sinai, and through the shaking of the mountains in Sinai, He shook the moral order of the world as He gave to humanity through His chosen people a Law. How good and great and wonderful a law it was is revealed in the fact that all modern civilizations have built their codes of ethics upon it. But in the fulness of time He came again, shaking that law, setting it at one side, sweeping away its ceremonial observances and symbolism, as He gave to the world the new moral ethic in the coming of His Son, and thus moved forward toward the final accomplishment of His will. He was working for the destruction of things which, having served their generation and His purpose in human history, might become, and, indeed, had become to some people, the very grave clothes that prevented their growth and advancement. Thus God is ever shaking to destroy the transient and to reveal the abiding, the things that are not shaken and which remain. The one Kingdom, which is His Kingdom; the one ideal, which is His ideal; the one law, which is the law of love; these are the things that are not shaken and cannot be shaken. In order that men may find them, turn back to them, God is forever shaking, disturbing. The things that are shaken are the things, either good or ill, which are transient. The things that are not shaken are the things that are eternal.

From that general attempt to understand the inner

thought of the text, let us lift our eyes to the circumstances in the midst of which we live.

What are the things that are being shaken in the world today? Dynasties, thrones, national boundaries, international relationships. I might speak of all these. They are full of interest, but they are incidental and not essential. The insecurity of certain men upon their thrones, the change of the map of Europe in the matter of national boundaries, the new methods of international relationships; all these things are incidental, and I do not propose now to tarry with them. God has been shaking to their very foundations false conceptions of humanity, false methods in diplomacy, and false emphases in religion. In the understanding of these things, we shall at least gain some gleams of light revealing the need for constructive work.

False conceptions of humanity are being shaken to their very foundation. The first is that widespread conception which had mastered the whole of Europe—and more, of the world—which may be expressed in the statement that Humanity is self-sufficient. God has so dealt with us during this period of war that we are face to face with the fact of humanity's insufficiency as within itself to arrange its own course, or make its own plans, or conduct its own efforts to anything like success. We are being taught today that human cleverness is entirely at fault and that human strength at its uttermost is defeated. We are being taught this by the experience of our enemies and by our own. Everything of human cleverness has broken down. Every plan that was peculiarly of men, and peculiarly clever, has been smashed in the course of two years. The illustrations that come to us most readily are those of all the ingenuity and terrific cleverness and marvelous comprehensiveness of the thinking of the powers with which we are at war. Yet they made no single plan that has not already been wrecked so that it never can be realized. Then, when we think of ourselves, I wonder how far we are prepared to boast of our own cleverness. How have we been delivered? If it be true that there are gleams of light upon the eastern sky for us, if we are beginning to feel a greater sense of security, if in our hearts we feel a new day is coming, how has this all come about? If we have learned nothing else, surely we have seen our smug self-confidence rocked to the center by the hand of God. If we have not seen this, then we are blind indeed.

Is there not, however, another false conception of humanity that God is shaking? The idea was prevalent that humanity was hopelessly degenerate; the idea that everything that was essentially fine had gone; that there was nothing left in man to which any appeal on high and noble lines could be made. Are we prepared to say that today? Are we prepared to say that for our own country as we look back? I confess I cannot altogether understand men who can look back over these two years without being made to think again in the presence of the quick and marvelous response to the high call, ringing out of the spiritual realm, that has characterized the going forth of our sons. Moreover, we have seen humanity able to endure the uttermost strain in its devotion to these high things. I am not saying for a single moment that anything that has happened in these two years is making any one of us think that we can do without Christ and His Cross. I will put the matter bluntly, as my own soul feels it when I say that as I look out upon these two years, I feel more than ever that His estimate of it is right, that it is worth dying for however much it may be bruised and weakened by the way. God is shaking us to the center, and so shaking these false conceptions of humanity.

Again, have we not seen, are we not living in the midst of the shaking of false methods in diplomacies? That is a great theme on which I dare not speak in detail. I speak as one who is looking out over the clouds and mists and trying to see clearly through any light that breaks through. Diplomacy has been conducted for many years under the inspiration of selfishness. Our phrases give us away. Here is one. Inferior races! That is a phrase we have heard in much of our diplomatic discussion, and because inferior races, they are to be mastered and managed, or let us tell the blunt truth for once, they are to be oppressed in the interest of the superior races. That has been the underlying inspiration of a great deal of diplomatic activity.

Or take another phrase that is not ours; we never made use of it although we did a good deal which seems to suggest that we believed in it. The superman! That means the right to conquer. These phrases reveal the inspirations of our arrangements. Our international plannings have been based upon the conceptions that there are such things as inferior races and supermen.

Where are we today? By the shaking of God we are coming at last to know that we have no right to speak of any race as inferior. We are at least beginning to think it is the superman who is inferior and that in every way.

Based upon these false conceptions, our methods have been the methods of cunning. The law of much diplomatic activity has been the law of outwitting someone else, quietly, secretly, no one other than the plotters knowing until it was done. God is shaking this to the very center, compelling us to a nobler way of thinking, bringing back to us words we have quoted day by day to our children but now applying them to national things and international:

The lip of truth shall be established forever:
But a lying tongue is but for a moment.

During these two years, false emphases in religion are being shaken to their very center. Our persistent and perpetual discussion of forms and media and channels is being challenged. We fight for the supremacy of some ecclesiastical form. The question of media has been considered more important than that of grace, and this has meant the destruction of the power of grace. One man says that grace comes through one media, and one man says it comes through another media. This man says that grace comes through certain forms and channels, another says that it does not come so, it comes directly. The matter of supreme import is not media. I believe that again and again grace is communicated to a man in connection with the laying on of hands. I believe that grace is found of some men through high ritual. But grace does not reach me that way. For the reception of grace into my own soul, I prefer the simplest place of meeting or the lonely quietness of some hillside. We of the opposing views concerning media quarrel with each other, and the result too often has been the destruction of grace!

Another false emphasis has been that of the finality of human opinion. We have been more concerned about formulæ than about truth; about the things men say about truth rather than about the truth itself, and so truth has been hidden. God is shaking these things. But it seems to me that it takes a profounder earthquake to shake these things than any others. I see more evidences of hope as I look round on false conceptions of humanity, as I look round upon false methods of diplomacy, than I do in this realm of religion. Nevertheless, God is shaking to the very center these attitudes toward religion.

Are there any things that are not being shaken? There

are, and they are the only things that matter. First, the relation of humanity to God is unshaken. He has the over-ruling of all human affairs. Take that map of yours and sit down and look at it, as it was, as it is, and, so far as you can, as it is going to be. Mark well the significance of what you see. Nation after nation is appearing before the bar of God and making its decision all unknowingly, and all unknowingly before that bar is receiving verdict and sentence. How many nations of Europe in these two years have chosen deliberately upon the basis of righteousness? How many nations of Europe within the last two years have chosen upon the basis of selfishness? I am not going to answer my questions. But this I say: God is judging. The nations have not escaped from the grip of God, and that impossibility of escape is the one hope of the dark hour.

The Lord still reigneth, and the fact of the reign of God is being demonstrated by the victories that faith has won. Take your eleventh chapter of Hebrews again. It is a wonderful chapter. I need not tell you that. The most wonderful part of the chapter is not that which gives names and shows us men, but the little brief sentences concerning the unknown heroes and the greatness of deeds. In the eleventh of Hebrews I find these words: "who through faith . . . waxed mighty in war, . . ." That is what has happened during these two years. That is the story of the hour. How have these armies of Britain been raised? In that glorious response of the earlier days what was the inspiration? Did your sons go out to bring more territory to Britain? Never! Those armies would not have been raised to accomplish that end. Did they leave university and court and office and desk in order to give commercial supremacy to Britain? Never! They would never have gone for such reasons. They went for righteousness and truth. They went by faith in God, and by the victories that are being won at cost of suffering and sacrifice enough to break the heart, faith is being vindicated and so the relation of humanity to God is being proved. That is something that cannot be shaken.

The supremacy of righteousness and truth as a national foundation is unshaken. Nations built thereon cannot be destroyed. All other ground is sinking sand. As national policy also it is unshaken. Nations acting thereby pass through travail to triumph. All other policies are folly.

Finally, I find unshaken still the centrality of the Cross as the way of human salvation. To this all spiritual ministry agrees in spite of forms or opinions.

All over the world the story is coming to us of men going back to the Cross who thought the world had outgrown it or been mistaken about it. The Cross is also found to be the law of victorious life, not armies or munitions, but the spirit of sacrifice in the consecration of high devotion to righteousness. These are the unshaken things.

For every shaking of the earth the man of faith thanks God. Only the things which are not vital can be shaken; only the transient can be destroyed. The real things of life abide; faith, love, and hope. Through the shaking these are manifested. Or, as Haggai said, through the shaking the desirable things of all nations come, which means that by this shaking comes the desire of the nations which is Christ Himself. By these shakings He ever comes. He comes again to take the kingdoms to be His own. May He direct our hearts into that patient waiting for Him that is born of our sense that the shaking of all things is of God, and that only that which can be shaken can be destroyed.

CHAPTER XIX

TRIBULATION, KINGDOM, AND PATIENCE

... the tribulation and kingdom and patience ... in Jesus. ...

REVELATION 1:9.

THE TEXT IS ONLY A PHRASE. BUT WHAT A PHRASE IT IS. TAKEN thus, in separation from its context it is full of suggestiveness. Its opening word, "tribulation," is tremulous with sadness. It speaks of stress and strain and sorrow. Its central word, "kingdom," is pregnant with majesty. It speaks of government and order and strength. Its final word, "patience," is vibrant with heroism. It speaks of courage, and fidelity, and endurance. Final word, did I say? I was wrong. There is yet another, and it is supreme. "In Jesus" are the final words, and they qualify, interpret, glorify, all that have gone before. ". . . the tribulation and kingdom and patience . . . in Jesus. . . ."

All this becomes far more arresting and illuminative when the phrase is considered in relation to its context. Therein it is the description of an experience; the experience of the writer; the experience of those to whom, or for whom he was writing; and—as the phrase itself reveals—the experience supremely of Jesus Himself.

The writer thus describes himself and his situation:

I John, your brother and partaker with you . . . was in the isle that is called Patmos, for the word of God and the testimony of Jesus. I was in the Spirit on the Lord's Day, . . .

His writing was addressed to ". . . the seven churchs which are in Asia. . . ." To Ephesus in danger of false teachers and bearing persecutions; to Smyrna, in tribulation, poor, suffering, some of them imprisoned; to Pergamum, dwelling where Satan had his throne and where Antipas was martyred; to Thyatira, in danger from the false prophetess and patiently enduring; to Sardis, overwhelmed in death, only a few remaining undefiled; to Philadelphia, keeping the word, not denying the name, under the most difficult circumstances; to Laodicea, made tepid by prosperity, that gravest of all perils that ever threatens the holy church.

Moreover, his writing was by the direct command of the One Who, speaking of His own experience said, ". . . I was dead; and behold, I am alive for evermore, . . ."

Our phrase then describes the experience of John, of the church, and of Jesus. It presents two outlooks which qualify each other. The first is the outlook on circumstances, and the whole of that outlook is condensed, compressed, packed into one throbbing word, tribulation. The other is the outlook on life, and the whole of that outlook is expressed in the two words, the kingdom, and the patience.

Let us then consider first this twofold Christian experience; the experience of circumstances and the experience of life. Let us then attempt to consider the mutual relation of these two phases of the Christian experience which cannot be separated in this present time and age and dispensation.

First, then, the twofold experience itself. The first phase is that of the experience of circumstances, expressed in one word, tribulation. What is tribulation? The thought of the word is that of pressure producing actual suffering. I can do no better than illustrate its meaning by reference to our Lord's use of it, when in the Upper Room He was discoursing with His own, prior to His departure. In the course of that conversation He said: "In the world ye have tribulation: . . ." In the same discourse a few sentences earlier, our Lord employed a most arrestingly suggestive figure which helps us to understand what tribulation is;

> A woman when she is in travail hath sorrow, because her hour is come: but when she is delivered of the child, she remembereth no more the anguish, for the joy that a man is born into the world.

The word there rendered anguish is the same word. We are brought by that flash of intimate understanding and tender grace, to an interpretation of tribulation; it is the pressure that means agony, but it is the travail that issues in life and joy. That is the experience of the church, of John as it was of Jesus, in this world.

Mark the persistence of it, taking first of all that which must be supreme in our thinking, the experience of our Lord Himself. His whole life was a life of tribulation; to quote the prophetic word uttered concerning the Messiah long ere He came, He was ". . . a man of sorrows and acquainted with grief: . . ." As we observe Him from babyhood to boyhood, and from boyhood to manhood, and through full maturity to the completion of His public ministry, in ever-increasing measure we see Him always feeling the pressure of circumstances.

This was so in material things. He was homeless. ". . . foxes have holes, and the birds of the air have nests; but the Son of Man hath not where to lay His head." Mentally it was so. He had no comrades. He had no peers in the realm of thought. There were no great philosophers in His age;

philosophy had become decadent before He came into the world. The great philosophers under the influence of whose teaching men were professing to live and act; Socrates, Plato, Aristotle, were not comrades for Him in their thinking. He was alone. Among the men of His own age and of His religion after the flesh, there was none able to enter into His conception of things or to soar to the height of His outlook.

Spiritually, He found no sympathy in the world at all. His spiritual concepts were not accepted by men, not understood of men. He stood alone. Such was His loneliness; materially without home, mentally without comrades, spiritually without sympathy. Life to Him was the bearing of a testimony to the essential and eternal things; the bearing of a testimony that men never apprehended, would not apprehend or receive. From the beginning to the end there crushed and pressed upon Him the false concepts and false ideals of men, which at last found their supreme expression in the words so often quoted and yet so terribly revealing: ". . . we will not have this man to reign over us." This pressure upon Him of circumstances found its culminating expression and experience in the Cross of Calvary.

The persistence of this experience of tribulation in the history of His people has been equally definite. The story of loyal-hearted discipleship has ever been, and still is, that if a man will live godly in this world he shall suffer persecution. The church forever contradicts the world. That is its business. That is what it is in the world for; to contradict it in its fundamental conceptions, in the conduct that grows out of its fundamental conceptions, and in the character which results from the persistent conception expressing itself in conduct. The church in the world is an eternal negative to the things which are supremely of the world.

With what result? The world is forever opposed to the

church. It is against the church. It will bring all its pressure to bear upon the church. It will do everything to silence her voice and destroy her influence and end her propaganda. If this is not so, it is because the church has forgotten her message. If the world now is making friends with the church, then alas for the church. The world has not changed. Its central conception of life, its ideal, is still that of the magnificence of mastery and the glory of the material. The church's ideal is still that of the magnificence of service and sacrifice and the beauty of the spiritual. These things cannot merge and mix without the quality being changed entirely on the one side or the other. The church is in the world to affirm the things of the beginning, the original things of truth, the meaning and the reason of things; to tell man what man has honestly sought to discover for himself but never has been able, the reason, the truth behind everything. The world is still saying: "We will not have these things"; the world is still against the church. The church stands in the center of this pressure, bearing her witness and feeling the agony of her loneliness and her strife with the things against which she is called to protest. This is a persistent experience.

But this is not all the truth about the experience of the church's Lord and of the church. We need the other two words of my text; not only is it an experience of tribulation, it is also an experience of the kingdom and the patience. Two thoughts are suggested by these words, and yet they are so closely related that they describe one supreme fact. In the one case, that of tribulation, we have the experience of circumstances. In the other, that of the kingdom and patience, we have the experience of the church in her very life, that which constitutes her what she is, that which differentiates her from all other societies, that which makes a distinction clear, sharp, between a man of God and a man of the world. What then do these words connote? The word "kingdom" connotes the rule and the realm of a king. Here, of course, the reference is to the Kingdom of God, and not to any dispensational interpretation of the phrase, not to any dispensational application or value, but to the fact of the Kingdom of God. It is the static, unchanged, abiding fact. It is static, that is, it is the one fact that has never altered, never changed, the fact that abides. The Kingship of God, the Divine sovereignty, holds all things in the grasp of its power and within the authority of its management. The whole fact of the universe is included, whether it be heaven above, or the earth beneath, or the depths of the underworld below. Nothing escapes from the operation of that one fact. Satan himself must report in the Divine Presence ere he goes upon any mission of persecuting the sons of God. The arch enemy of mankind cannot touch one single piece of your property, not so much as a hair upon the back of a camel that you possess, until he has asked permission. Satan desires to sift you. Then he must ask before he can do it. Satan desires to plunge a continent in war. Then he cannot act save under a Divine control. If in the Divine control there be a process of judgment, it is judgment proceeding toward the accomplishment of a purpose of mercy. The true experience of the whole church of God in its life is fundamentally an experience of that Kingdom of God.

And closely related, indeed growing out of it as an inevitable sequence, there is the experience of patience. The word literally means, "staying under"; but the staying under always means staying on. If we are to stay under the pressure of circumstances, we must stay on the kingship of God. Patience is the experience of the soul that relates itself to the Kingdom of God and relates all circumstances to that selfsame fact. The soul, keen and sensitive to the fact of the

Divine Kingship, is able to remain under the pressure of circumstances, tribulation, affliction, persecution, as it relates them all to the underlying fact. In use the word always connotes cheerful, hopeful endurance. It is never used of that state of mind that says things are as they are and cannot be helped. That is not patience, that is stupidity. Patience will feel the agony, shudder at its appearance, and be conscious of its pain; but patience will hear the undertone of the eternal music and express it in song even when circumstances press and grind upon the soul.

In the experience of our Lord the persistence of this sense of the Kingdom and of patience is most clearly marked. The whole truth was expressed in His own words in this same discourse to which I have already referred. When He said: ". . . In the world ye have tribulation, . . ." He also said: ". . . but be of good cheer. I have overcome the world." The victory of His life was gained by submission to the static fact of the Divine Kingship and by consequent sovereignty over all circumstances.

He gave us the supreme exemplification of the experiences of life. His life was homed in the centrality of the Divine government and expressed itself in infinite patience and so mastered all tribulation.

And that was not only the experience of our Lord Himself. By His grace and through the ministry of His Spirit, it is the experience of the Christian church. If her experience is that of fellowship with His sufferings, it is also that of fellowship in His triumph. There was one man who knew perhaps more of these things than any other man who appears upon the pages of the New Testament. I refer to Paul. When he was writing his second letter to the Corinthian Christians, he spoke twice of his own experience in this regard.

> We are pressed on every side . . .—and that is the same word, tribulation— ". . . yet not straitened; perplexed, yet not unto despair; pursued, yet not forsaken; smitten down, yet not destroyed; always bearing about in the body the dying of Jesus, that the life also of Jesus may be manifested in our body."

And again;

> . . . in everything commending ourselves, as ministers of God, in much patience, in afflictions,—(that same word)—in necessities, in distresses, in stripes, in imprisonments, in tumults, in labors, in watchings, in fastings;—(that is the experience of tribulation)—in pureness, in knowledge, in long-suffering, in kindness, in the Holy Ghost, in love unfeigned, in the word of truth, in the power of God; by the armour of righteousness on the right hand and on the left—(this is the experience of the Kingdom)—by glory and dishonour, by evil report and good report; as deceivers, and yet true; as unknown, and yet well known; as dying, and behold, we live; as chastened, and not killed; as sorrowful, yet always rejoicing; as poor, yet making many rich; as having nothing, and yet possessing all things—(this is the experience of patience).

The church always overcomes the world. In the case of every individual martyr, the victory is with the man slain and not with the men who slay him. In every hour of persecution it is the church that is victorious, not the oppressive power that persecutes. Following in the pathway of her Lord and Master, Who death by dying slew, the church bends to bonds and stripes, is battered and bruised to death, to rise again in life immortal, and to triumph. Tribulation! yea verily, but also the kingdom and the patience that are in Jesus.

The mutual relation of these phases of experience has already been seen in our consideration, yet it is so important, as it seems to me, that it demands separate statement. Let us think of tribulation then in its relation to life, and then of life in its relation to tribulation.

Tribulation is caused by life. The sense of the kingdom and the sense of the patience of the soul makes the world's opposition inevitable. It is impossible to have a man or a society utterly sensible of the Divine government, utterly faithful to the Divine government, living in a world like this, but that man, that society, becomes a center of opposition. Consequently, it is the kingdom and patience that create the tribulation. If we relax our conviction as to the kingship and our patient fidelity to all that kingship inevitably connotes, then the pressure weakens. We shall not feel it so much. If we abandon our attitude and our fidelity toward the kingship of God, the pressure of the world will cease altogether. We need not have persecution if we do not desire it. All we have to do is to abandon our loyalty to the Kingdom of God. The world will not persecute us then.

But not only is it true that tribulation is caused by life; it is also true that tribulation strengthens life. The very forces that are against us are making us stronger. This is the strange and wonderful experience of all Christian souls and of the Christian church. Deepening loyalty increases patience. Growing pressure increases the strength of the life which it strives to destroy until life becomes forever and finally victorious.

From Antioch in Pisidia Paul was driven out. At Iconium they put him outside the gates. At Lystra they stoned him, leaving him for dead. After a while the broken, bruised body revived and he went to Derbe. When he had been there a while he went back to Lystra, the place of the stones; back to Iconium where they drove him out; back to Antioch in Pisidia. He went back to teach the Christians something that it was important they should know, that "Through many tribulations we must enter into the Kingdom of God."

The very pressure of the stones had deepened and intensified the sense of the real and the spiritual. He went back to tell those people that by these things we enter the Kingdom of God in all its fullness. The old saying is indeed true, that "The blood of the martyrs is the seed of the church." The church hidden in the Roman catacombs overcame the gross and devilish materialism of Rome. The church seated and patronized by Constantine on the Seven Hills, became weak, paralyzed. It has ever been so. It has been by the pressure and agony of tribulation, that the forces of the church's life have been increased and renewed and made powerful. The church persecuted is the church powerful because then she is true to her life and realizes her strength.

Life is surrendered to by tribulation. The sense of agony and the sense of patience in the soul makes opposition contributory to the very life which it is persecuting. Here again I quote from Paul in his letter to the Philippians: ". . . the things which happened unto me have fallen out . . . unto the progress of the gospel," as the Revised Version has it.

The things that have happened unto me—the bonds, the imprisonments—have turned out for the beating forward of the gospel.

Life transmutes tribulation, and so (in effect) Paul writes: "Let us also rejoice in our tribulations. Tribulation worketh patience, patience worketh conviction, conviction worketh hope!" Wherever we find life in its strength, we find tribulation in its pressure, but if we watch the process we see life transmuting tribulation.

These are dark days for the church of God. Are they? Think again! What has provoked this world conflict? The opposition of the world to the church. Exchange that for other words if you like and say it is a conflict of ideals. That is but another way of saying that it is a conflict caused by the opposition of the world to the church. This is a testimony to the power of the church. The passion for the mastery of the earth by brute force is the hatred of the world for the ideals of Christ.

What is the issue to be? Let us ask another question. For the moment what is happening? The church is led into a wilderness in which she looks the world squarely in the face and shudders. That is great gain. Too long the church has been playing fast and loose with the world, and now God has permitted a situation when the church is once again compelled to look at the world and see what it really means. As she does it, if she is true to God, she shudders and is ashamed.

But she is not only brought into a wilderness in which she can look the world squarely in the face. The church is brought to the place where she looks God in the face anew. There will happen to the church that which happened to Jacob at Jabbok; she will be able to say, presently, after the night and the darkness have passed: "For I have seen God face to face, and my life is healed."

That thing is true individually. Here is a boy back from the war, marvelously preserved from anything more serious than a wound that has incapacitated him for a month or so. This is what he said: "I never really knew God till I was at the front." No, he was not a heathen and a publican. He belonged to the church. But he saw God there. That experience is being multiplied, and the vision will heal. There will come to us a new sense of the powers of our life, a new experience of the agony and of the patience.

Are we in tribulation? are we in Patmos? Let us also be in the Spirit on the Lord's day. So shall we know the kingdom, so shall we know the patience. It may be we shall hear behind us the voice of a trumpet, and being turned to look we also shall see the Son of Man, girt about the paps with a golden girdle, with feet that shine like brass burnished in the furnace, with eyes that flash as with a flame of fire, with hair white as the driven snow. The thing He will say to us amid the carnage and the darkness is this:

". . . I was dead, and behold, I am alive for evermore. . . ."

CHAPTER XX

THE HARVESTS OF THE WORD OF GOD

For as the rain cometh down and the snow from heaven, and returneth not thither, but watereth the earth, and maketh it bring forth and bud, that it may give seed to the sower and bread to the eater; so shall my word be that goeth forth out of my mouth: it shall not return unto me void, but it shall accomplish that which I please, and it shall prosper in the thing whereto I sent it.

ISAIAH 55:10-11.

THE FITNESS OF THE SYMBOLISM OF THIS TEXT IS APPARENT even to the most casual observer.

Snow and rain are characterized by gentleness which merges into force. One drop of rain falls upon my hand, and I brush it away, and it is not; but when the drop is multiplied and the great storm sweeps along the valley, it is almost resistless in its onrush. One feathery flake of snow falls through the atmosphere. I touch it and it passes and is lost, its crystal beauty destroyed forever by the rudeness of my human hand; but let that flake be multiplied and the falling snow will take hold of the thundering locomotive, clog its wheels, check its progress, bury it beneath its soft and noiseless whiteness.

Rain and snow are characterized by helplessness which grows into beneficence. We ask: "What can this drop of rain do for man? What can this flake of snow do for humanity?" And yet we know that when we pass from the individual drop to the great rain, that this in falling makes the earth laugh back in harvest and crowns the labor of the hands of men. There is no more exquisite word in all Scripture about nature than that simple and sublime passage: "He giveth His snow like wool." Like a warm mantle, it wraps the earth in winter time and keeps it from the penetration of intenser cold. And so we find that rain and snow, helpless as they seem, are the very messengers of beneficence to men.

Again, rain and snow come to us characterized by unfruitfulness, yet generating fruitfulness wherever they fall. Life cannot be sustained by the one or the other. Neither is there in either any element of reproductiveness. Yet in their cooperation with the forces of "old mother earth" and with the ministries of light and air, all that is needed for life's sustenance is produced.

This is but a surface application of the truth. As we watch the rain and the snow and think upon it more carefully, we find a most suggestive symbol of the Word of God. By the Word of God at this moment I mean all that phrase can possibly mean; the written Which reveals the Living, the Living Which seals the written; the written Which is still ours, the Living Which lies behind it and speaks through it in power to the sons of men.

This Word of God in the history of the race, what has it been? Symbols becoming substance, letters advancing to life, that which has seemed to kill becoming, presently, that which has bestowed life everywhere. In order that we may understand the value of this Word of God and learn the true method of appreciation of such value, let us take this symbolism of the prophet and consider it exactly as he has stated it; first, as to the similarities suggested; second, as to the principles revealed; and finally, as to the responsibility entailed.

Let me first tabulate the phrases which we are to consider in this verse: "Cometh from heaven; returneth not thither; watereth the earth; maketh it bring forth, and bud; that it may give seed to the sower; and bread to the eater."

The rain and the snow come from heaven. Man has nothing to do with the coming of the rain and the snow. You will remember how in that great theophany of the Book of Job when, after the human eloquence of his friends has providentially been silenced, God Himself begins to speak to the suffering man. He speaks to him in the midst of his sorrow and his suffering by making all His glory in creation pass before him. In the midst of that wonderful questioning of Job by God occur these two inquiries; "Hast thou entered into the treasuries of the snow . . . ?" which, being translated from poetry into prose means, do you understand the snow? Do you know from whence it comes? Can you analyze the mystery of its crystallization and deposit? Then, "Hath the rain a father? . . ." which, by some process of translation means, are you able to generate it, to produce it? With those questions in mind, let me read again this statement of the prophet. "For as the rain cometh down and the snow from heaven, . . ." The Word of God is a message from God to man which no man was able to find out for himself. It is never a philosophy formulated by human wisdom; it is always a revelation made, a something declared that man could not by searching find out. The supreme quality of the Word of God is that however men may occupy their time in discussing the methods by which we have come into possession of these documents, there is stamped upon every page of them the sign manual of Jehovah. They are great unveilings of His nature, great revelations of the deepest secrets of human life, great illumination of the problems that confront men by Divine revelation. The Word of God is the gift of God and not the contrivance of man.

But it ". . . returneth not thither. . . ." The snow and the rain pour themselves out on the face of the earth, they melt and pass, and within a very few hours of the great rainfall, which has sweetened everything in its coming, the roads are dusty again and we say, "How soon the rain has passed." So also, soon after the snow has once come under the influence of the sun, it is gone. It has seemed to pour itself out in magnificent waste. Judged by first appearances, it seems as though this gift of heaven had been poured upon earth to be spoiled, contaminated, soiled, wasted.

So also with the Word of God. The Word of God has been given to men in figure and symbol, in prophecy and song, and at last in the Person of Jesus, and since He came, in exposition and explanation, for centuries; and, ah, me! how perpetually it seems to us as we watch the openings and processes of the decades and even of the centuries, as though this great outpouring of Divine revelation was lost, falling upon man only to be spoiled. How often have we thought of it as wasted? Nay, have we not thought so of it sometimes when we have been preaching it? Have we not looked out with almost passionate desire upon audiences that have listened and passed away apparently to frivolity and forgetfulness and have said, Yea, verily, "as the snow and the rain from heaven . . . but it returneth not thither"? That is the first effect upon us after observing what happens as God gives His Word.

But there is another statement needed to complete and explain this; it ". . . watereth the earth. . . ." Take this dust as it lies upon the highway and over the furrowed field, and know that within the dust is the making of everything that is beautiful and fruitful. But the dust does not of itself laugh in flowers; it is capable and incapable. Lying within it are all the forces of life. All the mysterious magnificence of your personality on the physical side lies within the dust at your feet, and all flowers that bloom lie there in potentiality. As the rain and snow water the earth, which is at once characterized by capacity and yet unable to fulfil the possibilities that lie sleeping within its own being, it makes all nature laugh with new beauty.

So also the Word of God comes to men in whose nature are the potentialities but not the realizations. The Word of God falls upon the centuries, upon society, upon individuals, and we thought it touched them but to be spoiled and soiled and pass, but we watched and we found that by its falling the soil became productive. There is in every human being the capacity for Deity. There is in every human life the potentialities of the highest and the noblest and the best. I am not discussing the question of man's ruin. I know the ruin; I know it in my own life. But that which is ruined is not destroyed. Without some beneficent ministry external to itself it will be destroyed. Given that ministry it is still capable of realization. The very ministry it needs is that of the Word of God. As is the rain, as is the snow to the dust, so is the Word of God to humanity in its ruin. God has not been wasting His Word. As He has given it by prophets, seers, and psalmists, by His Son, in many a symbol and by many a sign, in many a dispensation; given it to the mocking, laughing, scoffing crowds; He knows that in all the dust that lies about Him there are potentialities; and as He gives His rain and snow to smite the dust into laughter, so He has given His Word that the Word coming to men may touch the unrealized capacity into realization.

The prophet now adds a further truth concerning these elements in the statement, ". . . maketh it bring forth, . . ." After the rain and the snow the dull russet ground becomes beautiful with emerald and opal and ruby and diamond, and thus we know that when God's rain and snow touch the dust it makes the dust bring forth.

So with the Word of God. The Word of God makes the dormant forces in man move to fulfilment. All men that have ever realized the possibilities of their own life have done so in response to some part of the Word of God, to the Word spoken, to the Word written, to the Word lived, to the revelation granted; and as the snow and rain coming upon the earth make the earth answer by bringing forth, so the Word of God in the centuries, as they come and go, has provoked into realization the dormant capacities of life.

Yet another word that I have taken separately, because I think it really is separate. It is a stronger word than the former—". . . maketh it bring forth, and bud, . . ." I feel inclined to use here the literal Hebrew word, "and sprout." That is to say, the rain and the snow not merely touch the dust into generation but actually come again in the grass, the flowers, the fruitage. You saw that rainstorm as it swept the field yonder. You watched it come; you smiled at the helplessness of the first few drops as they fell. You were appalled at the rush of the storm as the clouds broke and swept that field. Then you watched it as the clouds passed and the sun shone. As you watched the field it seemed as though all was lost and of no avail, and you went to sleep—and God gives unto His beloved in sleep—and you came back again and looked at your field, and there was the sheen of the emerald all over it. First the blade and then the ear, and then the full corn in the ear, and so on and on, until russet had become green and green had become golden harvest. And in that waving harvest of gold what do I find? The rain that I thought lost, the snow that I thought perished. It touched the dust with the alchemy of God, and it brought back the glorious, gracious harvest.

It is equally true that the Word of God that He has been giving for centuries has never been lost. It has come from Him to touch the failure of human life, and it has been returning to Him laughing with the harvest of ransomed souls. The Word was incarnate in the Christ supremely, and in a less and different degree but nevertheless as truly, God's Word has been re-incarnate in human lives in all the passing centuries. Do not let us be afraid of the word. I make no comparison finally between the incarnation of our blessed Lord and the incarnation of truth in the life of the believer. Nevertheless, in degree every Christian soul is a re-incarnation of the Word Who became incarnate in Jesus of Nazareth. Is it not so? That which is true and beautiful and of good report in you, in others, what is it but God's great Word which has touched the fibre of your being and reconstructed your broken lives to the realization of His purpose and so to the glory of His Name. The transmuted rain makes the earth not only generate by the touch of beneficence; it makes it sprout and bud and answer back in harvest. So also, the Word re-incarnate in believing souls is the harvest of the earth which supremely satisfies the heart of God.

Yet that is not all. ". . . that it may give seed to the sower, . . ." What is this harvest for? You say for the sustenance of human life. That is not the first thing. What is the harvest for? "That it may give seed to the sower" comes before "bread to the eater." Bread to the eater is a secondary thing. Bread to the eater is provision for the toiler that he may continue his sowing and reap his harvests. But the first thing is that, in the new form in which the rain and snow return to God, there is always found the potentiality of propagation waiting for new showers and new transmutations and new harvests. This is the perpetual story of the harvests as they come and go. Always first, seed to the sower.

So with the Word of God. The Word of God taking hold of human life, changing it, becoming incarnate in it, communicates propagative power; it makes a new wealth of seed which may be scattered still further afield. From every life re-made and sanctified by the Word of God, there must go forth the seed that will affect yet other fields and stretch out toward the consummating glory of the final harvest.

Finally we come to the last phase of the symbolism, ". . . and bread to the eater." The issue then is also sustenance to the toiler. The man that plowed and sowed and reaped, feeds. So surely also is it with this Word of God. It comes, as we have seen for the larger purpose, the creation of new seed that may be scattered still for the uplifting of man, but the Word of God is also the bread of life to the toiler. By it his own life is sustained, both in health and strength, and so he is enabled for the service for which he is created and to which he is called.

Let me pass now from these similarities to take the broader outlook and consider the great principles that are revealed.

The symbolism of this great prophetic Word teaches me, first of all, that the Word of God is purposeful. Rain and snow come certainly not for nothing and not for the display of their own wonders but for purpose. The symbolism teaches me, second, that the Word of God is powerful. The rain and snow come to victory always; they are never defeated. And the symbolism of my text teaches me, finally, that the Word of God is prosperous. It accomplishes, it prospers, as do also rain and snow.

The Word of God is purposeful. All this is seen by the various similarities which we have rapidly surveyed. The Word of God is not given to be possessed; it is given that it may possess. The truth of God is not given that men may hold it. Oh, I am tired of the men that want to know if I "hold the truth." Of course I don't "hold the truth"; no man can "hold the truth." It is too big for any man to hold, and God has never given His Word to men that they may "hold the truth." The facts are truly stated in quite another way. The truth must hold the man, wrap him around, change the very fibre of his being, permeate his complete life, and unless the Word of God is doing that for me it is failing in the first intention that God has for it. Not for our good only does it come. It is seed as well as bread. Unless we come to receive the Word as the earth takes the sun and the rain, then I am not sure that we had better not absent ourselves from every occasion when the Word is opened. If I come with my notebook to write down all I can learn about the Word of God in order that I may know it, then I am absolutely failing. But if I come to strip from my soul all the things that hide me that the Word of God may search me, if I have come to lay my life out in the light of the Word that the Word may correct it, then I shall find the Word in me is fruitful as is the snow, as is the rain upon the earth. It is a purposeful thing.

Then, thank God, it is powerful. He says it shall not return to Him void. And why not? May I not reverently say as in the presence of the inspired declaration, God's Word never returned to Him void because it never comes void from Him. Do you remember the word of the angel to the blessed Virgin?—". . . no word of God is void. . . ." Every word of God thrills with fruitfulness. If we but know how to receive it and how to respond to it, then it shall return to Him not void but fruitful, in lives changed, remolded, re-fashioned, sanctified.

And finally, then the Word of God is prosperous. It is so because it is His Word. "It shall not return unto me void, but it shall . . ."—and mark the two words—". . . accomplish . . . prosper. . . ." The word "accomplish" means it does something, it makes something, it realizes something; and the Hebrew word "prosper" literally means it "pushes forward." It is a great dynamic force. It is prosperous, moreover, by selection. ". . . that which I please, . . . the thing whereto I sent it."

These are the principles which we must bear in mind as we take up our Bibles and come to listen to the teachings of the Word of God. It is given for a purpose; it is full of power; it accomplishes the purpose by reason of the power.

In conclusion, it is important that we inquire as to the responsibilities that are entailed? Rain and snow might fall upon the earth a long time, and there be no harvest unless the earth is prepared. The rain and snow may fall in all their prodigal munificence and magnificence upon the earth, and there will be no harvest unless the seed is sown. And rain and snow may fall and make the earth laugh with harvest if the earth be ready and the seed be sown, and yet men get no benefit unless the harvest be reaped, the seed be sown again, and through the process the bread be eaten.

Here, then, are three things at least that I would say: the earth must be prepared; take heed how ye hear. The seed must be sown; preach the Word. The bread must be eaten; let the Word of Christ dwell in you richly.

Take heed how ye hear. In all tenderness and yet with

great earnestness and great conviction, I would sound that word in the hearing of all. Take heed how ye hear. How shall we hear? Prayerfully, obediently, and in faith. The spirit of criticism never produces the result of power. Let us pray that in our lives God will plow up the fallow ground, give us the receptive heart, the child heart, willingness to hear and learn, deliver us from preconceived notions and prejudice, make us ready when He speaks to obey, make us simple-hearted at His feet, for as the rain and snow demand an earth plowed, broken, prepared, so does the Word of God demand a condition in those who hear, if it is to bring forth a harvest.

The true seed must be sown, and it must be by the preaching of the Word if the work is to be done. We are not to criticize the Word of God, not to account for the Word of God, not to defend the Word of God. We are to preach it and hear it. And there is a yet fuller application of that truth. The final preaching of the Word is not that of the lips but that of the life. Fundamentally the Word is the seed in the hearts of men, but functionally for the sake of the world, the seed is the sons of the Kingdom, the men in whom the Word has had its true effect.

Finally, the Word, the bread that comes, must be eaten or the toiler will grow weak. We are to let this Word of Christ dwell in us, take it into our life. The Word must come into the intellect, the emotion, the will; and when we take the Word of God into our whole life and answer its every claim, then in that moment God's purpose will be fulfilled in us.

One of the greatest instruments of God in the world today is the British and Foreign Bible Society. It sends out no preachers, but it accompanies the preacher with his message in the tongue of the people to whom he goes. It cannot issue statistics of conversion, but it pours forth the great stream of living water over all the earth and by such action quenches the thirsts of humanity as with the river of God. Alone, however, it would soon fail. As the Word circulates it becomes the sustenance of human lives, and so over earth's wilderness wastes the green appears which merges at last into the golden glory of the harvests of the Word of God.

CHAPTER XXI

THE ASCENSION

Now this, He ascended, what is it but that He also descended into the lower parts of the earth. He that descended is the same also that ascended far above all the heavens, that He might fill all things.
EPHESIANS 4:9, 10.

THESE WORDS ARE PLACED WITHIN BRACKETS BOTH IN THE Authorized and Revised Versions, and rightly so, for they constitute a distinct parenthesis in the apostolic argument. We can omit them, and the main teaching is not interfered with in the slightest way, but it is made more radiant by reason of the light within them. The passage helps us to come to a clear apprehension of the supreme importance of the Ascension, which was at once the culmination of our Lord's earthly ministry and the initiation of His heavenly service. It consists of a question and of a statement: "Now this, He ascended, what is it but that He also descended into the lower parts of the earth?" and "He that descended is the same also that ascended far above all the heavens, that He might fill all things."

The question emphasizes a fact and is a question that does not require an answer. The fact, which is not in dispute, is that the Ascension of our Lord involved descension. Now that assumption arrests attention. One is inclined to challenge it. Does ascension necessarily involve descension? It certainly is not so in the case of any other human being of whom we have any knowledge, either personally, or in these Sacred Writings. We think of the blessed dead as ascended and properly so. Of course, the words "ascension" and "descension" are figurative terms enabling us to think intelligently of facts in a realm where dimensions are more than we are familiar with. I say then that we may properly speak of men of the past as having ascended, but their ascension does not involve their descension. If the first man had never fallen, all we know of humanity would lead us to believe that he would have ascended. After the period of earthly, probationary life, the school time of the soul, man would have passed to the higher and the larger life for which this life is forever a preparation. But this ascension would not involve descension. If the first man after having fallen, by reason of his confidence in God, ascended, it does not at all involve the idea of his descent. We think of Moses passing to the Mount and dying, as one has said, of the kisses of the lips of God, he himself ascended; but that ascent does not involve descent. The fiery prophet of Israel was caught away in a chariot of fire, a fitting vehicle for the conveyance of his spirit to the realms of light, and thus he ascended, but that does not involve descent. Enoch, the quiet man who walked with God, and was not, for God took him, ascended; but descent was not involved. These men began their being here in the world. Human life begins here, serves it probation here, and if it fulfils the ideal, it ascends, but that does not involve descent. Why then does the apostle say, in interrogative form, what he conceives will be at once admitted: "This, he ascended, what is it but that he also descended into the lower parts of the earth"?

If ascension involves descension, it involves much

more. If the Ascension of our Lord must include the fact that before His Ascension there was a descent, something far more is included. If ascension involves descension, it is patent that ascension is a return to a place originally occupied. Therefore, involved in this declaration is the central truth concerning the Person of our Lord. Whereas the Ascension lays emphasis upon the Resurrection and the passing into heaven of a man of our humanity, this statement warns us against thinking of Him merely in the terms of our own humanity. "He that descended is the same also that ascended . . ." is another way of saying that in the Ascension He passed back to the place from which He came. "In the beginning was the Word, and the Word was with God, and the Word was God." Then came His descent: ". . . the Word became flesh and tabernacled among us, and we beheld His glory, glory as of the only begotten from the Father, full of grace and truth." The Ascension was the passing back of this One into the presence of God. In this declaration of the apostle is involved the truth which he declared in another letter in which the descent is described in the most wonderful language. He said of Him, that being in the form of God, He did not count this high dignity a prize to be snatched at and held for His own enrichment but emptied Himself. That is the descent. Continuing, the apostle said that being found in fashion as a man He humbled Himself and became obedient to death, even the death of the Cross, wherefore God hath highly exalted Him. That is the Ascension, but it is the Ascension of One Who descended, and the One Who descended is the One Who in all the mystery of the past ever existed in fellowship and cooperation with God.

The whole emphasis of the question is on the descension. All the values of the Ascension—the human values which are ours, the things in which we make our boast and our trust which are of the very anchorage of our hope and faith—resulted from the descent.

"He . . . descended into the lower parts of the earth. He . . . ascended far above all the heavens, . . ." These two statements take us to the uttermost reaches of our thinking with regard to humanity. The first takes us to the uttermost depth. I am aware that there have been differences of opinion as to the real meaning of this phrase: ". . . the lower parts of the earth." There have been those who have suggested, and not without reason, that it is merely a reference to the earth simply placing it in contrast with the higher places of creation, ". . . all the heavens, . . ." which are subsequently referred to. But I do not so read the passage. Here I believe the apostle was referring to the ultimate depths of human experience resulting from sin; the lower parts of the earth, Hades, Sheol, the prison house of spirits. Involved within the phrase, of course, is the Incarnation itself. He descended; He took upon Him the form of a servant; He was made in the likeness of man; He came into all the circumstances and experiences of humanity; He lived His life among sinning men amid all the degradation of humanity which resulted from sin. He passed to the uttermost bound of that degradation in the mystic marvel of His dying. When His body lay in the grave, His Spirit descended into Hades and so He passed into the lower parts of the earth.

It is that to which the apostle draws attention. He declares in effect that the Ascension—while it involves descent and while, therefore, it further involves the prior existence of this Person, the Son of God—gains its values from that descent into the lower parts of the earth.

Now let us pass from this examination of the question, to consider the statement which immediately follows it and which is so closely related to it; "He that descended is the same also that ascended far above all the heavens, that He might fill all things." As in the question our attention is focused upon the descension, here it is kept focused there, but we are asked to interpret the Ascension by that descension. The statement first reveals the relation of that descent of our Lord to His Ascension. Apart from that descent and the accomplishment therein of a Divine purpose, there would have been no ascension in spite of the fact that the One Who descended had occupied a place in eternal fellowship with God. Ascent was the return of the One Who had accomplished His mission, and the last glory of the Ascension is that it sets an eternal seal upon the victory won in the mystery and the darkness of the descent. The One Who was from the beginning, the One Who became flesh, the One Who took our humanity and entered into it, entered into it for the purpose of ransom and redemption. That One could have found no way back into the place of power and fellowship with God had He failed to fulfil the Divine purpose. Let us at once admit that we are imagining the impossible. Nevertheless, here is the tremendous fact—which, trying to grasp with our human minds, we have to state it in this way—that God's adventure upon saving men was an adventure upon which He risked everything. The self-emptying of the Son of God was no easy thing even to Him. It was indeed self-emptying, the risking of everything upon the venture of dealing with sin, abolishing death, rescuing and ransoming a race, and bringing it back to the place of Divine intention and desire. This statement reveals to us the issue of that descension. Notice the superlative nature of the terms of which the apostle made use. ". . . far above all the heavens, . . ." Above the heavens. That is unthinkable, and because it is unthinkable it is written. In order that our estimation of the place which He now occupies should be superlative, Paul employed the phrase, "... above all the heavens, ..." I repeat, we cannot think beyond the heavens. This is a poetic figure and a most daring one. Paul speaks elsewhere about being caught up into the third heaven. In Scripture we are familiar with three heavens. The heaven of the atmosphere; the stellar spaces and the heavens beyond, the dwelling place of angels and of the spirits of the just made perfect. To that third heaven Paul said he was caught up upon one occasion. Now he said that this One ascended above all the heavens. It was a poetic figure intended to emphasize the high place, the final place of authority and dignity and power and glory to which this One passed. It means that He is elevated to a position which is above every form of creation. His Ascension was to the place of supreme and final and eternal authority.

Moreover He ascended above all heavens that He may fill all things. There are two possible meanings of that phrase. It may mean that He might fill all things by His presence, His sovereignty, His activity. Or it may mean that He might fulfill all things, realize the original purpose of God in all His creation. I believe that both ideas are included.

Yet, if we speak of Him as filling all things with His presence, His sovereignty, His activity, we seem to be contradicting the whole doctrine of the Ascension. The doctrine of the Ascension is that a Man of our humanity has passed to this central place of power and glory. But if He be a Man of our humanity, how can He fill all things? The mystery is admitted, but the admission of a mystery does not deny the actuality of the fact which is mysterious. Have we no glimpses of light on the subject in the stories of the days of Jesus between His Resurrection and Ascension? Was He not then preparing our hearts for an understanding of this fact? He appeared again and again to some group of disciples, and He did not come by the usual ways of human coming! The doors were shut for fear of the Jews, and they were not opened, but He was there. He talked with them in human speech and held out human hands and invited them to touch His human hands. Then again, without the shooting of a bolt, or the opening of a door, He was not! Not what? Did you think I was going to say not there? I was not. He was there, but He was not visible.

Two men were walking to Emmaus, and a third joined them. Their hearts burned within them while the Stranger talked with them. At last they invited Him in and offered Him the hospitality of their home for the night. He went in to abide and sat at the table with them. He was a Man of their own humanity, the very Man they had seen and beheld and handled, to use John's words. Suddenly, as He broke bread, they discovered Who He was, and then, with equal suddenness, He was not visible, but He was there! Let there be no Sadduceeism in our thinking. He can most certainly, suddenly, gloriously appear upon the field of battle to a dying soul. I believe with all my heart and all my soul that some of our boys have seen Jesus actually.

And yet, He filleth all things. This is not new in the history of Jesus. It was true of Him when He was here in the world. He spoke of Himself once in language that is very suggestive, as being in the bosom of the Father even while He was still here. For the three and thirty years that the Son of God walked the ways of earth, heaven lost its manifestation of Deity. It did not lose the presence of God, but it lacked His manifestation. While He was here, walking our ways, the roads of Judæa and Galilee, He was still in high heaven. When upon the green hill outside the city wall, He hung upon the brutal Roman gibbet, dying to save men, the chief pain and agony was felt in heaven in the heart of God.

That which is new is the assurance that comes to us as we remember that in that descent He won His victory, accomplished His purpose, carried out the great Divine campaign to finality and so went back again to heaven to be forever the medium through which God is to be known. Not yet do we see the glory of the victory, not yet do we see all things put under Him, but we see Jesus, the Man of our humanity, exalted thus to the right hand of God.

Now let us turn from textual examination to the theme itself. Let us think of the glory of the Ascension. The simple fact is that above all heavens is the One Who was forever there, but now He is there as Man, as well as God. That is new in heaven. When Jesus of Nazareth passed to the supernal heights, heaven entered upon a new phase and a new experience. Heaven then regained the One through Whom alone God manifests Himself to creation, but He was changed. The manifestation of light and love and life and of the glory and the beauty of Deity was the same, but there were new unveilings. At the center of the universe is a Man and withal a Man bearing in His body wound prints. The seer of Patmos, amid all the flaming and the flashing of the glorious revelations that came to him then, saw the throne, the light-girdled throne of the Ancient of days, and was ever more wonderful thing said concerning that throne: "I beheld in the midst of the throne . . . a Lamb as it had been slain, . . ." There at the heart of the universe is a Man of our humanity Who is a Redeemer.

By that Ascension, humanity is explained, and by that Ascension the place of man is secured in spite of his failure. By that Ascension, I say, humanity is explained. It is when we see Him ascended, that we know what was in the heart of Deity when God said: "Let us make man in our image, after our likeness." What dreams we dreamed as we read the

Genesis story. How we have tried to think out the meaning and the purpose of God in the creation of a being so wonderful. When God created humanity, He created it capable of close and intimate fellowship with Himself. Now all this is made plain by the fact that at the center of the universe God Himself remains incarnate, manifesting Himself to all creation through humanity.

But the Man there bears wound prints. Therefore, by the Ascension we know that the place of man is secured in spite of his failure. Our human need is joined forevermore with the grace of Deity. These then are the things that are verified to us by the Ascension of the Man of Nazareth.

But let this be interpreted by the context. This parenthesis, this excursus was called forth by the fact that Paul had just quoted from a Psalm. The quotation is not exact. It is marked by a verbal alteration which gives a new turn to the thought. The Psalm reads:

"Thou hast ascended on high, Thou hast led captivity captive. . . ." So far Paul's quotation does not vary. The picture suggested by the Hebrew poetry is that of a king returning, bringing with him a band of captives. ". . . Thou hast led captivity. . . ." Thy captives, Thou hast led them captive.

Then the Psalm says: "Thou hast received gifts among men, Yea *among* the rebellious also, . . ." We get nearer to the heart of the statement if we read it thus: He received gifts consisting of men, yea, consisting of the rebellious also. The King as he returns carries with him a band of captives. These are his gifts, not gifts he bestows, but gifts bestowed upon him. This idea Paul changes. With a fine daring, by a verbal change, he gives a new view of the situation. He says: "He led a band of captives captive; He gave gifts unto men." This verbal departure of the apostle is not a contradiction, but a fuller interpretation. The captives He led captive were His possession, according to the Messianic Psalm. "He led them captive, who were His possession, in order that He might bestow gifts upon them," is in effect the apostolic statement. They were given to Him by the right of His conquest, and He took them, not to put them into the galleys, not to oppress them, but to give them gifts, to crown them. Paul is not denying the teaching of the prophetic Psalm. That is all included in his sentence: He led His captivity captive. Paul says yes, but He did this in order to bestow gifts upon them.

This then is the contextual exposition. When He ascended, He ascended leading with Him a band of captives that were now His rightful possession. In His own words in that great intercessory prayer He called them: ". . . the men whom Thou gavest Me out of the world: . . ." He received gifts from among men. They were of the rebellious, they were of the stubborn; those who by their own sin had violated the order of His universe, had introduced deformity and ugliness, and were against God. But this One had by His descent won them, captured them, made them His captives, and when He ascended, He ascended representing them, carrying them with Him to the same supernal height, leading His band of captives captive, and that in order that He might bestow gifts upon them.

The first gift He bestowed upon His band of captives was the gift of the Holy Spirit. Then He gave some apostles, and some prophets, and some evangelists, and some pastors and teachers. Then He gave helps and healings and all the varied gifts that His captives need to lift them out of the degradation of their captivity and prepare them to reign with Him in life and glory and beauty forever and forever. In that Ascension of our Lord we also ascended. If indeed we are among the number of His captives, we are already in the purpose and plan of God, seated with Him in the heavens. Our life is hid with Christ in God even now. The life we live here in the flesh is the life risen, ascended, exalted of the sovereign Lord of life and glory. If for a little while we remain where the storms are sweeping and the long and dark and difficult journeys have to be undertaken, where the furnace is heated seven times, we are not alone; for while we are seated with Him in the heavens He is walking in us and with us, the way of sorrows.

From the heights, the mysterious heights of eternal oneness with God and fellowship with Him, He descended to the lower parts of the earth to be numbered with transgressors. He passed down into death in fellowship with humanity. He descended into the prison house of souls. Thence He ascended, and the glory that comes to Him is that of those men whom He receives as His gifts. Who are they? The rebellious!

> See how the plated gates unfold,
>   How swing the creaking doors of brass!
> With drums and gleaming arms, behold
>   Christ's kingly cohorts pass.
>
> Shall Christ not have His chosen men,
>   Nor lead His crested knights so tall,
> Superb upon their horses, when
>   The world's last cities fall?
>
> Ah, no! these few, the maimed, the dumb.
>   The saints of every lazar's den,
> The earth's off-scourings—they come
>   From desert and from fen.
>
> To break the terror of the night,
>   Black dreams and dreadful mysteries,
> And proud, lost empires in their might,
>   And chains and tyrannies.

There ride no gold encinctured knights
    Against the potentates of earth;
God chooses all the weakest things
    And gives Himself in birth.

With beaten slaves to draw His breath,
    And sleeps with foxes on the moor,
With malefactors shares His death,
    Tattered and worn and poor.

See how the palace gates unfold,
    How swing the creaking doors of brass!
Victorious in defeat—behold,
    Christ and His cohorts pass.

CHAPTER XXII

LIFE IN THE LIGHT

While ye have the light, believe on the light, that ye may become sons of light.

JOHN 12:36.

THESE WORDS OF OUR LORD WERE SPOKEN TO CRITICAL AND UNbelieving men, and as their context shows, their intention was that of urging these men to yield to the light which was so soon to be withdrawn. They virtually constituted the last public utterance of our Lord.

Let us think first of the assumption of our Lord which we know is so certainly fulfilled; that we have the light; second, of the true attitude towards the light, ". . . believe on the light . . ."; and finally, of the issue of such belief, ". . . that ye may become sons of light."

First, then, as to the assumption of our Lord. Light is peculiarly a word of John, and the sense in which he uses it is made perfectly clear in his prologue. Therein he said, ". . . the life was the light of men." Dealing with the relation of the Word to the whole creation, he declared inclusively that in Him was life. Then, marking the distinction between human life and all life below that in the scale of being, he said, ". . . the life was the light of men." That is to say that in man there is a spiritual and moral understanding. In the great process of creation when life reached the height of man, it looked back into the face of God and was conscious of Him. In man life became light.

Then further he declared, "The light shineth in the darkness, and the darkness comprehended it not. . . ." In that statement there is a recognition of the fact that this light in human life has never been wholly extinguished, but there is also recognition of the fact that this light is shrouded in darkness. The darkness and the light are both recognized.

At last he came to what was the supreme thought in his mind. His eyes fixed upon his Lord and Master with Whom he had walked the holy fields, with Whom he had become so intimately familiar, he said, "There was the true light, . . . which lighteth every man, coming into the world." It had always been in the world, it had been in every man; but there it was, coming into clear shining and clear observation. In the Incarnation, the hidden light that had been shrouded in darkness but never wholly extinguished, came from the darkness into visibility so that Jesus could and did say, "I am the Light of the world."

Light is that shining of truth which interprets life; the capacity for apprehending that light is in every human soul, and through man, as he receives the light, believes on the light, becomes a son of light, the effects of that light pass to the whole creation. ". . . I am the Light of the world, . . ." said our Lord, and He also said to His disciples in the days of His flesh and thereafter to all who believe on His Name, "Ye are the light of the world."

The light then, for us, has been focused in a Person and that a Person of our own humanity. Jesus was a human being, a perfect human being. That is not all of the truth concerning Him. There are deeper and profounder truths concerning the Person of our adorable Lord than can find expression in that statement. To that, this very prologue bears witness in the mystic sentences with which it opens; "In the beginning was the Word, and the Word was with God, and the Word was God." But we must remember that the completion of that statement is found in the fourteenth verse: "And the Word was made flesh, and dwelt among us (and we beheld His glory, glory as of the only begotten of the Father,) full of grace and truth." For the purpose of understanding the light then, we are not called upon to think of Him in the terms of the eternal and the mysterious. These He came to reveal, but He came to reveal them through the things that are temporal and through our own humanity. Therefore, when we think of the Light, we think of Him, our Lord, as a perfect human being.

What shining forth of light was there in that human Being with regard to the physical, with regard to the mental, with regard to the spiritual?

First, as to the physical. When He, the Word, came into human history as a human being, all conditions were open to Him for His coming. He might have come into any sphere or condition of human life. He might have come into the courts of kings; into the fellowship of learning. He might have entered life amid all its material splendor or, on the other hand, He might have come into the most abject and absolute poverty. All conditions were open to Him. How then did He come? Into what conditions did He come?

The conditions that He chose for Himself in order to give us light upon the physical side of human life were those which may be described as simple and sufficient. We often speak of the poverty of our Lord. It is a comparative and relative term. In certain senses, yea verily, He lived a life of poverty. But we never ought to think of Jesus with pity when we think of His poverty. His was not the grinding poverty which is a tragedy. His life was characterized in His boyhood, in His young manhood, and through the years of His public ministry, by a stern simplicty, but He had all things sufficient. In the Book of Proverbs we have the wonderful prayer of Agur,

> Remove far from me vanity and lies;
> Give me neither poverty nor riches;
> Feed me with the food that is needful for me;
> Lest I be full, and deny *Thee*, and say, Who is the Lord,
> Or lest I be poor, and steal,
> And use profanely the name of my God.

That prayer was answered perfectly in the case of Jesus of Nazareth. He was removed in the material surroundings of His life from vanity and lies; He had neither poverty in the extreme sense of the word, nor riches. He was fed throughout His life with food that was needful for Him. He was never full having to face the temptation that comes from repletion, of denying God and saying, "Who is He?" He was never poor having to face the temptation to steal and to use profanely the Name of His God. He chose to enter human life and live as to the physical in circumstances that were characterized by simplicity and by sufficiency. That is light upon human life. It is the interpretation of the true place of the physical therein; it should be without poverty and without riches.

Then as to the mental. So far as the thinking of Jesus is revealed in His teaching and in His acting—and surely these are the means by which thinking is perpetually revealed—His mental outlook was that of a perpetual apprehension of the spiritual and appreciation of the material. He was forever conscious of the spiritual, forever acting as in the presence of the abiding and the eternal, but never withdrawing Himself from the material or treating it as though it were unimportant or valueless, appreciating it everywhere, in flowers, in children, in all the commonplaces of life. Of course, that was the trouble created in the minds of certain men of religion concerning Him; so much so that exaggerating their language as men in criticism usually do, they said, He is ". . . a gluttonous man and a winebibber. . . ."

His whole mental outlook, however, was most evidently that of the apprehension of the spiritual. This, of course, is in some senses difficult to speak of. The spiritual is so difficult to reach, to understand in other human lives. It is so profoundly difficult that I question whether one human soul can ever, even after long comradeship, know perfectly the spiritual secret of another human soul. We become acquainted with physical and material manifestations; we pass by dint of friendship into fellowship with the mental attitudes and movements of mind; but that most strange dignity, the spiritual being, dwells always in an inner shrine. Sometimes we get a little nearer to it in the case of each other and then some day are surprised to discover how little we know of the spiritual fact. I believe that this is wholly beneficent and gracious, for God deals with us alone and none other can intrude. Yet we must know something of the spiritual fact if we are to understand life. As we look at this Man, and follow Him on His journeyings, and listen to Him in His teachings, we become familiar with His mental expression and with the physical fact. But how shall we describe the spiritual truth about Jesus? I think we may do so by saying the same things that we have already said concerning His mental outlook, only attempting to say them in the deeper and profounder terms that express the spiritual.

He lived in unbroken fellowship with the eternal and, consequently, in unceasing control over the temporal. He was never mastered by anything temporal, because He was always mastered by the eternal. He reigned over circumstances, because He was reigned over by the static facts of God and eternity.

The fact that He lived in perpetual fellowship with the eternal was manifested in that there was no evidence of haste or of panic. His complete control of the temporal was proved by the fact that there was no evidence of delay or of paralysis. No haste, no panic, because He was dealing with eternity; no delay, no paralysis, because in the conscious power of eternity He dealt with time and mastered it.

There are many of His words which might illustrate these two things. I shall make two selections. That fellowship with the eternal, which meant no haste and no panic in the case of our Lord, always seems to me to have had wonderful expression when He said to His disciples:

> Are there not twelve hours in the day? If a man walk in the day, he stumbleth not, because he seeth the light of this world.

There is something wonderfully Eastern about that. The Eastern mind is the mind which is conscious of eternity, of the vastness of things, and, therefore, cannot be hurried. This attitude of mind is expressed in the highest sense in these words. His disciples were afraid for Him, afraid that He should go back to Jerusalem. He said in effect, "There is no need for haste, there is no need for fear. When a man walks in the day of God's own measurement, he does not stumble; he walks in the calm, hasteless freedom from panic which is the result of the spirit life in fellowship with the eternal." He was a Man in time, in the midst of the running hours, mastering the whole of them in their movement because living in fellowship with God with Whom one day is as a thousand years, to Whom a thousand years are but as one day.

Yet let us hear Him again upon another occasion, and we shall find another note balancing this first one and showing that when a man touches the temporal, there must be no delay and there need be no paralysis. Said He to His disciples:

> We must work the works of Him that sent me, while it is day; the night cometh when no man can work. When I am in the world, I am the light of the world.

That is singularly Western. That is the language of movement, that is the language of haste that cannot brook delay, that is the language of the soul that seizes the present opportunity for the doing of the present duty. In the Old Testament are two statements, far separated and in some senses having no connection. Nevertheless, I borrow them in this connection. Jesus lived so in fellowship with the eternal that it might be said of Him, ". . . he that believeth shall not make haste"; and He so lived mastering the temporal that it might be said of Him with equal accuracy, "The King's business requireth haste." He was free from all haste but always hasting; free from any panic and paralysis but seizing every hour and doing the thing appointed therein. Every hour presented to Him an open door of opportunity, only open in that hour, and He, girded with the strength of eternity and acting in cooperation with the impulses of Deity, passed through the open door, met the opportunity, and fulfilled the duty.

If this is the Light of the human personality and being of Jesus, let us see the light that came through Him on human activity. Here we need to remind ourselves that all human activity is fundamentally spiritual. There is nothing that I do with my hand that is not the outcome of my spiritual life. The spiritual life may be degraded, or it may be noble; it may be true, or it may be false; but every physical activity is the outcome of spiritual activity. Processionally, human activity therefore is mental. Out of that deep unfathomable mystery, the spiritual life, the mind forms its conception of things external, and spiritual life and mental process become manifest in things material and physical. We must observe, then, as far as we are able, the mental attitudes of our Lord a little more carefully. Things we have already said will be repeated, but with a new application. The intelligence of Jesus was characterized by the seeing of the whole instead of the part. Does that seem a poor thing to say? As a matter of fact it is a big thing. There are men who see this earth only, and men who see this earth only are sensualists. There are men who strive never to see this earth at all but to see the heavens only and the spiritual only, and they practice their endeavor alone and live the ascetic life. Both outlooks are false, and each is as false as the other. The man who sees the earth only becomes a sensualist but never destroys the harrowing, hungering cry of the spiritual life; he simply refuses to listen to it or attempts to drug it. The man who attempts to realize the spiritual at the expense of the material, thinking of the flesh in a vulgar material sense which is never the New Testament sense, never escapes from his flesh, never escapes from the material. He was not intended to escape thereby. In the long issue the ascetic becomes as sensual as does the voluptuary. Our Lord saw the whole of things. He saw God and His creation. He saw all ages as well as an age. Perhaps nothing more beautiful was ever written than Thomas Whytehead's poem on the Second Day of Creation. Let me remind you of two or three stanzas from it:

> This world I deem
> But a beautiful dream
> Of shadows that are not what they seem,
> Where visions rise

> Giving dim surmise
> Of the things that shall meet our waking eyes.
>
> But could I see,
> As in truth they be,
> The glories of heaven that encompass me,
> I should lightly hold
> The tissued fold
> Of that marvellous curtain of blue and gold.
>
> Soon the whole
> Like a parched scroll
> Shall before my amazed sight uproll,
> And without a screen,
> At one burst be seen,
> The Presence wherein I have ever been.

May I reverently say that all that Thomas Whytehead so beautifully imagined was the commonplace experience of Jesus. Wherever He looked He saw the creation and the God of creation. He never abused the material. He never flagellated Himself. That was an iniquity wrought by his enemies. He realized the glory of the physical and the material because of His keen understanding of the glory of the spiritual.

Emotionally we ever discover in Jesus the feeling which resulted from the vision. He knew the beauty of holiness, and He knew the possibility of renewal even in the case of that which was degraded. He loved the true, He hated the false. He was passionately moved and provoked and consumed by a desire to end the ugliness and restore the beauty, to destroy death and release life, to banish the darkness in the shadow of which He lived and flood the world with light.

Volitionally, all His choices were consonant with that emotion and that outlook.

Thus we have light upon life's activities. There are senses in which we cannot have light upon the activities of today by looking at Jesus. There is a sense in which there is no activity of today on which we cannot have light by looking at Jesus. In the mere external and local facts of the day, we are not in Judæa, we are not in Galilee, we are not living in that strange hour of misery when all the world lived under the incubus of the Romans. Nevertheless, in the deeper things of life, Jesus is still the light of human activity.

What then, must be our attitude toward the Light? Said Jesus: "While ye have the light, believe on the light, . . ." I could very much wish that this had been rendered, "believe into the light." Activity is suggested. It is infinitely more than believing in the light. That is fundamental, but being only intellectual it may stop short there. That is not what our Lord meant. We are to do more than believe in the light; we are to believe into it. He calls us to action in consonance with conviction. Already in this discourse He had interpreted His meaning as He said: "Walk while ye have the light." To walk in light is to make use of it, to yield ourselves to it. To believe into the light is not to admire the glory of it, it is to obey the call of it.

Those who have the light have this responsibility, that they must seek it. This Light is shining, is shining clearly. Our business is to seek it by considering Him, by giving ourselves to holy contemplation of this Person. If we are to believe into the light, we must acquaint ourselves with the light. We need to get back again and again to Him to understand that light.

Then it means also the trusting of the light as it shines, trusting His ideals, consenting to His conceptions, and refusing to postpone to a more convenient season any great command of Jesus. We are to trust the light and to act in accordance with it.

In our case it will mean perpetual spiritual re-adjustment; the constant activity of mind that brings it into conformity with the spiritual re-adjustment. In our case it will mean the perpetual watchfulness over all material and physical expression that these things shall be in harmony with the mental conformity to spiritual re-adjustment.

If we will do these things, what then? Then we shall be sons of light. Sons of light, not children. There is a difference. There is a difference in the New Testament, and there is always a difference. Canon Westcott says that the word "child" in the New Testament indicates community of nature; the word "son" always connotes the dignity of heirship. Dr. Erdman, of the United States, says: "Sonship relates not to nature but to legal standing. A son is no longer a minor, a son has attained his majority. That is the force of the word 'sons.' All sons are children." Yea verily! but all children are not sons. All children have not attained their majority; all children have not entered into the dignity of heirship. Our Lord did not say "children of light"; He said, ". . . sons of light." We have the light. Let us believe into it, seek to trust it, obey it, and we shall come into the full dignity of our heirship in light. That means that life will be interpreted, service guided, suffering transfigured.

CHAPTER XXIII

SONGS IN PRISON

> ... *about midnight Paul and Silas were praying and singing hymns unto God, and the prisoners were listening to them; and suddenly there was a great earthquake, so that the foundations of the prison-house were shaken: and immediately all the doors were opened; and every one's bands were loosed.*
>
> ACTS 16:25, 26.

THIS IS AN ARRESTING AND WONDERFUL STORY, AND THE MORE carefully it is considered the more the wonder grows. At first we wonder at the singing. Then we wonder so much at that which inspired the singing, that we should wonder more if these men had not sung. At first we are amazed with the cheerfulness and heroism of these men, and then we find out that their singing was not abnormal but normal. It was not the result of a transient emotion. It was the expression of a constant experience of the soul.

Let us, then, first look at the picture presented by these two verses; second, recognize the one central value of the story in order that third and finally, we may consider some of its particular teaching.

These are the things that arrest attention. First the men, Paul and Silas, then the circumstances in the midst of which we see them, then their occupation in the midst of the circumstances and finally, the issue of the story as it is contained in all that remains of the chapter.

Paul and Silas were Jews and were held in contempt in Philippi because they were Jews, as is most evident from this story. Yet, as emerges in the course of the story, they were Roman citizens. But preeminently they were Christians, the one an apostle and the other a prophet.

Their ministry and their message necessarily challenged effete Judaism and paganism wherever they came. They were calling men to a new way of life both as to ideal and power. Consequently, wherever they went they created disturbances. ". . . These that have turned the world upside down have come hither also!" That is always the note of true Christianity. It always challenges effete religions and paganism. Organized Christianity which fails to make a disturbance is dead. It is equally true that they created love for themselves wherever they came. What tender heart affections fastened around this man Paul!

Now observe their circumstances at this time. "But about midnight. . . ." That disjunctive sends us back as it suggests all that had gone before. They had been charged with sedition. They had been beaten with many stripes. Beating with rods was a terrible experience. When Paul was writing to the Corinthians, he referred to such beatings as amongst the things he had endured. "Thrice was I beaten with rods. . . ." It was physical brutality of the worst kind. Their backs were bruised and bleeding and unwashed. They were cast into the inner prison, some inner chamber or dungeon from which light was excluded and probably almost all air was shut out. The final barbarity was that their feet were made fast in the stocks. All that before the "But." Immediately following it are the words, "At midnight!" That accentuates everything. It accentuates the loneliness, the weariness, the suffering.

We now come to that which is central; the occupation of these men. They were praying and singing hymns. This is not a description of two exercises. It does not mean that they were offering petitions and also singing hymns of praise. The word translated praying covers the whole ground of worship; asking for gifts, rendering of adoration, continued supplication, offering of thanksgiving. In this story the word "worship" is qualified by the word that follows. They were hymning the praises of God. The Greek word here employed is one that had long been reserved to represent the praises offered to heroes or gods or to the one God. The worship of these men was that of adoration. It was the expression of the gladness of their hearts. Two were gathered together in the Name and in the midst was the Lord; all unseen by the eyes of sense, unapprehended by any who were round about, undiscovered even after the jailer himself had come back to look at the prisoners. That Presence was the supreme sense of these men. They did not ask for anything, they gave. They were exercising their Christian priesthood on its highest level, which is not intercessory but eucharistic, the priesthood of thanksgiving. In the dungeon, in the darkness of the night, their feet fast in the stocks, their backs all bloody, they offered praises. They gave and their giving was the outcome of their gladness.

Immediately we ask, "What was there to make them glad?" I am inclined to answer the inquiry by saying that if we had asked them they probably would have said, "Nay, what is there to make us sad?"

Finally, we must glance at the issues. The prisoners were listening! Here again a word arrests us. It indicates attentive listening. It is a word that is almost invariably employed for that listening which gives pleasure, the word used when men listened to perfect music and were charmed by its sounds, or when men listened to some oration that swept them away.

In all this story there is revealed that which is peculiarly Christian, the victory of the soul over all adverse circumstances and the transmutation of all opposing forces into allies of the soul. Think of some of the sayings of this man Paul who sang that night. He (in paraphrase) says: "Tribulation worketh patience, therefore rejoice in tribulation." He says: "Afflictions work a far more exceeding and eternal weight of glory, therefore we will rejoice in our afflictions." Yet again he says: "Godly sorrow worketh repentance." These are all the things from which the soul of man shrinks; tribulation, affliction, sorrow! These things are made the allies of the soul, they work on behalf of the soul. Out of tribulation comes patience which leads on to confidence and hope of ultimate victory. Afflictions which can be dismissed in the light of eternity as light afflictions, which are but for a moment, are seen working out the weight of glory. Sorrows of the soul are working toward the change of mind which means its transformation into perfect harmony with the mind of Christ Himself. This is the central value of the story. This is the central truth concerning Christian experience.

What then was the secret of this experience in the case of these men? It was the outcome of their knowledge of God. He was known as compelling all things to work together for good to those who love Him. The experience is not stoicism. The Christian man does not say: "What cannot be cured must be endured." I am afraid I have often said it, but when I have done so, it has been because for the moment I have forgotten my Christianity. To say that what cannot be cured must be endured is paganism. It is wonderful that paganism ever climbed to that height. It is a great attitude, it is heroic up to a certain point, but it is not Christianity. Christianity does not say what cannot be cured must be endured; it says, rather, that these things must be endured because they are part of the cure. These things are to be cheerfully borne because they have the strange and mystic power to make whole and strong and so to lead on to victory and the final glory. Christianity is never the dour pessimism which submits. Christianity is the cheerful optimism which cooperates with the process, because it sees that through suffering and weakness, joy and triumph must come. That always and only results from a clear vision of God. Wherever this clear vision of God comes to the soul through Christ—through Whom alone it can come—there follows the ending of bondage to all secondary causes, and the sense of relationship to the primary and final cause is supreme. Two men were in Philippi, in prison, in the inner prison, in the stocks, in suffering, in sorrow! All true, but the final thing is not said. They were in God! Their supreme consciousness was not that of the prison, or the stocks, or the pain, but of God. They were not callous or indifferent; pain was pain to them; confinement was confinement; loneliness was loneliness; but they realized how all these things were yet held in the grasp of the King of the perfect order, Whom they knew as their Lord and Master and, consequently, they sang praises. They did not ask for anything, not even for an earthquake. They gave Him praises. That is Christianity. Because of this vision of God and because of this sense of the soul, the experiences which otherwise would have depressed and led to despair became wings of hope, the inspiration of song.

All this took place at midnight! That accentuates all the difficulty, the loneliness and weariness and pain. Yet the phrase is not really "At midnight." This very slight alteration in the Revised Version is not to be passed over lightly.

"About midnight!" To these men midnight was not a definite moment at all. Midnight is never a stopping place. It is coming, and lo! it is gone before we know it. Time is transfigured. There is no long, deadly moment with all the agony of eternity pressed into it to these men. They are traveling, and they are traveling in the spirit of the hymn:

> We are marching through Immanuel's ground
> To fairer worlds on high.

Through Immanuel's land; not to Immanuel's land, but through it. John Bunyan puts the river his pilgrim had to cross in Immanuel's land. The pilgrim did not cross the river to reach Immanuel's land; the river was in it and ere he knew it, he had passed the river. So to these men all these things were in Immanuel's land. Midnight, that deadly hour, that most terrible hour, wherein some people seem forever to dwell; anticipation of it makes it a perpetual presence, and the memory of it an abounding agony. But for these men there was no such actual time. It was about midnight, and then they sang, and they sang praises to God.

What then are the things of value here for ourselves? In attempting to answer this inquiry let us keep our mind upon these men. First, we learn that men who sing while they suffer are men who have learned the profound secret that suffering is the method by which joy is perfected. That declaration is limited by human history as we know it. I am not prepared to say that we can make a statement like that, and apply it to the whole universe of God. It is conceivable that there may be abounding joys in God's great universe that have never been reached through suffering. I cannot tell. I do not know. I do not ask to know. I am dealing with humanity as the result of our own experience and in the light of the biblical unveiling. Suffering is always the method by which joy is perfected. In the midst of the Paschal discourses our Lord said: ". . . your sorrow shall be turned into joy." That is an entirely different thing from saying that your sorrow shall be exchanged for joy. Without desiring for a moment to be censorious in criticism, yet it is true that half our hymns suggest that we should look on to heaven where we shall find a joy which is a compensation for the sorrows of life. There is truth in that view, but it does not get to the heart of the Christian revelation. The truth is that all the ultimate joys of the heavenly state are joys that have come out of the agonies of the earthly tribulation. Is that a startling thing to say? Then listen to these most revealing words: ". . . Who for the joy that was set before Him, endured the cross, despising shame. . . ." With infinite reverence I say that He had never reached that joy save through His sorrows. That which was wrought out in the experience of our Lord on our behalf is a revelation of what all this pain means—this abounding, palpitating, poignant agony. Your sorrow shall be turned into joy. Again and again we have glimpses of it, outworking into the present of immediate experience. Look back over the years. There they are, travel-worn years; much of light is upon them, but much of darkness also; many days of triumph, marching with the band playing and the flags flying, and many days of disaster and defeat. Already you know that the greatest things of life have come, not out of the sunlit days, but out of the darkened hours. Your sorrow has already been turned into joy. When your sorrow that seemed unendurable at the hour, blossomed with beauty, your sorrow was turned into joy. Christianity as an experience is the ability to know that this will be so even while the agony is upon us, and so we are able to sing in the midst of it. Men who sing while they suffer are men who have learned the profound secret that suffering is the method by which joy is perfected in human life and human history.

But again, men who sing in prison are men who cannot be imprisoned. It was impossible to imprison Paul and Silas. But they were imprisoned. They could be shown in that prison, in that inner chamber, with their feet fast in the stocks. Ah, but they were not imprisoned. Fellowship with God is the franchise of eternity. You may put these men within your stone walls, you may make their feet fast in the wood of your brutal stocks, but they are not there. They are sitting with Christ in the heavenly places. They are ranging themselves with the living ones. They are swinging the censers of their heavenly priesthood in high and holy places. As to bodily presence, they are there in the prison, but as to spiritual essence they are with God. Men who sing in prison are men who cannot be imprisoned.

Therefore we may add: men who sing at midnight are citizens of that city of which it is said they need no light of sun or moon, for the Lord and the Lamb are the light of it. But they are in Philippi! Yes, as to bodily presence but not as to spiritual experience. Abraham left Ur of the Chaldees to find a city but never found it. He died without seeing it. Those who have followed in his steps have still been seeking it. It has never been found. It is not found yet. But it is clearly seen; it will be built; it will be established. Abraham lived in it though he never saw it; he walked its streets though it was never built; he held communion with its inhabitants though he never reached it. Paul and Silas, where are you living just now? In Philippi? No, in the City of God! In the City of God there is no night. These men were children of light, they were stars of the morning, and the morning stars sang together long ago, and they will sing together through all earth's midnight until the last shadow is melted. Men who sing at midnight are citizens of the city in which there is no night.

And finally, men who sing when their work is stopped are men whose work is never stopped.

They have put Paul in prison. His beloved work is stopped. He cannot preach in prison. But they sang praises, and the prisoners were listening. A man who can sing in prison is a man whose work is never done. When the missionary journey has to be abandoned and the preaching services are all canceled and there is nothing more to do, he will sing and the prisoners will hear his singing. The singing of a prisoner is a message to prisoners and they will listen. I cannot go any further. I do not know what happened to those prisoners afterwards. If you will allow the speculation, I believe that some of them were brought to Jesus Christ as the result of that singing. Cancel that if you do not agree. At least one man was won for Christ; the hard brutalized man who had been able to put these men in the stocks in the inner prison and leave them all bleeding from the rods and faint with loss of blood. He had left them and gone to sleep. He was asleep. If you want to know how brutalized he was, get that upon your heart. What is the next thing we see him doing? Washing their stripes, his whole nature revolutionized, his whole being completely changed with a suddenness equal to that of the earthquake that shook the prison to its foundations. He is washing their stripes; he is putting food before them. Men who sing in prison when their work is stopped are given to see that their work is never stopped; it runs on through bondage to liberty, and the gospel is preached anew.

All I have so far said has had to do with one verse of my text. There is another verse. ". . . suddenly there was a great earthquake; so that the foundations of the prison-house were shaken: and immediately all the doors were opened; and every one's bands were loosed." That was very wonderful, but we will not dwell upon it. I made it part of the text in order to say that it does not matter. It does not at all affect our story. It does not rob from it; it does not add to it. The glory of our consideration is in the other verse. That earthquake does not always come. We shall miss a great deal if we imagine that when we are in prison and sing, there will be an earthquake. Prison doors may not be opened at all. Thousands have been left in prison and died there, but they sang, and they sang through until they joined the new song on the other side. That earthquake does not matter. Do not let us fix our minds upon the earthquake. Probably we shall never have a deliverance like that. That is not the point of the story at all. Two or three years passed away and Paul was in prison in Rome, and then he wrote to these very people, to this jailer, and these Philippians. Read his letter, the letter he wrote to these very people from another prison. It is a song from beginning to end. He was still singing, and there was no earthquake. But probably he was liberated. Yes, I agree. Possibly he expected to be liberated. Indeed, he surely did as that letter shows. But he was not singing because he was to be liberated. Read the letter through, and you will see that the inspiration of his song was not the expectation of deliverance. It was the realization while he was in prison of the fact that he was a prisoner of Jesus Christ. That is the secret of the singing in the Philippian letter. That sense of relationship to Jesus Christ transfigured everything else. The chain? He looked at it, but it flashed with light. He was the prisoner of Jesus Christ. Let us go on. Presently, he was in prison again, and he was never coming out, and he knew it. His last writing was the letter of a man in prison never to escape. He knew it perfectly well. Things had not gone well with him in the first part of his trial, and he was assured that the issue of the second part of it would be death. How then did he write? What is he doing? Listen to him for a moment:

> For I am already being offered, and the time of my departure is come. I have fought the good fight, I have finished the course, I have kept the faith: henceforth there is laid up for me the crown of righteousness, which the Lord, the righteous judge, shall give to me at that day; and not to me only, but also to all them that have loved His appearing.

He was singing still; still an anthem, still a paean of praise! They were very dark days. Listen!

> Do thy diligence to come shortly unto me: . . . Demas forsook me, having loved this present world, and went to Thessalonica; Crescens to Galatia, Titus to Dalmatia. Only Luke is with me. Take Mark, and bring him with thee; for he is useful to me for ministering. But Tychicus I sent to Ephesus. (It is colder here.) The cloak that I left at Troas with Carpus, bring when thou comest, and the books, especially the parchments. Alexander the coppersmith did me much evil. . . .

Do you see the conflicting circumstances? Was he singing now?

> At my first defence no one took my part, but all forsook me: may it not be laid to their account. But the Lord stood by me and strengthened me; that through me the message might be fully proclaimed, and that all the Gentiles might hear: and I was delivered out of the mouth of the lion. The Lord will deliver me from every evil work, and will save me unto His heavenly kingdom: to Whom *be* glory for ever and ever. . . .

He was singing still. Ah yes! and the singing that we have listened to in Philippi was before the earthquake. He had no idea that the earthquake was coming. He did not sing because he was to be let out of prison. He sang because prison did not matter.

> Your harps, ye trembling saints,
>   Down from the willows take;
> Loud to the praise of Love divine,
>   Bid every string awake.
>
> His Grace will to the end,
>   Stronger and brighter shine;
> Nor present things, nor things to come,
>   Shall quench the spark divine.
>
> When we in darkness walk,
>   Nor feel the heavenly flame,
> Then is the time to trust our God,
>   And rest upon His Name.
>
> Blest is the man, O God,
>   That stays himself on Thee!
> Who wait for Thy salvation, Lord,
>   Shall Thy salvation see!

CHAPTER XXIV

WAITING FOR GOD

For from of old men have not heard, nor perceived by the ear, neither hath the eye seen a God beside Thee, Which worketh for him that waiteth for him.
ISAIAH 64:4.

Things which eye saw not, and ear heard not, And which entered not into the heart of man, whatsoever things God prepared for them that love Him.
I CORINTHIANS 2:9.

THE SIMILARITY BETWEEN THESE TWO PASSAGES IS PATENT. There is, however, an equally definite disparity. In the letter of Paul the words constitute a quotation. He introduced them by the formula, "As it is written. . . ."

Now, there has been much discussion as to where the apostle found these words. Jerome affirmed them to be found in the Apocalyptic literature, with which Paul would certainly be familiar, but did not suggest that he quoted them from that literature. If they were quoted from the Hebrew Bible, this passage in Isaiah is the only one in the Old Testament which could in any way be looked upon as that from which Paul quoted. But there is a difference between the thing that Paul quoted and the passage which we are bound to notice. It is possible that he quoted from some other manuscript than that from which our translation was made. It is interesting to Bible students to observe in passing that both in Isaiah and Corinthians the revisers in the margin have not referred to these passages as being direct quotations but have indicated the relation by the use of the word "compare." By that method they suggest that it was not necessarily a direct quotation, but that it moves in the same realm of ideas.

Let us observe, then, the disparity between the two passages. In that in the prophecy of Isaiah, the emphasis is on the marvelous God Who works for those that wait for Him. ". . . from of old men have not heard, nor perceived by the ear, neither hath the eye seen a God beside Thee, Which worketh for him that waiteth for him."

In the Corinthians the emphasis is not upon God at all; it is upon the marvelous things which God does for them that love Him. "Things which eye saw not, and ear heard not, and which entered not into the heart of man, whatsoever things God prepared for them that love Him." Isaiah says that no other such God has been heard of or seen. Paul says that such wonderful things as those which God prepares have not been seen, or heard, or apprehended by the human heart; so wonderful are they that they can only be made known by the Holy Spirit. In Isaiah the cause of wonder is that God works for them that wait for Him. In Corinthians the marvel is caused by the things that God does for those that love Him.

This recognition of disparity moves toward a recognition of the true spiritual relationship between the two passages which makes it more than probable that Paul was indeed quoting this very passage, only he did as New Testament writers perpetually did—changed the literal wording of the Old, caught a higher spiritual harmony, went further than the suggestion of the Old, modified it while not contradicting it in order to bring out a fuller and richer phase of truth. In each of them it is evident that the thought is moving in the same realm of ideas. In one it is occupied with the marvelous God Who works for them that wait for Him; in the other it is occupied with the marvelous things that God prepares for those that love Him. And so it seems to me that we may weave these two things into one statement: Our God is marvelous in that He does marvelous things for those who wait for Him because they love Him.

Now let us observe the similarity between the two declarations, in the light of the circumstances under which they were uttered or penned.

Historically the passage in Isaiah is not easy to place, but the nature of the circumstances is most clear. It was a day of darkness and of difficulty, when it seemed as though God had abandoned His own people and had ceased to act. Glancing back at chapter sixty-three, in the fifteenth verse, we find these words: "Look down from heaven, and behold from the habitation of Thy holiness and of Thy glory: where are Thy zeal and Thy mighty acts? The yearning of Thy bowels and Thy compassions are restrained toward me."

Or again in the close of verse eighteen and in verse nineteen:

". . . our adversaries have trodden down Thy sanctuary. We are become as they over whom Thou never barest rule; as they that were not called by Thy name."

It was a day, moreover, when there were those among the people who with passionate desire were making appeal to God:

"Oh that Thou wouldest rend the heavens, that Thou wouldest come down, that the mountains might flow down at Thy presence; as when fire kindleth the brushwood, *and* the fire causeth the waters to boil: to make Thy name known to Thine adversaries, that the nations may tremble at Thy presence."

Then suddenly the prophet seems to have taken a backward look which was born of his intense desire that God should thus appear, and the backward look was one which brought to mind God's past appearances:

> "When Thou didst terrible things which we looked not for, Thou camest down, the mountains flowed down at Thy presence."

It is as though the prophet had said: "I am not asking for things that have never been; I am asking Thee to return to Thine ancient attitude towards us, and to the activities of the past." In that very note of memory an idea was born. ". . . Thou didst terrible things which we looked not for. . . ." Then he enunciated a central philosophy of life, as he declared: "For from old men have not heard, nor perceived by the ear, neither hath the eye seen a God beside Thee, Which worketh for him that waiteth for him." Thus we discover the value of the declaration. God's words for a waiting people, and they only fail when they try to manage without Him.

Now let us turn to the New Testament and look at the circumstances that were in the mind of the apostle when he wrote. In this Letter to the Corinthians he was dealing with the difficulties that were confronting the Christian church, and in his mind was the fact of the darkest day in all human history. He was thinking of the day in which the cleverness of the world had crucified the Lord of glory. That was the day, that very day of unutterable and unfathomable darkness, in which God was preparing things for those that loved Him, too wonderful for human understanding, apart from the interpretation of the Spirit. This, then, is the second phase of the truth. God prepares in darkness and in mystery things for those that love Him that are so wonderful that they can only be understood by the interpretation of the Spirit.

From the wealth of ideas suggested by these two kindred passages I propose to make two simple deductions and to apply them.

The deductions are these. In the hour of darkness and difficulty the true attitude of those who believe in God is that of waiting for Him. The only strength sufficient to enable men to wait for God is that of love to Him, for love is the capacity for receiving the interpretation of the things which He is doing.

Waiting for God is not laziness. Waiting for God is not going to sleep. Waiting for God is not the abandonment of effort. Waiting for God means, first, activity under command; second, readiness for any new command that may come; third, the ability to do nothing until the command is given.

The Hebrew word translated "waiting" here has a pictorial affinity which is peculiarly suggestive today. It has affinity with a word that means "to entrench." We do no violence to the real thought of the text if we read it in that way. God worketh for him that entrenches himself in Him. The idea of waiting for God here is that of digging ourselves in to God.

Waiting for God, then, is the adjustment of our lives to the truth concerning Him which we know. When circumstances are chaotic, when it is impossible to understand their movements and to know what will be the outcome of this or that combination of circumstances, that is the hour in which we are to wait for God. God is certain; the one and only certainty of which we have any knowledge; far more certain than the fact of our own being. There is a sense in which we are sure of ourselves, we are sure of our existence, but there are infinite mysteries behind us as to the how of our being and far more unfathomable mysteries lying ahead of us as to the issue of our being; and as to its present continuity, there is no certainty. God is the one unchanging fact from everlasting to everlasting. Waiting for God means putting this life, of which I am so uncertain in a thousand varied ways, into right relationship with Him of Whom I am absolutely and everlastingly certain. Waiting for God means that I adjust my life to Him rather than to circumstances, and that I set my hope on Him rather than on the wit and the cleverness of men. Waiting for God means that definite personal activity which is busily occupied in adjusting the whole fact and circumstances of life to the unchangeable and unalterable fact of God.

Waiting for God means, therefore, readiness for any command; that state of perpetual suspense which listens for the word in order that it may be immediately obeyed. Those who wait for God are pilgrim souls that have no tie that will hold them when the definite command is issued; no prejudices that will paralyze their effort when in some strange coming of the light they are commanded to take a pathway entirely different to that which was theirs before; having no interests either temporal or eternal, either material or mental or spiritual, that will conflict with the will of God when that will is made known. Souls who wait for God are such as have their loins girt about, their lamps burning; they are alert, awake, ready.

Waiting for God, then, means power to do nothing save under command. This is not lack of power to do anything. Waiting for God needs strength rather than weakness. It is the power to do nothing. It is the strength that holds strength in check. It is the strength that prevents the blundering activity which is entirely false and will make the true activity impossible when the definite command comes.

For those who thus wait, God works; and as surely as men wait thus for Him while He works for them, there will come to them, presently, the clarion call to arise and co-operate. When it comes, the plan is almost invariably a different one from that which had been expected. "In ways we looked not for," said the prophet, "Thou hast wrought for us in the past."

Is not that the history of every forward movement in the economy of God? A period of darkness, a period of desolation, a period of difficulty in which His people were brought to the point of knowing that they did not know and understanding that they could not understand. A period of being clever enough to be done with their own cleverness, and then, while they waited, a period of adjusting their lives to God, severing all ties that held them, abandoning all prejudices that paralyzed, putting an end to every effort that was likely to conflict with the practical definite command and program and plan.

When the call comes, it is almost invariably to something new and surprising and startling, in the doing of which we seem to have to go back upon things that we have said and done in the past. The peril of the people of God is always that they shall be so wedded to yesterday that they are not ready for God's tomorrow; or that they shall be so busy today making their programs that when God brings His program, their own arrangements interfere with the carrying out of His will.

This is no easy conception of life. Waiting is far more difficult than working. It would be a much easier thing for the church of God at this very hour of her darkness to call conferences and councils and make plans for tomorrow than to wait. Waiting requires strength. It demands the absolute surrender of the life to God, the confession that we are at the end of our own understanding of things, the confession that we really do not see our way and do not know the way. The waiting that says: "Until God shall speak we dare not move and will not move, we will not be seduced from our resolution to wait"; requires strength. There is only one motive that is sufficiently strong to bring us to the place of true waiting and that motive is love. Isaiah in effect said, "God works for men that wait for Him"; Paul in effect said, "Marvelous things does God prepare for men that love Him." Love is confident in the authority; love is eager for the command; love rests in the wisdom of God; love is the alertness that waits and moves immediately. No fear of God will produce this waiting in the soul. There may be a waiting which is the result of fear, but that will be the waiting of inertia, the waiting of incapacity, and the waiting that, presently, when a call shall come, shall have no preparation for advance. The waiting that is to have the alertness and eagerness and strength enough not to do must be the outcome of love.

This is an hour and power of darkness. The supreme hour and power of darkness came two millenniums ago when the world in its cleverness crucified the Lord of glory. That was a darker hour than this. The situation was more hopeless and helpless than anything the world had known before or since when the rulers of this world, knowing not the wisdom of God, crucified the Lord of glory. So far as our lifetime is concerned, this is the hour and power of darkness. The similarity of our condition and those of the days in which Isaiah's word was spoken is perfectly patent. This is a day in which it seems as though God had abandoned men and ceased to act. This is a day in which the cry is going up from many hearts, "Oh that Thou wouldest rend the heavens, that Thou wouldest come down." This, then, is a day in which God is surely acting in ways that we cannot see.

Gleams of light there have been. Great principles have been discovered, and in the light of them we have lived through all these weary months. Yet I do not believe there is any man in the Christian church who is prepared to tell us exactly what God means and what God is doing. But faith affirms its conviction that God has a meaning and that God is at work. There is a similarity between this hour and that condition of darkness to which Paul referred. Today the rulers of this world are crucifying the Son of God afresh and putting Him to open shame. Then, by the sign and token of Golgotha and the unutterable darkness of the Crucifixion, we affirm our faith that this is a day in which God is preparing for those that love Him, things that eye has not seen and ear has not heard, things that have never entered into the heart of man and which can only be interpreted by the Holy Spirit.

What, then, is our duty today? Our duty is to wait for Him. Every activity which brings us into more perfect adjustment with Him is to be the eager occupation of our busy life and that combined with the resolute refusal to take any action which may prejudice His purpose.

During recent days the Congregational ministers of London have been gathering together to pray and to wait on God in the very sense which we have considered, that of seeking the adjustment of their own lives to the will of God. They are not creating machinery but seeking to be ready for God. That is the true attitude.

It is impossible for us to have lived through these months, critical as they have been and still are with new and sinister evils in our midst assaulting our souls with fear, without wondering.

That day of new conditions in this England of ours! That day of the new problems! Are we ready for it? Letters lie upon my table from men in the war and most of them speak of the new sense of life that has come to them. They are coming back presently. Shall we be equal to the call?

One peril that confronts us is that of making our plans and setting up our organizations. As surely as we do, we shall make ourselves unready for the day of God. What, then, shall we do? Wait for God. Our activity must be that of setting our own lives in right relationship to Him, of placing all our organizations at His disposal. Waiting for God means being free and alert so that when the breath of God moves over us and the voice of God sounds, we shall be ready for departure along the new highway which He will mark out for us. While God works and we wait, He is preparing for a working in which we must cooperate. The new working of God will be revolutionary, the breaking up of our ideals, the scrapping of our mechanisms. Today we must get ready for this. If we are thus to wait for God, we must love Him as we have never loved Him. The question that comes to us as we look honestly within our own souls is the question, "How are we to increase our love to God?" The central need of the moment is a new and passionate love for God, burning and flaming in His holy church. In proportion as that love comes, the church will be able to wait with the waiting that means alertness and readiness for service. Our love to God will be deepened by two things: a new and earnest cultivation of our fellowship with Him and a new and simple and definite obedience to Him.

How are we to cultivate our fellowship with God? By the contemplation of Christ. No man hath seen God at any time. The Son Who is in the bosom of the Father hath declared Him.

> Would we see God's brightest glory?
> We must look in Jesus' Face.

There must be a new contemplation of the Christ. There must also be a new consideration of human history from the standpoint of the Divine over-ruling; an attempt to focus upon the present situation the light of past situations. Do you not think that when Israel of old came down to the river which prevented her crossing into the land and the command was given to her that she should go across that river and take possession, that she was greatly helped in the interpretation of the problem by the history of the divided sea at the exodus? We are altogether in danger today of looking out with the men of the world, with the men of affairs, with the men whose only look is horizontal and never perpendicular. We are in danger of looking at things on the level, and there is no light anywhere. It is for us to be cultivating our fellowship with God by climbing to the heights and looking back and seeing how God has acted in the past, not in Bible history only, but in all history, for all history is divine. God has abandoned no nation utterly in all time. The man of faith who knows God, especially through Jesus Christ, will look out on the history of the past and the whole history of humanity and see it as a history of the denial of human cleverness and the proving of the folly of the wit and wisdom of the world even when it seemed at the point of victory. He will see everywhere an over-ruling providence, or, better, he will see the over-ruling God.

Let us cultivate our fellowship with God by considering the past and interpret the present hour of stress and strain and darkness, not by the things that are at our disposal in the material or the mental world, but by the activities of God in human history through the running centuries and the cycles of the years. Let us cultivate our fellowship with Him by practicing that which we hear referred to in every Christian service at its close: the communion of the Holy Ghost.

The final responsibility is not a communal responsibility. It is an individual responsibility. It is a responsibility that rests upon me. The cultivation of God must be personal, it must be lonely, and it must be intense. It demands time, it demands effort, it demands endeavor. The waiting for God of the whole church depends finally upon the waiting upon God of the individual members of the church. Through the busy rush of these terrible days, when every hour must sweat its sixty minutes to the death, we are failing unutterably if we do not find the hour of retirement, of separation, of quietness, that we may find God and cultivate our fellowship with Him. Waiting upon God, we shall learn to love Him more, and by loving Him more, we shall be more perfectly prepared to wait for Him.

That which must accompany that individual fellowship is quick, simple, ready obedience to every shining of the light at whatever cost and to every inspiration of the love at whatever cost.

In proportion as we thus love Him and wait for Him, we shall be ready for whatever may be the plan of God in the days to come.

CHAPTER XXV

THE LOOKING OF JESUS

And He entered into Jerusalem, into the temple; and when He had looked round about upon all things, it being now eventide, He went out unto Bethany with the twelve.
MARK 11:11.

THIS WAS THE FINAL INCIDENT IN A WONDERFUL DAY, AND IT was as remarkably suggestive as anything that happened on that day. In the morning Jesus had ridden toward the city amid the plaudits of the multitudes. On the way He had paused, and beholding the city, had wept over it and had pronounced its doom. Then He had entered the city and at last had come to its very heart and center, the temple itself. There He ". . . looked round about upon all things, . . ." and departed. That looking of Jesus arrests our attention. The word which the evangelist employed to describe it is a compound word and our translators, in order to convey its significance, have become almost redundant in their use of words; ". . . he had looked round about upon, . . ." and the four words constitute the translation of one Greek word. The prefix of the Greek word suggests a looking everywhere and all round everything, and the idea is expressed by our words *round about upon.* The base of the word suggests thoroughness in looking. It does not indicate the gaze of wonder.

There is such a word in our Greek New Testament—looking with wide-open eyes as does a child—but that is not the word of my text. Neither—and this I would enforce even more carefully—does it suggest the inspection of one not familiar with what he is looking at; it is not the inspection of one who desires to discover. There is a word in our Greek New Testament which stands for exactly that kind of looking, but this is not that word. This word suggests, rather, the voluntary contemplation of what is already known. The idea is that of looking thoroughly at the whole of the facts before His eyes, the kind of looking which suggests thought.

What did He see as at that eventide He looked round about upon all things? What did He think as He looked? The answer to both inquiries may be gathered from His subsequent actions. He came to the temple again, certainly twice, probably three times. I am going to take it for granted that He came three times and if the third coming is not established, at least we shall see that on the occasion to which I shall refer His mind and heart were there. What we shall find Him doing will reveal to us what He saw when He looked round about upon all things, and what He thought as the result of what He saw. He came the next day and cleansed the temple and for a few brief hours guarded it against all defilement and intrusion. He came the day after and spent the whole day there, judging the rulers, condemning them, and as He left He prophesied the doom of the temple, declaring that not one stone should be left upon another of all the great and glorious building. He came again, as I believe, on Passover night. When in the midst of the paschal discourse He said: ". . . arise, let us go hence," I think He led the disciples back toward the temple, and there at its most glorious entrance, under the shadow of the golden vine, He uttered His teaching concerning the vine and offered His great intercessory prayer. In the light of these facts therefore, let us answer our questions; what did He see? What did He think?

What then did Jesus see? That is our first question. Let me give an answer from the three incidents briefly, before dwelling upon them at greater length. He saw a den of robbers. He saw a destructive force already at work which would never end its operations until the whole temple was demolished. He saw the Divine victory beyond the demolition.

He saw a den of robbers. He came back on the following day into the temple, cleansed and guarded it and proceeded to teach, giving reasons for His strange and wonderful action in these words: ". . . It is written, My house shall be called the house of prayer: but ye have made it a den of robbers." In these words of Jesus His conception of what the temple ought to be is revealed; ". . . My house shall be called the house of prayer: . . . The emphasis was not so much upon the fact that it was to be called the house of prayer, as upon the fact that it was to be the house of prayer for all the nations. He was by no means concerned to defend the temple as a peculiar place of worship for the Hebrew people. He was making His protest against that very misconception. Part of the defilement of the temple lay in the fact that men looked upon it only as a place where Hebrews might worship. Let it be distinctly remembered that what Jesus saw as He looked round about was that a traffic was being carried on within the temple courts but not within the holy places. This traffic was prosecuted in the courts which in the Divine provision had been set apart for the gathering of the Gentiles, the men of other nations who desired to worship the God of the Hebrews. The inner courts into which went the priests or the Hebrews bringing sacrifices were held sacred against the profanation of Gentile feet. The courts appointed for the Gentiles were filled with traffickers. They were making religion easy for the Hebrews. They were setting the Hebrew free from the responsibility of selecting his offering of a lamb or turtle dove. The moment men begin to make religion easy, they cut its nerve.

They were doing more, they were making religion difficult for the Gentiles who ought to have occupied that particular court. The temple courts were being used as a short cut from one part of the city to another. These people were going to and fro through the courts, carrying vessels and merchandise, thus making religion easy for the Jews and difficult for the Gentiles. These were the surface things, but the things upon the surface tell the story of the things that underlie them. As our Lord looked out upon that scene, He knew that the rulers of the temple were guilty in that they encouraged the traffic and permitted this crossing of the courts in order to reach a place in the city more easily; and He knew that the people who employed the method were guilty also. It was not only that they were wronging the Gentiles, in the wronging of the Gentiles they were wronging the God Who was the God of the Gentiles as surely as He was the God of the Jews. He went into the temple, and He looked round about upon all things and He saw the temple as a den of robbers.

Further, He saw a destructive force at work. When, next day, He came to the temple, He challenged the rulers while the rulers thought they were challenging Him; He tried the rulers while the rulers thought they were trying Him; He found a verdict against the rulers while they were trying to find a verdict against Him; He sentenced the rulers and the nation while they thought they were passing sentence on Him. By parabolic method of investigation and denunciation, He compelled these men to find verdicts against themselves and pass sentences upon themselves. Again eventide came and as He was leaving the temple, His disciples drew His attention to the beauty of the building. He looked at them as one who should say: "You need not show Me the beauty of the building, I know it well; Do you see it? Not one stone shall be left upon another, that shall not be thrown down." I need not stay to dwell upon the literal and absolute fulfilment of that prophecy within a generation when the armies of Titus surrounded Jerusalem and not a single stone was left upon another of that temple. That is not the point now but rather what Jesus saw. He saw what Isaiah saw. He saw the whole city, the whole temple, and the whole audience therein, enwrapped in fire, the fire of the immediate nearness of Deity, the slowly burning but surely destructive fire which destroys only that which is perishable, and purifies, ennobles, and beautifies that which is in itself noble, high, and true. We remember Isaiah's great passage: "The sinners in Zion are afraid; trembling hath seized the godless ones: . . ." Why? ". . . Who among us can dwell with the devouring fire? Who among us can dwell with everlasting burnings?" In the prophet's question there was no reference to the hell that lies beyond. There was reference rather to the very conditions in the midst of which they were living. The prophet saw that God forgotten was not God distanced; God disobeyed was not God defeated. He saw that God was there as the slowly burning fire of which there is a parabolic illustration in all nature. Scientists tell us of the eremacausis, a slowly burning fire in nature which oxidizes iron or steel if we leave it out in the dew, and paints the trees with their autumnal tints, as it destroys the effete for the perfecting of that which really lives. Jesus saw this fire everywhere. He saw the inevitable end therefore. He knew that the symbol, the temple, must be destroyed when its meaning was denied. Material strength and beauty were doomed when they were not the vehicle of spiritual interpretation and moral appeal. Therefore, as He looked round about upon all things He saw, not only the den of robbers, the desecration of the Divine ideal; He saw also doom and destruction, because God is not mocked, neither can He be distanced from human affairs.

He saw more, He saw the Divine victory. If He did not actually come to the temple on Passover night, He was certainly there in spirit. I personally believe He actually came there on that night and that the last great discourse, the allegory of the vine, was uttered there. At Passover time the gates of the temple were open for pilgrims that they might enter and meditate. The main entrance was never closed. Josephus tells us in his "Antiquities" that over the entrance Herod had constructed a thing of infinite beauty, the wonder and amazement of all who looked at it, the golden vine, the vine being the scriptural symbol of the Hebrew people. Under that golden vine then it is probable that Jesus stood with His disciples when He said: "I am the true vine, ..." What then did He see as He looked round about upon all things? He saw a city without a temple. He saw the realization of the Divine ideal symbolized in the vine which Israel had never succeeded in fulfilling. He saw the vine bearing fruit for the nations. Israel had failed and He must curse and denounce the city. But if it be true that God is not distanced, it is also true that God cannot be defeated. Looking out upon all things in the temple, He saw with great clearness a city wherein there should be no temple. The woman of Samaria had said to Him: "Our fathers worshipped in this mountain; and ye say, that in Jerusalem is the place where men ought to worship." Jesus had answered her: ". . . Woman, believe me, the hour cometh, when neither in this mountain, nor in Jerusalem, shall ye worship the Father. . . . the hour cometh, and now is, when the true worshippers shall worship the Father in spirit and truth: . . ." He saw beyond the doom and destruction of the temple, the glad, glorious, wonderful day, when the temple should be unnecessary in the perfected city of God. John saw that city in Patmos, the city of God with no temple therein. Looking through the darkness, He saw a sanctified life in which worship would no longer be special, occasional, but normal and persistent. Looking round about upon all things, He saw a den of robbers, a destructive force, but a Divine victory.

What, then, let us ask in the second place, did He think as He saw these things? Here again we are instructed by the things that followed. When He saw the house appointed for worship, a house of prayer for all the nations, desecrated, He knew that the Divine ideal must be maintained at all costs. Therefore, He returned on the morrow. He cast out the moneychangers and overthrew their tables, and more, He would not suffer any carrying a vessel to pass through those courts. Look at the scene. How long it lasted I cannot tell, probably some hours. Jesus is seen holding the temple, guarding it against intrusion, and turning it to its rightful uses. First of all, He cleared away abuse; turned men out, overturned tables, halted every man who tried to take a short cut through the courts to some other part of the city. Matthew says that two things were going on during the time He held and guarded the temple. It is a beautiful picture; Jesus the Lord and Master of the temple is seen healing sick folk, and all the while the children are singing round about Him—a musical obligato to Divine healing. For a moment He gave the city and the world for all time to see what a house of prayer is; not a place where we go to ask for things for ourselves, but a place where the halt and maimed are healed while children sing. If man has destroyed the Divine ideal, the Divine ideal must not be lost. He gave us a picture in a flash of what He is still doing and what He will continue to do until He has completed the work of driving out the traffickers and overturning the money tables and guarding men's right of access to God.

But He came again and argued all day long with the rulers and condemned them, and as He left He pronounced the final doom upon the city and declared that not one stone should be left upon another of the temple. What then did He think as He looked round about upon all things?

That the human degradation must be destroyed. That human degradation was complete He knew full well as witness His parables in that long day's teaching. These men would kill, not merely the servants sent unto them, but the very Son Who came out from the Father's heart. Because the degradation was complete, nothing must be left which would be of the nature of false security. There are times when the best thing we can do with a church is to close it. Better abandon a sacrament and close a church than traffic with the church and with the sacrament in an unholy way. The temple must be destroyed because if it remain it becomes a false security and a libel on God. Consequently, we find that the fierce fire of His wrath is kindled by the deeper passion of His heart in mercy. He will destroy all false security that the soul in its nakedness may be driven out toward Himself for help, healing, and blessing.

As He looked round about upon all things, He knew not only that the Divine ideal must be maintained and human degradation destroyed, but that the Divine purpose must be realized in the Divine way. When He came back on Passover night, after He said: "I am the true Vine, . . ." He began to pray. ". . . Father, the hour is come; glorify thy Son, that the Son may glorify thee." He was praying for strength for the Cross. As He looked round about upon all things, He knew that in order to the final establishment of the Divine ideal and in order to move toward the Divine purpose in spite of destruction, it was necessary that He should gather up into His heart and life in a mystery utterly beyond the possibility of human analysis, all the sin that had wrought the havoc and quench it in His blood.

So He still observes. So He still looks round about upon all things. There are no questions more important for us individually, socially, nationally, ecclesiastically, than those we have been asking in the presence of this old-time story. He looks down upon men wherever they foregather, whether it be a church or in a theatre; whether it be in the halls of commerce or in places of amusement; whether in the capitalist club or the labor church; He looks, He observes, He sees. He looks at the national attitudes and activities and understands them in their profoundest depths, in those depths that no diplomacy will ever discover to statesmen, and yet with which statesmen must deal if nationality is ever to be anything worth the name. He still looks round about upon all things in the church, upon all its worship and upon all its work. We need to remember that when Jesus looks He sees everything thoroughly. He sees the good, and He sees the bad. He sees that which is high, and that which is low. He sees that which is true, and that which is merely formal. He knows whether, when our lips recite the prayer He taught His disciples, we are indulging in the talk of parrots or praying. He sees thoroughly the internal as well as the external, the motive as well as the manner, the aspiration as well as the achievement. If this be a scorching, burning truth, there is yet more comfort in it than in anything else I know. He sees everything. Your neighbor listens to your profession; He knows the truth about you. Your friend knows how you blundered, failed, sinned. He knows why you did it, and how you did not want to do it, and how your aspiration was a great deal better than your achievement. He knows all about you, the fire in the blood, the deadly, dastardly, devilish poison that drives you; He takes it all into account. He sees everything and sees thoroughly.

Remember, in the second place, that when He looks, He measures everything by the Divine standard. He does not measure anything by the standards of human convenience, or selfishness, or by that of vested interests. They had vested interests in the temple, and He hurried them out overturning their tables. He does not measure the drink traffic today by the standard of vested interests. We ought to be filled with shame that we are not taking out of the way of our sons the possibility of temptation and from devilish men and women the chance of tempting them.

Neither does He measure by the standard of our ability. You say, "I am doing the best I can." He does not measure us that way. That is not all the truth of life. Doing the best we can is a poor business. What then are the standards of His measurement? The purpose of God and the power of God as available for every man. It is not enough that I do the best I can. I am to do the best that God and I can do. "I can do all things in him that strengtheneth me" said Paul. He expects, not that I shall do the best I can, but that I shall avail myself of all the power that is at my disposal in God. He measures by Divine standards.

Again, when He looks, He always agrees with God in His destructive judgments. His parable of the barren fig tree teaches this. The hour comes, according to that parable, when the vinedresser after long provocation to fruit bearing has to say with the proprietor: "Cut it down." He ever agrees with God. The building must go even though it be the temple, be it never so ancient, never so strong, never so beautiful. It is leprous, it must go. If that be true of a building, it is much more true of the men who have caused the pollution.

One thing more. I would not have said all I have said if I had not something else to say. When He looks, He pities and He provides a way of escape, even from the pre-determined judgments. That was the goal of all His journeyings and that the explanation of the pathway of His choice, the pathway that led Him ultimately to Calvary. When there was no eye to pity, He pitied. When there was no arm to save, He saved. So mighty was His pity and so profound His compassion that when He had to curse the city, he wept over it. Robert William Dale once said that Dwight Lyman Moody was the one and only man he knew who had any right to preach about hell. When asked what he meant, he said: "Moody never talks of hell except with tears in his voice." Jesus never talked of destruction except with tears in His voice. O man, under the destructive judgment of God because of thy pollution, remember there is pity in His heart, and if thou wilt but avail thyself of His provision, He will deliver thee even from that pre-determined judgment. He looked upon all things with love-lit eyes, eyes illumined, irradiated, by the infinite compassion of His heart.

I will end our meditation by grouping one or two Scriptures together. ". . . He looked round about upon all things. . . ." Then in the last picture of Him in the New Testament, I find this sentence: ". . . His eyes were as a flame of fire." In a letter written by one of His apostles, I find these words: "Each man's work . . . is revealed in fire; and the fire itself shall prove each man's work, of what sort it is." Then I read again, with new understanding: ". . . Who among us can dwell with the devouring fire? Who among us can dwell with everlasting burnings?"

Then I come back from the apocalyptic word, the apostolic declaration, and the prophetic inquiry, and standing again in the presence of the One Who looks I hear Him saying: "Come unto me, all ye that labor and are heavy laden, and I will give you rest." Then I feel as though I must go, and I hear Him say one other word: ". . . him that cometh to Me I will in no wise cast out." Under the scrutiny of those eyes of fire may we hear the sweetness of that voice of love.

CHAPTER XXVI

THE WAGES OF SIN—THE GIFT OF GOD

For the wages of sin is death; but the free gift of God is eternal life in Jesus Christ our Lord.
ROMANS 6:23.

IN THE PREVIOUS CHAPTER WE CONSIDERED THE TREMENDOUS declaration of Paul that where sin abounds, grace does more exceedingly abound. Continuing in this chapter, we lay emphasis upon the individual and particular responsibility of that truth and upon the responsibility which it involves. There can be no statement more clear in this regard than that of the text. In these words we have the revelation of the alternative which is offered to every soul who has heard the gospel of the grace which abounds more exceedingly than all the multiplying of sin. To many men, that alternative has never been presented. There are those who sit in darkness and under the shadow of death in lands to which the gospel has never come. They are not in view when we speak of the alternatives of this text. There are multitudes of people in London who are not in view, for we make a great mistake if we imagine that London is evangelized. There are people in the west and in the east who know nothing of the gospel. The alternative of the text is that which is offered to a soul who has heard the gospel, who knows its terms, who is familiar with its message. Such a soul will either yield to sin, serve it, and earn its wages; or it will yield to God, receive His gift, and live. No soul can escape from sin. Sin is inherited. One of the first emphases of the gospel is the emphasis it lays upon the Lordship of Jesus Christ, and where this Lordship is truly understood, it becomes the revelation of sin in the life of the soul. A man may stand, by reason of his early education and training, under Mount Sinai without trembling. No man can come consciously into the presence of Jesus Christ without finding his own guilt and his own unworthiness.

But if this soul who knows the gospel cannot escape from sin, it is equally true that it cannot escape from the gift which is placed at its disposal in the gospel. The gospel is the announcement of the fact that God has placed at the disposal of every soul the gift of eternal life. A man can ultimately escape from either sin or grace, but not from both. He can escape from sin by yielding to grace, or he can put himself outside the operation of grace by yielding to sin.

This presentation of an alternative is according to the perpetual method of God. In this text there are two statements: first, ". . . the wages of sin is death"; second, ". . . the gift of God is eternal life in Christ Jesus our Lord." If I found these two statements entirely separated in my Bible, they would both remain true; but the fact that they are together is in itself more than a suggestion of the love of God. It is in harmony with His perpetual method. In nature every poison has its antidote. When we turn from nature to the literature of revelation, the whole message is concerned with the one poison and the one antidote. It is the literature which reveals the poison; it is the literature that declares the antidote. The Bible is not a Book that gives us any light upon the universe in detail. It tells us enough to compel us forevermore to set the universe to its uttermost bound in relation with the God from Whom it proceeds. The Bible has to do with a world where sin is, and if we want to know what is the nature of the poison that blasts life, we must turn to this literature. Outside it, we shall find the fact of sin recognized and called by all kinds of high-sounding names, but here it is stripped to the nakedness of its actuality.

But grace is here also; the antidote is discovered from first to last. The Divine compassion is its supreme message; the Spirit of God brooding over the chaos; the wealth of the love of the Eternal, demanding: ". . . Adam, . . . where art thou?" "How shall I give thee up, Ephraim? . . ." God is the God Who makes a way by which His banished ones may return; He is the God Who so loved the world, that He gave His only begotten Son.

In our consideration of this very old and familiar text, let us first observe the contrast in the alternatives; second, ponder the two courses described; and all that, in order that as God shall help us we may in this very hour face the crisis created.

First, then, as to the contrast. The very reading of the text suggests it, and a closer consideration of it shows how perfect it is. In the first part of the text we have three terms: wages, sin, death. In the second part we have three terms: a gift, God, eternal life. They stand over against each other in each case. Wages—a gift; Sin—God; death—eternal life.

What are wages? Wages are earnings. A man has a right to wages. Wages are the equivalent of work, or at least they ought to be. When a man takes his wages by common courtesy he will say, "Thank you." He really need not do so. He has nothing to thank any one for when he gets his wages. He has earned them. They are the answer in equity and justice to what he has already given in toil and in effort.

Wages lie within the realm of law, or order, of accuracy, of justice.

What is a gift? The revisers have accurately translated the one Greek word by two words, for it is a word that emphasizes the freedom of the gift. What then is a free gift? Something that cannot be earned. That which no man can claim as his right. That which cannot be bought. A free gift must be received of grace, of favor, of love. A free gift is in the realm of grace.

Let us take the next stage of contrast: sin and God. In our text the term sin is in some senses qualified by the term wages. Its appeal is made personal and direct by that word. Sin is considered here as an individual act. It is the act of a free agent. It is not merely the missing of the mark; it is wilful missing of the mark. It is not merely failure; it is the choosing of failure. If wages be the payment for work, sin is the work that earns the payment. Here sin is considered as definite volitional choosing of the wrong with all which that involves of guilt and of paralysis.

Now what term is set over against sin? The term God. That is a very arresting fact. Even in the inspired writings in which the words were chosen under the direction of the Spirit of God we always find that when they are dealing with the things of God and Christ, language breaks down. Grace is bigger than literature; grace is mightier than language! In order to make this contrast complete, the lower level of perfect rhetoric and balance and proportion must be violated. It was easy to set the free gift over against the wages, but when we come to sin, the course of action demanding wages, what can be put over against it? No course of action is equal to dealing with sin. Then God is immediately placed in contrast with sin.

Another series of contrasts could be imagined. Let us

consider them. It would be possible to say, and it would be a perfectly true thing to say: the wages of sin is death, but the wages of holiness is life. That is a perfectly balanced contrast in its entirety. But therein is no reference to a gift; the first set of terms do not constitute a contrast, but a similarity. The contrast in that statement is between sin and holiness and between death and life. That, however, is not the text. If we go back to primitive man in the garden, we may say that the alternative before him may thus have been stated: the wages of sin is death, but the wages of holiness is life. That is the alternative before a sinless being. It was so in the case of God's second Man, the last Adam, Jesus. In His case the wages of sin would have been death and the wages of holiness life. The text was not written for the sinless; it was written for sinning men. In their case we can understand the declaration, ". . . the wages of sin is death, . . ." But what alternative is offered to sinning men? The answer of grace is: ". . . the . . . gift of God is eternal life. . . ." God puts Himself over against sin. In a man's new endeavor He does not say: the wages of sin is death, and the outcome of reformation shall be life. He does not say: the wages of sin is death, and the outcome of religious observance shall be life. These things are of no use. The man who is in the thought of God is a man who is incapable of reformation and whose religious observances would in themselves be sinful. Therefore, God put Himself over against sin. Sin—God. We are only looking at the terms, but mark the arresting grandeur of the contrast.

So we come to the last contrast in the text: death and eternal life. What is death? It is the end of sin, the righteous end. It is that which makes sin musical. It maintains the harmony of the universe. If in the universe of God, the breaking of a law could be permitted without check or hindrance, then all music would cease, the beauty missed, and the last victory never be won! Death is the necessary end of sin, the only answer to it, the only final harvest that men can reap who sow in sin. Death is that which every man chooses in the moment when he yields himself to sin. By that yielding, he chooses death, disintegration, corruption, ruin. To break law is to create anarchy; to create anarchy is to make hell necessary.

Over against death, our text places eternal life. Death is an end; life is a beginning. But life is more than a beginning; it is the energy for the development of that which is begun; it is the potentiality for the full realization of everything which is begun. The final contrast does not refer to the end only, but to the beginning also; not to the beginning only, but also to the end; not to the beginning and the end alone, but to the whole process of development.

Let us consider the two courses of life presented by this alternative. Here we must take them in the other order. First, we must consider the second part of the text: . . . the free gift of God is eternal life. . . . In our understanding of that, we shall find a new definition of sin which qualifies the first part of the text giving it a new meaning in view of God and His free gift. Sin, when the gospel is known no longer, consists of certain actions; it consists in the attitude of soul which results in these actions. No man who has heard this gospel will ever perish for the sins he has committed. If he perish, it will be because he has refused God's gift, the reception of which would have made him master over the sins that he has committed. Therefore, we must begin with the second part of our text.

Here, then, the first word to be considered is God. God is concerned of as One perfectly knowing the soul; as One Who is unutterably holy so that He cannot overlook sin or clear the guilty while the guilt remains; as One Who is unchangeably loving so that His love alters not when it alteration finds.

This God offers a free gift to the sinning man. That is to say, He offers a gift of His own will, a gift which is the result of His own operation, of His own passion. Moreover, He offers this gift as a free gift without any condition as to character in the person who is to receive it, without any pledge on the part of that person as to the future. God bestows His gift freely upon all such as will receive it. God does not ask that men bring a certificate of character with them. Neither does He ask us to make a pledge and a promise that we will always be good. He asks no such pledge; He asks no such promise. That is the grace of God. I speak in soberness of truth and under emotion when I say I would to God I knew just how to say "grace" as it ought to be said! Out of the very grace of His heart which in operation has involved His own unutterable pain and sorrow, God offers a free gift, and He offers it to a man without any promise whatsoever as to that man's character and without any pledge as to the future.

What, then, is this gift? It is the gift of life, age-abiding life. Our word "eternal," great and wonderful as it is, connotes in our thinking one element only, the element of quantity. The Greek word so translated has in it more than the element of quantity, though that is included; it rather suggests a quality which ensures the quantity. Literally, it is age-abiding life. Our imagination is helped by the writings of our New Testament. We may climb the heights, and watch the ages as they come and go. Glancing back over the few brief ages of the history of this world—for how few and brief they are in comparison with all the ages—we see the age of fellowship with God, the age of conscience, the age

THE WAGES OF SIN—THE GIFT OF GOD

of law, and the age of grace that has lasted now for nearly 2000 years. Looking on, we see the age of the reign of Jesus with His saints for a thousand years, and the more wonderful age beyond the millennium, the age of the Kingdom of the Son and the City of God. There the Bible ends its revelation because there is not room to tell all the story. Paul climbed to a great height one day, and he tried to say something and broke down in magnificent poetry in the attempt as he wrote of "The generation of the age of the ages." In the light of that suggestion we see them coming, age after age, out of the fathomless Being of God, profound in mystery, glorious in strength, new ages of which we can but dream in the highest moments of our spiritual illumination. Age-abiding life is life that includes them all, persists through all, harmonizes with all. That is the gift which God gives a man without asking him for a certificate of character or any pledge for tomorrow.

This gift is that of life won out of death, and therefore in its reception the soul is pardoned and cleansed. It is life in union with the risen Lord and ascended Lord, and therefore it is the life of power equal to all the demands that can be made upon it in this and every succeeding age. It is life in fellowship with God; ultimately, therefore, it must prove itself to be a life of complete realization; the perfection of the individual instrument in spirit, mind and body, and the accomplishment of the purposes of God, not merely in the instrument, but through the instrument.

This, then, is one course open to every man and woman who knows the gospel. It begins with God. The soul comes to Him, yields to Him, puts itself in relationship with Him, blunderingly, tremblingly, it may be; not necessarily understanding the doctrines of faith, for no man was ever saved by understanding the doctrines of the faith; not necessarily at the moment accepting all evangelical theology, for that is too vast for immediate understanding, but by yielding to God as He has manifested Himself in Christ. There we begin. When we do so, we receive a free gift in which there are qualities of cleansing, of peace, and of pardon; and as we answer its call and its demands and its guidance through the running days and the multiplying years we are brought by it into the realization of the eternal purpose of God. That is one course open to every soul who knows the gospel.

What is the other? Here we begin at the point where the soul begins. The beginning is sin. Sin is rejection of the gift. I halt to remind you of the careful emphasis which I laid at the beginning on the fact that we are dealing only with those who know the gospel. To such, sin is rejection of God's gift. That is what our Lord meant when in His Paschal discourse He said to His disciples that when the Holy Spirit came He would convince the world of sin, of righteousness, of judgment. Concerning conviction of sin, He said: "Of sin, because they believe not on Me." For the man who has heard the gospel, that is the whole heart of sin, it is the whole reach of it. Included in it are the desires that inspire the rejection. Why do men reject the Lord Christ? Because there are certain desires clamant in their lives which they wish to satisfy and which they know they could not if they yielded to Him. The things thus done in answer to desire are done at last under compulsion. Men cannot cease if they would. All this multiplying of sin grows out of the central sin of the rejection of Christ. Let us state this from the positive side. If this gospel means anything, it means that if a man will yield to God, there is power in the gift of life which He bestows sufficient to break the power of canceled sin. Consequently, sin is the rejection of the remedy.

Where this sin is committed wages follow as the necessary results of the things we decided to do; the harvest that must come from our own sowing; that which is righteously due to us by reason of our choice; that which must come to us as the result of the false effort we are putting into life.

The wages are described by the one word, death. The only wages that sin ever pays are the wages of death. They are paid immediately and continuously. Do not confuse, I pray you, appearances with facts. Someone may say, "Sin pays more than that. Sin pays some men wonderfully!" Sin does pay some men wonderfully to all appearances, but the gains of sin are the destruction of the sinner, always, and that not ultimately merely, but immediately.

The man who imagines that riches gained in the nefarious practice, the blighting traffic by which he is damning others that he himself may get rich, constitute the wages of sin, is blind. He himself is dying and never more so than when he is counting his gains and imagining that they are the wages of sin. The wages of sin is death spiritually; this first. Eyes that cannot see God, ears that cannot hear His voice, the heart that is insensate to His nearness, the life that is untouched by the movements of His grace; this is to be dead in trespasses and sins, and this eventually will mean death, bodily and mentally as well as spiritually; and at last it will mean eternal death, age-abiding separation from God, the second death. The second death is the ending of the possibility of dying, and that is the ultimate in sin.

So we come face to face with the crisis. These two ways of life are before every one of us now. God is close at hand; nearer is He than breathing, closer than hands or feet;

> Circling us with hosts of fire.
> Hell is nigh, but God is nigher.

Sin is also with us, it is close to us, but God is nearer than sin. Sin is here in the sanctuary. Satan cannot be excluded from the sanctuary. He yet has access to the heavenly places. There will come the day when he shall be cast out finally, but that day is not yet. Sin is here. Sin is bargaining with souls, and souls are bargaining with sin even now, wondering whether or not they shall yield to God or sin.

These are the only alternatives open to every human being who knows the gospel. There is no middle way. Moreover, there is no hindrance either way except the hindrance created by the opposite. I can choose sin if I will. Grace will appeal to me, woo me, warn me, but it will not compel me nor can it. I can sin if I will and take the wages if I will and die if I will. Grace is here. I can yield to grace if I will. Sin will lure me and seek to blind me and traduce the God Who is near, but sin can have no power over me if I will yield to God. Sin cannot compel me. I can yield to God now and receive His gift now and begin to live now. And that, in spite of all the past. I do not want to know the past. I would not have you tell me the past. There is only One ear that ought to hear the confession of sin, and that is the ear of God. Perhaps someone is saying: "The past is indeed with me; the sin of it, the shame of it, the smirch of it, the contamination of it, the horror of it, and the paralysis of it, and my trouble is emphasized by the fact that I once yielded to Christ and walked in power, but I have turned my back upon Him." Even if that be so, God desires to blot it out like a thick cloud and banish that past. He offers His gift without any reference to the past.

But something else must be said. There is no guarantee that this offer will continue. Therefore, the question is immediate; which way of life shall we take? The debate goes on in the human soul more subtlely, more powerfully, more rapidly than any words of the preacher can describe. If this congregation could be seen from the higher heights, as the angels I think see it, what a battleground would be seen as to which way souls shall go.

The preacher's work is done. He must now stand aside, for there can be no final interference between the human soul and its own choice and its own destiny. Where God declines to interfere, who is man that he should endeavor so to do? Sometimes the preacher closes the Sunday night's service and goes away into quietness. He thinks of his congregation again; the congregation reverent, kind in their attention; then dispersing, passing along the streets in all directions, going into houses and closing doors. Such different places, so many different circumstances, such different consciousnesses, and yet, that whole congregation so scattered has been united by the service, all having taken action in the central dignity of their own humanity, all having made a choice, all having made a decision. If they are united thus, they are also divided into two companies: those who have accepted the gift and live; those who have sinned and are dying while they live. How shall we go? May God help us in the hour of our decision.

www.ingramcontent.com/pod-product-compliance
Lightning Source LLC
Chambersburg PA
CBHW052143300426
44115CB00011B/1492